FIRE AND WATER

A LIFE OF PETER THE GREAT

ALSO BY ALEX DE JONGE

Nightmare Culture: Lautréamont & Les Chants de Maldoror

Dostoevsky & the Age of Intensity

Baudelaire: Prince of Clouds

The Weimar Chronicle: Prelude to Hitler

Alex de Jonge

FIRE
AND WATER

A LIFE OF
PETER THE GREAT

Coward, McCann & Geoghegan

NEW YORK

Copyright © 1979, 1980 by Alex de Jonge
All rights reserved. This book, or parts thereof, may not
be reproduced in any form without permission in writing from
the publisher.
First American Edition 1980

Library of Congress Cataloging in Publication Data

De Jonge, Alex, date.
 Fire and water.

 Bibliography: p.
 1. Peter I, the Great, Emperor of Russia, 1672–1725.
2. Russia—Kings and Rulers—Bibliography. I. Title.
DK132.D42 1980   947'.05'0924 [B]   79–23113
ISBN 0-698-11018-8

Printed in the United States of America

For Edward and James

CONTENTS

The government is absolute in the last degree, not bound up by any law or custom, but dependent on the breath of the Prince, by whom the lives and fortunes of all the subjects are decided ... However such as are employed in the state have their share of arbitrary power, their proceedings being without appeal all in the czar's name, which they often abuse to satisfy their avarice, revenge or other guilty passion.

Whitworth

Men who are not free always idealise their bondage.

Boris Pasternak

Nothing calms one as much as history.

Gogol

INTRODUCTION

The most celebrated statue in Russia is set on a solid 1600-ton block of granite and stands on the south bank of the Neva. A gigantic bronze figure sits on a horse rearing over an abyss. He sits firmly in the saddle, his right hand stretching out over space. He is every inch the master of his wild mount, and though we cannot tell whether it is rearing in terror, or about to cross the chasm before it with a monstrous thrust of its gigantic quarters, we know that whatever its rider may ask, it will accomplish.

The horseman is, of course, Peter the Great, riding his country into modern history. He was not the gentlest of riders, but nor was his mount the easiest of rides. The Russia he was born into was a country which for 250 years had been under the rule of a foreign power, the Tartars. This legacy of thraldom and oppression had stamped the profoundest of marks upon Russia, a mark it still bears to-day. For centuries it was either under the yoke of infidels or at war with them. This created something of a "frontier" mentality, together with a fierce sense of allegiance to the Orthodox Church and to Russia as a defender of the faith, long before any comparable sense of patriotism existed in the West. The Tartars also gave Russia the pattern of her government, a pattern based on unquestioning and total obedience to an absolute authority; whether under the oppressor or at war with him, Russia had no opportunity to evolve the kind of liberal institutions developed in the West. Right up to the revolution of 1917 Russia's ruling classes rejected out of hand suggestions that the czar abdicate his authority in favour of some constitutional régime, which they felt was quite unsuited to Russia. "The so-called democrats should remember," wrote one of the last Grand Dukes, Alexander Mikhailovich, "that at the time King John signed Magna Carta we were under the yoke of a foreign and pagan power."

Along with a fierce sense of patriotism and the unquestioning acceptance of a despotic pattern of government the Tartar occupation had a third vital consequence: it deprived Russia of a renaissance. Although by the middle of the 17th century she was "beginning to awake from her long sleep", as one foreign observer put it, Russia, in the age of Louis XIV and Sir Isaac Newton, was still a medieval country.

It was Peter Alekseyevich Romanov, the Bronze Horseman, who drove her headlong into modern history. A giant of a man, standing six and half feet high, he was endowed with energy and practical curiosity to a degree surpassing even his own physical stature. Although Russia would certainly have turned to the West in due course, it is very largely thanks to the actions and attitudes of this one man that medieval Muscovy became Imperial Russia within the span of some twenty-five years.

The reader can only get some inkling of the colossal scale of his achievement when he understands something of the Russia into which Peter was born. Steeped in sluggishness, inertia and narrow-minded chauvinism, it was a land in which tradition was everything. The old ways were the only ways, foreigners were fools, heretics, sorcerers, and anyone who departed from tradition by so much as altering the pattern of his dress or shaving off his beard was thereby endangering his immortal soul. Peter's achievements, his transformations, are remarkable by any standards, but when the raw material he had to work with is considered they defy belief – although it is true that a lot of that raw material fell by the wayside in the process.

For along with his energy, his vision, his determination to drive his country forward, Peter possessed a ruthlessness, a degree of cruelty even, which matched his energy and physique. He used forced labour on a massive scale, and it is impossible to count the innocent victims of his enterprises: war, public works, and the construction of a new capital city in a far northern swamp. Moreover he treated anyone he suspected of opposing his plans with terrifying savagery, flogging and executing with his own hand, shutting two half-sisters and a wife away in convents, and torturing to death his first-born son, who, he had decided, was not worthy to succeed him.

Yet though the story of Peter's life has its dark, bloodstained chapters, there is another more joyful side. For Peter loved to play, both with fire and with water; his favourite sport was the launching of a new ship accompanied by salvo after salvo of cannon fire. He also loved "firewater", which he consumed on the generous scale that marked all his actions. Despite his determination to drive his country at his own breakneck pace over any and every obstacle, and despite the cruelty with which he plied his whip and spurs, there was nothing solemn about this horseman, nothing remote or vainglorious about his style; no one could be further removed from the pompous ceremonials of a Louis XIV. Peter was the worker czar, who loved energetic companions and was proud of his calloused hands. He was happier drinking with Dutch seamen in a tavern than keeping royal company in the courts of Europe. Despising display and ostentation, he was endowed with a marvellous self-confidence which allowed him always to be natural, to be himself, and he possessed the kind of real greatness and sense of majesty which never needs look to trappings and ceremonies for support.

Peter's life is fascinating enough in itself, but it also helps us to understand Russia. The most casual study of that country's history will quickly suggest that in Russia some things do not change. Peter, for example, can be seen to exemplify a certain style of rulership which can be found in the three strong men who have imposed themselves on Russia with such force that they belong not to history so much as to myth: Ivan the Terrible, Peter the Great and Stalin. That the three have much in common is a truism. Stalin was a great admirer of Peter the Great; there have even been Stalinist sycophants who have tried to prove that Peter was really a Georgian. Equally it is tempting to draw analogies between Ivan's mindless, motiveless annihilation of Novgorod and Stalin's purges. Peter was the founder of the Russian secret police, while both he and Ivan had a son's blood on their hands.

There are other ways in which Russia has not changed much. The aggressive hospitality of Peter's day will be familiar to anyone who knows the official or unofficial Russia of to-day; guests needed hard heads and strong stomachs just as badly then as now. Peter's subjects were like their descendants in other respects. Although his reign had its brief moments of violence and cossack rampage, his people on the whole displayed an astonishing capacity for submissive acceptance of his violent and disruptive authority, as he imposed change after change that went quite as much against the grain as any Stalinist collectivisation. In *The Gulag Archipelago* Solzhenitsyn is bewildered by the "rabbits", the millions who submitted to the authority of Stalin's terror and went to the camps quietly. Blind submission to arbitrary authority is part of the Russian tradition – there were rabbits enough in Peter's day too, and in Ivan's.

Yet despite similarities between the leaders who have set the style of rulership in Russia, it must be said that Peter is by a long way the most attractive member of the trio. Although he had his share of murderous and paranoid suspicion, this never dominated his character as it did with the other two. In comparison with Ivan's *oprichniki* or Stalin's "operatives" his secret police were positively benign. Moreover, and above all, Peter's own motives were always benevolent. He never asked more of his people than he asked or gave of himself. Although he was savage in the demands he made of his mount, his kingdom *was* his horse, his pride and joy, his whole life, and if horse or rider should fail in their giant bound then both would perish together.

The reader can get some idea of the lag between Russia and the rest of Europe from the fact that at the time Samuel Pepys was writing in England, or Racine in France, Russia did not even possess a literary language. Accordingly there was no historical tradition, no contemporary observers who left abundant diaries and revealing collections of letters for the historian to draw upon. Peter himself was practically illiterate until his teens, while his most influential adviser, Alexander Menshikov, could never do more than sign his own name. Although Peter left a copious correspondence, his letters consist largely of formal instructions and announcements. It is only occasionally that a personal note comes through, for the language was simply not up to description, let alone the expression of finely articulated feelings. It consisted of a blend of highflown and formalised Church Slavonic and the purely practical vernacular of civil servants and clerks. There are, it is true, a handful of contemporary accounts of aspects of Peter's reign to be found in the compilations of Sakharov and Tumansky, also a few strangely unremarkable personal memoirs, and copious official records. But it is seldom that we can hear individual voices speak to us across the centuries.

For telling and vivid detail we have to rely largely upon the numerous foreign observers who write in often bewildered amazement of what they found in Russia.

In *Fire and Water* I have tried to tell the story of Peter's life, convey a feel for the man and for the Russia of his time, while never entirely losing sight of the subsequent turn of her history. When thinking of certain episodes which can challenge belief, such as the Red Army in World War II using penal battalions to clear minefields with their feet, there is a temptation to give one's head a shake and dismiss the incident, since it is impossible to understand that anyone could give or indeed obey such an order. To learn about the Russia of Peter's day may help us understand something of its subsequent history. In Russia the price of human life has always been modest and such orders have long been possible; although since Peter never asked of others more than he asked of himself one cannot help feeling that he would have led the battalions through the minefield in person.

CHAPTER ONE

Old Muscovy

To the 17th-century traveller who had spent weeks or even months on the road passing through miserable villages and the occasional poor town, Moscow appeared magnificent. "At this distance few cities in the world make a finer appearance; for it stands on rising ground, and contains many stately churches and monasteries, whose steeples and cupolas are generally covered either with copper gilt or tin plate, which shine blue, gold and silver in the sun."[1] The Jesuit Père Avril found it one "of the most beautiful sights I have ever seen – *viewed from afar*".[2] The qualification is vital, for Moscow did not live up to its first impressions. Visitor after visitor was startled to discover that for all its splendid appearance the city was a miserable place. The houses were crude and poor, "made of ties and pieces of timber let in with joynts, without any gentility or ornament. The town itself gives a noble prospect if you view it from without, but when you come within it it appears very ugly, the streets are irregular without uniformity and the houses built after multifarious manners so that the poorest village in the low countries is a paradise in comparison."[3] Its streets were "very spacious and handsome enough in dry weather, but after the least rain very dirty, and would for some time of the year be rendered quite unpassable were it not for the great quantities of fir posts which being laid across the streets serve instead of a pavement".[4]

The city was built almost entirely of wood, and this not simply through a lack of other materials. It was widely believed that

[1] Bell, p. 12.　　　　　　　　[2] Avril, p. 131.
[3] Struys, p. 121.　　　　　　　[4] Crull, pp. 7–8.

wooden houses were healthier to live in than stone ones, but the citizens of Moscow paid dearly, and often, for their health. When Adam Olearius came to the city in 1634 he "observed whole streets burnt down, the fire having been so violent that it had reduced to ashes some five thousand homes, in so much that most of the inhabitants were forced to live in tents and huts".[5] Homes were easily replaced, however; they could be bought in Skorodom, literally "Quick House", a quarter outside one of the city walls; the purchaser would simply take his new home to pieces and have it brought to the site of his previous residence. Fires were seldom fought; instead they were accepted as an inevitable hazard. When the danger threatened the best course was simply to dismantle one's home and remove it until danger had burnt itself out.

Fire was by no means the only hazard. Seventeenth-century Moscow was an extraordinarily violent city. Robbery and murder were commonplace, and every morning there would be a fresh batch of corpses to be found laid out in the streets. "No night passes without murder, and these come to a peak on Shrove Tuesday. On St. Martin's Eve we counted 15 dead bodies in the Court of Zemsky, a place where they are exposed, that their kindred and friends may know them and take them for their burial. If nobody owns them, they are dragged thence like carrion and thrown into a ditch without any ceremony."[6] In fact the body-count on Shrove Tuesday was a matter of some general interest. It was believed that the more murders there were that night the better the year would turn out, and a moderate death roll was known to inspire considerable discontent.[7] The streets were not exactly safe by day either, and one could expect no help if attacked: "The misery is that no citizen will so much as look out of his window, much less come out of his house, to relieve those that are affronted, so much are they afraid to come into the same misfortune they see others engaged in."[8] Foreigners were particularly subject to violent attack, which could take the most peculiar forms. Somewhat later in the century a certain Korb, secretary to an Austrian ambassador, tells of a foreign captain who dined together with his wife at the house of a boyar.*

[5] Olearius, p. 14.   [6] Ibid., pp. 83-4.
[7] Avril, p. 269.   [8] Olearius, p. 85.

* Strictly speaking the boyars were the highest rank of the so-called service classes, persons who held grants of land in return for service to the czar either military or civil.

After dinner his host invited him to go for a sleigh ride. On their return the captain discovered that his wife had been decapitated and all subsequent investigation failed to solve the mystery.[9]

Yet for all its casual violence and wretchedness Moscow remained a magnificent capital city, and its public life was the perfect expression of the values of old Muscovite culture. It was shaped by an elaborate sense of ritual and unchanging ceremonial. The great religious festivals were all marked by sumptuous stately processions in which czar, patriarch, churchmen and boyars all took their appropriate places, at the proper times and in the proper manner. On Palm Sunday, for example, the czar and his boyars left the Kremlin and proceeded to the *Lobnoe Mesto* on Red Square where they were met by the patriarch and handed palms and willow branches. After a service the patriarch mounted a donkey, which the czar would solemnly lead back to the Cathedral of the Assumption, with a procession of sledges each drawn by six grey horses behind him. Another major ritual was the blessing of the waters on the Feast of the Epiphany. The czar, guarded by twelve companies of musketeers and in full regalia, left the Kremlin together with his court, dressed in furs and cloth of gold, and proceeded to the frozen Moscow river, where again he was received by the patriarch and his retinue. After a service the patriarch blessed his congregation and moved on to a large hole cut in the ice where he stepped on to a richly decorated floating platform, from which he made the sign of the cross over the waters, dipped his crucifix in them, dripping water into a silver vessel, which completed the proceedings.

Such occasions were the very substance of the public life of Muscovy. With the set enactment of their rigidly prescribed patterns they signified, if not an aspiration to timelessness, then at the least a passionate belief in tradition and a fierce resistance to any notion of alteration, progression or change. Affairs were to follow the pattern which they had followed always, and nothing would ever alter. Moscow was the third Rome, the last defender of true Christendom, the successor to Rome and Constantinople, and a fourth Rome there would never be. The czar was of course the supreme figure in this pattern of ritual, his occasional public appearances rendering him a ritualised object

---

The boyars enjoyed the special privilege of sitting on the council which advised the czar. However, the term comes to be used loosely for any Russian nobleman of rank.

[9] Cht., 1866, no. 4, p. 120.

of veneration, as his subjects literally kow-towed before him. He imposed his authority through ceremony, and in this he was encouraged by the boyars who constituted his entourage, mediating between him and his subjects and cutting him off from all other elements.[10] Although the authority he wielded was absolute on a scale unknown to Western rulers, the czar was none the less himself caught up in the series of rituals which informed his public life and which could require him, for example, to spend up to eight hours daily in public prayer. To the rare foreigners that saw him he was the chief part of an elaborate and alien pattern of ceremony:

> The Grand Duke sat in his chair, clad in a long coat, embroidered with pearls, and beset with all sorts of precious stones. He had above his cap which was of marten skins, a crown of gold beset with great diamonds and in his right hand a sceptre of the same metal, and no less rich, and so weighty that he was forced to relieve one hand with the other. On both sides of his majesty's chair young lords, very handsome, both as to face and body, clad in long coats of white damask, with caps of a lynx's skin and white buskins, with chains of gold, which, crossing upon each breast, reached down to their hips. They had laid over their shoulders each a silver axe, whereto they put their hands as if they were going to give strike.[11]

The celebration of customary order was reflected in the rigid patterns set for state banquets at which dishes were brought in and served according to the strictest precedence. The czar would sometimes honour a guest by giving him a beaker of wine from his own hand. The actual food itself was less impressive than the ceremonial. The dishes took so long to arrive that they were frequently cold and almost invariably contained immoderate quantities of garlic. One English ambassador found the czar's banquet "All very handsome had not the silver dishes looked so black they seemed more like lead than silver".[12] The secretary to a Swedish ambassador in the 1680's found a similar blend of ritual and bad food poorly served, when dining with a certain V. V. Golitsyn, at the time the most powerful man in Russia:

[10] Perry, p. 142.   [11] Olearius, p. 17.   [12] Howard, p. 292.

The dishes were offered one by one in order of precedence;
when he had taken enough the boyar waved the dish away and
the next was presented. The dishes were taken down until they
reached the lesser nobles who stood at the foot of the table.
Onions were used generously instead of garlic, the dishes were
mere tin, the soup tureens copper plated with tin. Only the
boyar and his son had silver spoons, ours were of wood ...
The first dish was a raw sheep's head in vinegar, the last melons
and cherries ... Among those who waited upon the boyar and
helped themselves at the foot of the table was a Tartar prince
who had known better days.[13]

Foreigners found that matters were not improved by the Russians' rigid observation of their fasts – children were obliged to
follow the dietary laws from the age of two. In the mid
17th century failure to comply was allegedly punishable by
death. During Holy Week fasts were so severe and rigidly
observed that the entire country closed down. Abstinence
and regulation extended beyond the control of eating: "The
ecclesiastical law commands their abstinence from venery three
days a week, viz, Monday, Wednesday, Friday. After coition they
must bathe before they enter a church."[14]

Similar principles of strict conformity and regulation were
applied to dress and personal appearance. Beards were essential
to personal salvation: "It is most certain that the Russes have
a kind of religious respect and veneration for their beards, and
so much the more because they differ herein from strangers,
which was backed by the humour of their priests alleging that
the holy men of old had worn their beards according to the model
and the picture of their saints."[15] "Thus they will sooner accept
the word of a man who has a beard than the oath of one who
is beardless."[16]

Dress too was a part of the ritual of tradition, for dress never
changed; the notion of fashion was unknown in Russia and the
mode of dress had not altered for generations. "Their shirt they
wear over their drawers girded under the navel (to which they
think a girdle adds strength). None, neither male nor female must
go ungirt for fear of being unblest."[17]

[13] Posselt, vol. ii, pp. 21–2.   [14] Collins, p. 11.
[15] Perry, p. 196.   [16] Collins, p. 69.
[17] Ibid., loc. cit.

Conformity to traditional patterns of dress was actually enforced by decree, suggesting that their symbolic significance was fully appreciated by those anxious to preserve the old ways and protect Russia from the corruption of the West. In 1675 czar Aleksey Mikhailovich, father of Peter the Great, decreed:

> That no man should adopt the habits of Germans and other foreigners, that they should not cut their hair short, nor trim their clothes, nor wear foreign coats or hats, nor should they allow their followers to do so. And should anyone in their following cut their hair short and wear dress after the foreign fashion, they would incur the wrath of the czar and lose their rank.[18]

Everything about Russian culture aimed for continuity, the perpetuation of a secular and religious *status quo* which was held to be perfection, as the year's cycle was observed with the appropriate fasts and rituals both religious and secular. Thus at certain times such as Shrove Tuesday there were mass public walks, each of which involved particular customs and followed particular routes. It is not too much to claim that the cyclical pattern of the ritualised year, and the re-enactment of the past in the present, made for, if not timelessness, then a very particular sense of time and direction. Indeed the notion of time was still geared to the slowly shifting pace of the seasons, being counted in hours after sunrise. There was no attempt to emulate the West and impose the arbitrary rational pattern of human time upon natural time. Russia counted by the sun and not by the clock.

Seventeenth-century Russia displayed a degree of commitment to its traditions that could be total. When the patriarch Nikon sought to revise ecclesiastical ritual and the Old Church Slavonic liturgy which was full of inaccurate translations from the original Greek, he provoked a split in the church known as the schism or *raskol* which persists to this day. Rather than accept seemingly trivial adjustments, such as making the sign of the cross with three as opposed to two fingers, the schismatics fled to the wilds of Siberia, or burnt themselves alive, literally in their thousands – more than 20,000 within the first five years. This violent reaction to seemingly minor modifications can give one some hint of the hold of rigid orthodoxy and tradition upon the Russians of that age.

[18] Ustryalov, vol. iii, pp. 184–5.

It is this attitude which informs the most important and enduring feature of the Russian character; total acceptance and indeed veneration of the authority of the state, an attitude shared by peasant and boyar alike. It was this that accounts for what Tibor Szamuely has described as "the ecstatic rapture, the exaltation bordering on idolatry, with which Russians of all classes learned to regard their country and their state. Instead of 'my country right or wtong' it was 'my country never wrong'. The Russians' insufferable self-righteousness, their unshakeable conviction of moral superiority, the self-glorification that they carried to ridiculous lengths ... would have been less galling to foreigners had they not seemed so groundless, so utterly divorced from the harsh realities of Russian life. It has been hard for outsiders to realise that Russian national feeling is a spiritual emotion largely detached from the mundane things of life, that for centuries past Russia has meant for her people much more than just a country to be loved and defended: 'Russia' was a state of mind, a secular ideal, a sacred idea, an object of almost religious belief."[19]

Certain otherwise puzzling aspects of 17th-century Russia grow somewhat clearer when considered in the light of this fervent commitment. Blind unreflective adherence to their country and way of life made for an altogether uncritical acceptance of authority. Foreign visitors were constantly amazed, for example, at the low price that the natives set upon personal freedom: "Those who are freeborn but poor, do so little value that advantage that they sell themselves with their family for a small matter; nay they are so mindless of their liberty that they will sell themselves a second time after they have recovered it, by the death of their master or some other occasion."[20] In fact it was made a capital offence to sell oneself into slavery – as a means of tax avoidance since free men paid taxes while slaves did not. Korb's comments on Petrine Russia could equally well be applied to earlier times:

The Muscovite nation is closer to slavery than to liberty; all Muscovites whatever their rank, irrespective of person, are beneath the yoke of the most cruel tyranny. As for those who hold important office in the Privy Council, and bear the stately title of grandee, and are entitled to the highest dignities in the land, their very prominence reveals their slavish situation the

[19] T. Szamuely, *The Russian Tradition*, London 1974, p. 60.   [20] Olearius, p. 83.

more clearly; they are loaded with chains of gold whose very magnificence renders them harder to bear: the glittering situation of these slaves stands as a reproach to the baseness of their condition.[21]

Celebration of servility and the unquestioning acceptance of authority are well reflected in the peculiar institutions of Muscovite justice and law. This was derived from a strange sense of equality; all men were equal before the czar, in the very special sense that no one, whatever their rank or station, possessed either as an individual or member of a corporate body any kind of right or privilege which the czar could not revoke at will. The highest ranking noble in the land could be stripped of his wealth overnight, while peasant and noble alike were equal before the knout; *no one* enjoyed the right of immunity from flogging, or indeed any other kind of right or privilege. The rule of law ultimately meant neither more nor less than the arbitrary and unchecked exercise of the will of the czar.

Anyone familiar with the description of life under Stalin provided by Solzhenitsyn and Nadezhda Mandelstam will recall the very considerable contribution made to its quality by "*donos*", or denunciation. "Failure to denounce" was itself a criminal offence, a subsection of the famous clause 58 of the Soviet penal code dealing with political offences. The remarkable continuity of Russian culture is both well known and well founded, and the enduring importance of the *donos* is a case in point. Denunciation was thoroughly encouraged in pre-Petrine Russia, as it would continue to be. Anyone had the right, indeed the duty, to denounce anybody they suspected, regardless of differences in rank, and a successful denunciation could reward the fortunate informer with all that his victim possessed. However, there were drawbacks. In pre-Petrine times at least, unfounded denunciations could be severely punished, a sanction Peter removed when he made denunciation a positive duty. Moreover the actual process was not pleasant. *Both* parties would be arrested and imprisoned, and both subjected to identical processes of interrogation. Interrogation had to culminate in a confession and here again we find similarities between the 17th and 20th centuries. If justice was to take its proper course a confession was essential.

[21] Cht., 1867, vol. i, p. 277.

The accused cannot be condemned although a thousand witnesses come in against him except he confess the fact; and to this end they want not torment to extort confessions.[22]

In other words the essential instrument of interrogation and investigation was judicial torture – to which both denounced and denouncer could be and usually were similarly subjected, presumably until one of them broke. Confession was first sought through "diligent interrogation" and if that failed recourse was taken to the knout. This could be applied in various ways, simple flogging, flogging accompanied by strappado or dislocation of the arms, flogging, strappado and roasting over a slow fire, and occasionally the tearing out of ribs with red-hot pincers. A mere act of confession did not, in the case of serious crimes, enable the accused to escape torture. He would be exposed to it anyway to ensure that he had kept nothing back. Moreover, it was understood that in such situations testimonies were not always reliable, which is why it was generally held that the accused could only be believed when he had told the same story three times in three separate sessions of interrogation.

Beyond interrogation the actual penalties, including decapitation, breaking on the wheel and flogging to death, had a peculiar brutality. False coiners were dispatched by having molten metal poured down their throat, while rapists were gelded: "Of which if he recover well and good, but it is very rare that anybody does."[23] However, the worst fate was reserved for wives who had done away with their husbands. They were buried alive up to their necks in a public place and left to die. Husbands found guilty of an equivalent crime usually escaped with a fine.

A passionate attachment to tradition and authority, blind and unquestioning belief in the moral superiority of their ritualised patterns of culture, with its blend of magnificent public life, savage justice and no less savage casual violence, did not develop in the Russians qualities that impressed their foreign visitors favourably. One of the most intelligent observers of Peter's Russia heads a chapter looking back on earlier days with the question "Used the Russians to be as savage and beastly as reputed?" On reflection he concludes that they had been, associating their condition with an excessively uncritical attitude to their own ways. His opinion is shared by Olearius, writing some

[22] Collins, p. 72. [23] Struys, p. 156.

27

seventy years earlier. "If a man considers the natures and manner of life of the Muscovites he will be forced to avow there cannot be anything more barbarous than that people."[24] A particular aspect of that barbarity was the treatment of women. Marriages were invariably arranged, usually through a go-between, and not infrequently bride and groom would first meet at the altar. On marriage a woman disappeared immediately into the oriental confinement of the co-called *terem* or women's quarter, from which she seldom emerged and where she was kept under rigid discipline. The 16th-century text *Domostroy*, a handbook on the rituals of household management, encourages husbands to beat their wives *nezhno i prilezhno*, "gently and diligently", and always to maintain the strictest discipline in their home. The wife-beating habit died hard. Well into the 18th century a certain Prince Dolgoruky complained to the czar that his daughter had been severely flogged by her husband, who then attempted to starve her to death. The husband in question replied when charged with this barbarous behaviour that he "was not without fault, but whenever she opposed or disobeyed me I beat her personally; she was not well disposed toward me, never listened to my words and used much bad language".[25] Another observer found that:

> Muscovy may well be called the purgatory of women, they being kept under so rigorous a discipline by their husbands that in some places slaves be treated with less severity ... it has been alleged on behalf of the Muscovite house discipline that the women here have very lewd tongues, will drink many a cup of strong liquor, and upon an occasion will not refuse a kindness to a friend.[26]

However, a foreigner might have thought twice about accepting an offer of that kind, since in appearance at least, he would have found the ladies of 17th-century Moscow unusual:

> Muscovite women paint their faces red and white, their teeth black, esteeming blackening teeth an addition to their complexion, with the same intention as our ladies make use of patches. I am apt to believe that their teeth being generally spoiled by their mercurial paints, has obliged them to make

[24] Olearius, p. 177.　　　[25] Soloviev, vol, iv, p. 582.　　　[26] Crull, p. 162.

a virtue of necessity, and by a universal agreement, to cry that up for an ornament, which appears to us the greatest deformity.[27]

Love of "strong liquor" was not restricted to women, indeed it was a love that knew no restriction of any kind, and one which played its own part in Russian rituals:

> Their greatest expression of joy upon festivals is drink and the greater the day the greater their debauches. To see men, women and popes [i.e. priests] reeling in the street is counted no dishonour. After a very great entertainment among the grand ladies, the lady of the feast sends her chief gentleman the next day to inquire of their health and if they got well home, or slept well. The lady answers: "I thank thy lady for her good cheer which made me so merry ... that indeed I know not how I got home."[28]

Olearius reports that when women drank their men under the table, which was their custom, they would sit upon them and continue to drink until they too became unconscious.[29] "Chief gentlemen" were not sent to inquire after the guests' well-being out of mere politeness, since there was always a chance that the guests never got home at all:

> Some of them going home drunk, if not attended with a sober companion, fall asleep upon the snow (a sad cold bed), and there they are frozen to death. If any of their acquaintance chance to pass by, though they see them likely to perish, yet will they not assist them to avoid the trouble of examination if they should die in their hands ... 'Tis a sad sight to see a dozen people brought upright in a sledge frozen to death, some have their arms eaten off by dogs, other their faces, and other have nothing left but bones. Two or three hundred have been brought after this manner in the time of lent.[30]

Drink made for scenes of a quite remarkable coarseness, which one could not advance as being uniquely Russian, but which display that special blend of indelicacy and a brutal and uncaring

[27] Ibid., pp. 239–40.
[29] Ibid., p. 83.
[28] Collins, p. 19.
[30] Ibid., p. 23.

panache which is recognisably a Russian characteristic. Olearius, for example, writes of a drunken lady pilgrim who collapsed naked in the street; a naked man tumbled down beside her and possessed her in front of an admiring public before he too passed out.[31] Korb recalls a tale of high drunken idiocy reflecting a blend of stupidity and benevolence which may again be considered characteristic. A state official entertaining some friends grew very attracted to one of the women present. He proceeded to make everyone very drunk and when the women passed out he dowsed the lights and took the men off to drink some more. They returned to find what he believed to be the woman in question. The host first embraced her, was well received, so possessed her and then invited his friends to follow suit. It was only after they had all obliged that he discovered that the woman in question was his own wife. Whereupon he roared with laughter and congratulated himself on extending his hospitality beyond mere food and drink.[32]

Visitors were surprised by the immorality of the natives. Olearius tells of their licentiousness, bestiality and love of sodomy, which, another observer claims, was practised on a positively "Persian" scale.[33]

> We have seen both men and women come out of the public brothel house stark naked and incite some young people of our retinue to naughtiness by filthy and lascivious expressions.[34]

While it was also widely held that along with their immorality the Russians:

> Love their neighbours as themselves with as much warmth as might be extinguished by a single drop of water.[35]

It might seem too easy to try to explain such behaviour as being the consequence of the patterns of absolutism, and an arbitrary government that created something tantamount to a nation of slaves, yet this surely played its part in shaping national characteristics, particularly with respect to one vital trait: the

[31] Collins, p. 82.
[32] Cht., 1866, vol. iv, p. 85.
[33] Ibid., 1873, vol. ii, p. 22.
[34] Olearius, p. 81.
[35] Cht. 1873, vol. ii, p. 22.

complete lack of anything remotely equivalent to the Western sense of honour. One of the fundamental differences between Western societies and Muscovy was the tremendous importance played in the West by the notion of privilege. To a greater or lesser extent nobility, gentry, guilds, burghers, either individually or as corporate bodies, enjoyed more or less inalienable privileges. The aristocracy in the 17th century was still conscious of itself as a warrior or ex-warrior caste, and the notion of personal honour or "*gloire*" was vital to, say, the French aristocracy of the period. In Russia there was no equivalent distribution of privilege, since the sole privileged person was the czar. There was, it is true, a highly evolved sense of the relative importance of various families, which created the principle of priority of place, or *mestnichestvo*. This consisted of a strictly recorded order of family precedence. It was of such vital significance that a member of a particular family would sooner submit to disgrace and flogging than sit below a member of a junior family. This created problems enough in peacetime. In time of war it made the whole notion of chain of command impossible to operate. Thus in wartime *mestnichestvo* was deemed to be suspended; all officers were held to be *bez mesta*, without place, while the fighting was on. However, this evolved sense of relative dignity did not bring with it a sense of personal honour as this was understood in the West; there was nothing which could evolve into a sense of personal morality; no sense of the gentleman or *honnête homme*. Indeed personal dignity of that kind could scarcely be expected in a country in which there was no one who did not run the risk of a public flogging, and in which to be flogged was not held to be any kind of disgrace.

This lack of an equivalent to the Western sense of honour is reflected in a number of ways. Russians appeared to foreigners positively to pride themselves on dishonesty and sharp practice. "Russian conceptions of honesty are so corrupt that the art of cheating is held to be a sign of great mental capacity."[36] An example, of in this case somewhat bemused sharp practice, is provided by the case of one Prince Theodore Khoteshovsky, who was flogged for selling the same estate twice over.[37] Lack of a sense of honour had its advantages however. Duelling was virtually unknown to the Muscovites. The "*point d'honneur*" escaped

---

[36] *Ibid.*, 1866, vol. iv, p. 78.   [37] Sakharov, p. 68.

them entirely. They were ready enough to abuse one another savagely but did not often take matters further:

> They seldom come to fighting, or if they do, when their spirits are exalted by the strength of the liquor, it is done with their fists, or switches or a cudgel, or perhaps by soundly kicking one another about the belly, for in the height of their rage they are sure to aim for the codpiece.[38]

This lack of a sense of *gloire* did not encourage the Russian nobility to love war. When foreign officers reminded them that the nobility of Europe prided itself on its warlike virtues they tended to reply: "That just shows that there are more fools than wise men in the world. Always believing discretion to be the better part of valour they found the notion of fighting for one's honour derisory. Their land was fertile enough and they had all they wanted. The nobleman who has no knowledge of rich clothes and foreign delicacies was lucky to be ignorant of them. Their life was too comfortable to be abandoned in the vain pursuit of honour. They understood the virtue of defensive wars, and defensive wars alone. They saw no benefit to themselves in conquest and were utterly lacking in the *point d'honneur*."[39]

Their rejection of the Western honour code was only part of a more general and violent rejection of the values of the West. This was held to be heretical, pernicious and corrupt; its culture to be resisted at all costs, witness czar Aleksey Mikhailovich's decrees against the shaving of beards and the adoption of Western dress. Of course the rejection was by no means total. From the reign of Ivan the Terrible on we find Western architects, artisans, doctors and artists in Muscovy, while foreign merchants were accorded favourable trading agreements. Boris Godunov encouraged Dutchmen, Danes and Hanseatic merchants to come to Russia and by 1638 there were Muscovite troops "trained according to the German discipline" with French, German and Scottish officers.[40] However, foreign residents were segregated. They were confined to the Foreign Quarter, the *Nemetskaya Sloboda*, in the NW region of modern Moscow, then a separate settlement laid out like a small northern European town. Its inhabitants enjoyed considerable freedom within its limits, including freedom of worship, and the community of Scots, Germans,

---

[38] Crull, p. 142.   [39] Cht., 1873, vol. ii, p. 107.   [40] Olearius, p. 86.

Danes, Dutch and Englishmen all maintained their own traditions, modes of dress and local customs. They enjoyed more immediate access to the West than any Muscovite, and were able to run their households along European lines. However, there were restrictions designed to prevent them from diffusing the corruption of their ways; for example they were not permitted to own serfs or to employ Orthodox servants.

Foreigners were tolerated rather than welcomed, and regarded with a grave suspicion which could give rise to dangerous misunderstandings. When Olearius demonstrated the principle of the pinhole camera by blacking off a room and making a small aperture in the window, projecting an image of men walking upside down on the opposite wall, it was generally concluded that he must be a sorcerer. Olearius also tells of a Dutch surgeon, very popular at court, who was seen playing his lute while a skeleton hanging in his room moved slightly in the wind. That was enough. He was nearly burnt for sorcery, obliged to leave the country and the skeleton was publicly destroyed.[41] A Lithuanian officer serving in Moscow fell ill and was visited by a Polish doctor. They conversed in Latin and the doctor advised his patient to sprinkle *cramor Tartari*, cream of Tartar, on his food. A Russian soldier present at the interview concluded that they were considering defecting to the Crimean Tartars, and they had the utmost difficulty in establishing their innocence.

Suspicion of the West was clearly reflected in the almost total restriction on foreign travel. To attempt to leave Russia was an offence punishable by death:

> By travelling abroad they might grow enamoured with the sweet taste of liberty other nations enjoy ... They were not only prohibited to go abroad into other countries, but also persons of a high rank debarred from all converse with foreign ministers in their own country without the Great Duke's express permission.[42]

In fact the single experiment at sending Russians abroad had not been a great success. In 1603 czar Boris Godunov had dispatched four young noblemen to study in England. None returned and one became an Anglican priest. Despite repeated requests that they be repatriated, on that occasion at least the

[41] *Ibid.*, pp. 77–8.　　　　　[42] Crull, p. 176.

33

British government declined to return them to their almost certain death. So rare indeed was foreign travel of any kind that in 1698 a frontier post on the Livonian border, Neuhausen, recorded the passage of precisely two travellers in six months, and Livonia was the preferred route to Germany and Holland. By the same token foreign visitors had great difficulty in getting into Muscovy. They were only admitted if they could show that they were coming at the express invitation of a person of rank.

From time to time Russian diplomats did of course travel abroad on embassies, and were required to leave hostages behind them against a possible non-return. It must be said that when abroad their conduct was not invariably exemplary. In 1687 some envoys returning from a mission to the court of Louis XIV, where they had received an unfriendly reception, broke the royal seals on their baggage and began to trade openly in furs and fabrics: forgetting their ambassadorial rank to become merchants, "preferring their personal profit to the honour of their master".[43] When the king sent an officer to order them to desist he was insulted by their servants, one of whom took a dagger to him.

Rigid conservatism, passionate adherence to the ordained patterns and values of orthodoxy, total subjection to the unlimited power of the czar, a savage code of justice, no hint of the values of Renaissance humanism, and private habits and practices that appear brutish, vile and violent – the image of old Muscovy seems singularly black and cheerless. Certainly it appeared so to Western eyes. Yet one must recall how far removed these visitors were from the country that they observed in horrified amazement. For all its ignorance, superstition and seeming degradation, this was still the *Matushka Rossiya*, the Mother Russia, which has always inspired a savage attachment in its inhabitants that goes far beyond European conceptions of patriotism and nationalism, and which antedates these by centuries. Russia was after all Christendom's frontier, its bulwark against infidel Turks and Tartars. Russia had fought and would continue to fight the enemies of Christendom for centuries in regular and unremitting war. Moreover its traditions, its ceremonies, its ecclesiastical and domestic rituals, its manners, inspired and inspire in Russians a quite extraordinary love together with a strange yet deepseated sense of security and reassurance. It offered them the image of an organic society firmly rooted in its past, proof

[43] Coll., 1881, vol. xxxiv, p. 17.

against change and corruption, containing within it, for all its shortcomings, a kind of Christian truth, goodness, spirituality which were felt to stand in total and favourable contrast to the dispersed, materialistic and egotistic values of the West. It was felt to be a truly Christian culture which preferred to material progress and personal freedom an almost mystical sense of wholeness, rightness and emotional warmth.

Religious faith and belief in the culture were both inseparable and total. It is a kind of adherence which the outsider finds inexplicable nor can it be properly explained or justified. However, to understand virtually any aspect of Russian history, to the present day, it is necessary to accept the existence of this faith in the Russian idea, a faith which, quite necessarily, transcends all reason. As the poet Tyutchev wrote:

> Russia cannot be fathomed by the mind
> Or measured by a common yardstick
> She has a stature all of her own
> Russia can only be believed in.

CHAPTER TWO

The Early Years and a Mutiny

Peter's father, czar Aleksey Mikhailovich, 1645–75, enjoyed a reign that was anything but uneventful. It was an almost uninterrupted succession of wars, with Turkey, Poland, Sweden and rebellions, including the famous revolt of the cossack Stenka Razin, who set Southern and Eastern Russia alight, and whose name, like that of Pugachev a century later, has come to embody the spirit of a free wild life of cossack rampage. Aleksey Mikhailovich's reign also saw the *raskol*, the schism that has split orthodoxy ever since and which did irreparable damage to the orthodox church by driving so many of its most fervent adherents into dissent. However, one may seek to explain that singular degree of submissiveness which the church subsequently showed in its dealings with the state there is no doubt that over the years much of its energy was sapped by the shism.

For thirteen years Aleksey Mikhailovich fought a bloody and bitter war with Poland and with the Swedes. He proved singularly unsuccessful against the latter, and in 1661 the peace of Kardis was signed, a treaty which recognised Sweden's title to the Baltic provinces of Ingria and Livonia, and which ensured Swedish domination of the Baltic for half a century. Peace with Poland was concluded at Andrussovo in 1667. This gave Russia both Kiev and Smolensk together with effective control over much of the Southern Ukraine.

The relative success of Aleksey Mikhailovich's reign owes much to the role of two outstanding statesmen. The first, Afansiy Ordin Nashchekin, was a brilliant diplomat, who knew both German and Latin and was sympathetic to Western ways. He was also, uniquely, a supremely honest man. It was he who was largely responsible for negotiating peace with Sweden and Poland, and eventually he became what amounted to chancellor of Russia. He also brought about important domestic reforms. He encouraged trade with the West, and also commissioned, in 1667, the construction of Russia's first ship, the *Orel* or *Eagle*, which eventually sailed down the Volga to Astrakhan before being burnt by Stenka Razin. Among his other achievements was the creation of a postal system between Russia, Poland and Courland, and the introduction of bills of exchange to assist trade.

Ordin Nashchekin was disgraced in 1671 and retired to a monastery. However, his successor Artamon Matveev was in many ways no less able. By 1672 he was the chief adviser of the czar and he too was sympathetic towards the West. His house was arranged on Western lines, with painted ceilings, thick carpets, portraits and clocks; all these apparently being objects which the Muscovites viewed with wonder. Moreover his wife, who may have been of Scottish origin, was not confined to the seclusion of the *terem*. She drove boldly round Moscow in her own carriage, whereas Muscovite ladies usually went abroad in closely curtained litters. Matveev introduced the czar to Western culture – to the point of having plays and musical performances put on at court; traditionally all forms of juggling, games and acting had been considered the devil's work.

In 1647 the czar had married Maria Miloslavskaya, a member of a powerful and ambitious family. She died in 1669 having borne thirteen children, five sons, of which two, Ivan and Fedor, survived, and eight healthy daughters. Shortly after her death Aleksey Mikhailovich met in Matveev's house a seventeen-year-old ward and pupil of his, Natalya Kirillovna Naryshkina. The czar was very taken by her and in 1670 made her his wife. The family of a czar's wife could expect to benefit hugely from their situation, both in prestige and material advantage, so that the czar's second marriage was both a blow to the Miloslavskys and correspondingly favoured the Naryshkins; an insignificant but plentiful and ambitious family who flocked to court at once. They were regarded as pushy upstarts, and inevitably resented, but this did not prevent them from gaining their share of good fortune. Late in 1670 Natalya's father Kyril, together with Matveev, were raised to the second rank in the court hierarchy – the rank of boyar being the first. Matveev became one two years later. The promotion was to celebrate the birth on May 30, 1672, of a son, Peter Alekseevich, the future Emperor of All the Russias.

When one tries to understand how a man of such monstrous energy, savage impatience with tradition, passion for innovation and reform at any cost could have emerged from the steady, warm and conservative heart of old Muscovy, facts are precious little help. It is true that the reign of Aleksey Mikhailovich saw steadily increasing diplomatic and cultural contact with the West. Both his advisers were, by Russian standards, outstandingly cultivated men, and both persons of high intelligence to boot. It can never be seriously maintained that Peter was single-handedly responsible for turning his country towards Europe. It was a movement which he accelerated, violently, and it is in this that his achievement and the fascination of his style of rulership and personality reside. Without him Russia would have turned to the West in due course, but the movement would have been a more gentle one.

It is just possible that from early childhood onwards he might have enjoyed some awareness of the value of European ways. It would be tempting to suggest that his mother's contact with Matveev and his possibly Scottish and certainly liberated wife might have helped push the young czarevich in that direction. Yet in later years the Naryshkins were to prove diehard traditionalists, and there was no question of his mother displaying any kind of affection for Western ways. She was a stupid and extremely limited woman who would never have any understanding of her son's bewildering and unorthodox energies, which she continued to her dying day to view with suspicious alarm. Whatever her exposure to the Matveev household might have been she remained utterly committed to the values of old Muscovy.

The little we know of Peter's earliest years suggests that he enjoyed an intense version of ideal Russian childhood, a world of softness, indulgence at the hands of women and an almost stifling physical and emotional warmth. The baby is watched over by a bevy of adoring ladies whose whole life seems dedicated to its comfort and well-being and the avoidance of anything remotely approximating a draught. The mood will be recognised instantly by anyone who has enjoyed a traditional Russian childhood, and its atmosphere has been superbly evoked by Goncharov in the section of his *Oblomov* entitled "Oblomov's

Dream". Peter's early childhood appears to have been a time of stifling luxury if we are to judge by the objects which then surrounded him. His cradle was a blend of magnificence and softness, the perfect symbol of an overheated royal nursery world. It was covered with Turkish velvet, upholstered in yellow cloth, with straps trimmed in red Venetian velvet. Its eiderdown was edged with gold, as was the pillow, which might have been uncomfortable and indeed would have exposed the newly born Peter to possible suffocation. At six months he had summer and winter garments of white satin edged in ruby coloured moire, with sable britches stitched with gold, trimmed with lace and with pearl fastenings. His buttons were emeralds mounted in gold. His nursery was covered with red cloth and the furniture had white coverings with embroidered edges.

In short Peter was born into a soft, indolent and magnificent old Russia, utterly foreign to his temperament. One might even suppose that these childhood surroundings actually aggravated when they were designed to soothe. At all events whatever his early response may have been, Peter would never feel tempted to relapse into the secure and comfortable world of old Muscovy.

Yet even now his nursery world was by no means entirely one of indolence. At the age of three Matveev gave him a little Western-style closed carriage, sprung, with glass windows. Trimmed with gold, lined with velvet and with wheels of gilded bronze, it was drawn by a couple of diminutive bay ponies, and the three-year-old was accompanied by an escort of six dwarfs similarly mounted. We find more tangible evidence of an early sense of energy in Peter's choice of toys. Play would always remain an essential feature of Peter's life, to his last month, and would provide the mainspring of many of his most important actions. Certainly by the age of three his interests are already turning towards war games. In June 1675 he is made two bows decorated in red and gold, a little single-headed axe, a plain axe, a quiver, an ambassadorial axe, a hammer, and a series of maces and clubs. By December he is getting little cannon mounted on carriages. The quantity of toys made for him continues at the same impressive rate and the emphasis is without exception upon war.

We know little enough about his early education, probably because there was precious little of it. The need to educate a possible future ruler of Russia carefully and elaborately did not appear to have been acutely felt. Certainly at the age of sixteen

Peter was almost completely illiterate and innumerate, while his knowledge of literature never extended far beyond the Scriptures and his spelling would always remain at the mercy of his whim.

His first known tutor was an amiable drunk not entirely lacking in ability. Traditionally Nikita Zotov was believed to have been summoned to attend on Peter's father in 1677. He was so frightened that he fainted in the antechamber but started work on March 12 of that year, being rewarded by two sumptuous outfits, into one of which he changed immediately. Peter was apparently interested in works of history, illustrated and with a military emphasis, and learnt the New Testament by heart.[1] However, it has recently been established that Zotov, who was to play an important part in Peter's subsequent rituals of ceremonial intoxication, could not have started tutoring before 1683, so that we must assume that any early education Peter may have received has simply passed unrecorded – an indication in itself of the modest degree of importance attached to it.

Peter probably spent a lot of time in these early years with his parents at their country "palace" in Preobrazhenskoe (The Transfiguration), a village on the left bank of the Yauza river beyond Sokolniki and some $4\frac{1}{2}$ miles distant from the Kremlin. There Aleksey Mikhailovich had plays performed and could also indulge his passion for hawking and hunting. The palace itself was by all accounts a modest enough building. Some years later a visitor considered it an old-fashioned wooden house scarcely worth 100 thalers, with no more than six rooms of any size, standing in a poor and narrow street.[2] However, Peter was to spend much of his youth there, and the village of Preobrazhenskoe was to be the birthplace of the Russian army.

We get occasional glimpses of him as a boy, although these are all suspiciously consonant with his future character. Thus when he and his mother were watching the czar receive an Austrian ambassador from their apartments, the three-year-old Peter is said to have impatiently opened a door, breaking protocol by permitting the foreigners to see the czarina and her son.[3]

Peter's father died suddenly in 1676. His reign had been a remarkably successful one. Known as "the quiet czar" in contrast to his youngest son, he was well loved for his gentleness and humanity, although like Peter he was capable of violent rage and had been known to tear tufts from his councillors' beards. He

[1] Sakharov, pp. 19–21.   [2] Busching, 1786, vol. xx, p. 355.   [3] Ustryalov, vol. i, p. 10.

was a conscientious and diligent ruler, although he never stepped beyond the patterns of tradition. An extremely devout man, well read in ecclesiastical literature, it has been estimated that he spent some eight months of the year fasting.[4] Moreover he had a gift rare enough in absolute rulers, who have more need of it than most, the ability to find able and honest advisers. In this respect he seems to have done better than his son Peter.

On his deathbed he named his eldest son Fedor his successor. Fedor was fourteen at the time and, like his full-brother Ivan, suffered from very poor health. He was of course a Miloslavsky on his mother's side, and his succession meant the eclipse of the Naryshkin faction. It has been suggested that Matveev attempted to secure the nomination of the four-year-old Peter to the throne, but this is not likely. However, there can be no doubt that the Miloslavskys were suspicious of Matveev, whom they had exiled for crimes against the state within six months of Fedor's succession. He went into exile protesting his innocence furiously, but it is clear that innocent or guilty the Miloslavskys would have ensured his disgrace.

The situation of Peter's mother was now considerably altered. No longer the czar's wife, she was confined, at the least, to the obscurity of the *terem*. Her public role was ended and the Miloslavskys were in the saddle once again.

For all his physical shortcomings, which were considerable, Fedor was an educated and enlightened young ruler. He instituted certain important changes. For the first time a clear distinction was drawn between military and civil service. Where in the past all nobles had served in the army in time of need, while some of their number had also played their part in the civil administration, the two forms of service were now distinguished; a distinction which would be further clarified and defined by Peter in due course. Fedor also abolished the preposterous practice of *mestnichestvo*, solemnly destroying the books recording relative rank upon which the entire system was based. This made it easier to make appointments based on merit alone, and here too we may see a pale anticipation of the future policies of Peter.

Fedor was encouraged by the advice of yet another remarkable councillor, Prince Vasiliy Vasilievich Golitsyn. A member of one of the oldest families in Russia he was an intelligent, able and enlightened man. He knew German, Greek and Latin and was to

[4] Collins, p. 123.

play a prominent part in Russian life throughout the next thirteen years.

Fedor's first wife died in 1681 and their only son died soon after her. Against all medical advice Fedor re-married some nine months later, February 24, 1682. By April 27 he was dead, dying without nominating his successor.

Order of succession was not established by law. It was universally held that the czar must come from the descendants of Mikhail Fedorovich Romanov, but it was up to each czar to nominate his particular successor. This was usually his eldest son, who tended to be declared the heir at his majority, and who would receive the formal blessing of his father on the latter's deathbed. Fedor had made no such provision and although Ivan, his full-brother, had reached majority Fedor had not designated him since his health – he was almost blind – clearly put his ability to rule in question. Thus on Fedor's death Russia was left without a ruler, the choice being between Ivan and Peter, a Miloslavsky and a Naryshkin.

Support for Peter extended well beyond the Naryshkin family. Ironically enough it was the more conservative elements that rallied to him. The boyars who chose Peter were hostile to the late Fedor Mikhailovich for "having abandoned the ancient ways, favouring Polish dress and ornament and above all for abolishing *mestnichestvo*".[5] They looked to Peter and the Naryshkins as a conservative force which would restore the old ways, as did the patriarch Ioakim, another staunch traditionalist. When the news of Fedor's death was tolled out an assembly of all office holders was called in some haste. Peter's supporters expected trouble, and some of them wore armour under their robes as the crowd gathered in front of one of the Kremlin cathedrals. The patriarch accompanied by persons of high rank went out to them, announced the death of Fedor and asked them which of the two half-brothers should be czar. Although official history would have it that the assembly called with one voice for Peter Alekseevich, there were in fact also those who tried to acclaim his brother. But for the moment the Naryshkin faction prevailed, and it was announced that the ten-year-old Peter had been chosen to rule Muscovy.

Peter's supporters now made a serious mistake. They were content to allow effective power to rest with Peter's mother and her

[5] Pogodin, p. 65.

family rather than appoint a strong regent at once. Peter's mother did not have the capacity to cope with a potentially explosive situation while no member of her family had ever displayed significant political ability of any kind. It is true that Natalya seems to have recognised her own limitations quickly enough. One of her first actions was to recall Matveev from exile. However, it took him the best part of three weeks to get to Moscow, by which time the damage was done.

The effective leader of the Miloslavskys was a twenty-four-year-old woman of remarkable energy and resolve. Peter's redoubtable half-sister Sophia Alekseevna was anything but a lady of old Muscovy. She rejected out of hand the passive and secluded role that Russian traditions reserved for her sex. An intelligent, in many ways open-minded, and fiercely ambitious person, she was out for power, combining a good sense of political tactics with determination, not to say ruthlessness. A contemporary describes her as follows:

Although she had neither read nor studied Machiavelli she knows his principles instinctively, particularly the one which maintains that there is no crime that may not be justified in matters of politics.[6]

Another observer, Matveev's own son, suggested that she envied foreign princesses able to rule in their own right, and that her heroine was the Byzantine empress Pulcheria, who seized the throne from her weak brother Theodorus and reigned successfully for many years.[7] An 18th-century historian of Peter's reign described her as a princess of "masculine spirit, unlimited ambition and great parts".[8]

The medium for her bid for power was to be the *streltsy* (literally shooters or musketeers), the only force in Muscovy approaching a standing army. (In those days the nation relied on an annual mass levy of all those with service obligations with their attendants as the basis for its army.) The only permanent organised force of the time, the *streltsy*, combined the function of soldiers, riot police and firefighters. They were divided into regiments and wore uniforms: scarlet, dark blue or green over-garments, with red or gold sashes, caps of yellow velvet trimmed with fur, and boots. They constituted something tantamount to

[6] *Russ. Star.*, 1891, vol. lxxi, p. 258.   [7] Ustryalov, vol. i, p. 27.   [8] Gordon, P., p. 87.

a separate and hereditary estate, in which sons succeeded their fathers. They also recruited, taking only free men, while they were officered by members of the nobility. Their chief means of support were the special trading privileges they were granted, and these appear to have given them a steadily increasing sense of autonomy. In the early 1680's there were signs that the *streltsy* were beginning to get out of control. Admittedly hostile observers describe them as having become a law unto themselves. They had grown increasingly concerned with trade, as opposed to the defence of the realm, had purchased prominent stalls in the best sections of the merchants' quarter and were growing more and more insubordinate and confident in their own power and immunity. "They made themselves so independent of all authority, that they ruled over themselves as if they had, so to speak, established their own republic, forgetting all their allegiance and obligation to serve."[9]

By the spring of 1682 they had grown restless and insubordinate to the point of mutiny, while Sophia and the Miloslavskys worked hard to increase the agitation, going to them secretly and turning them against the Naryshkins. At the time there were nine regiments of *streltsy* in Moscow, numbering some 14,000 men. In fact they were by no means all won over to the Miloslavsky cause, many of them were wavering. However, the Naryshkins did not help. One of Natalya's first actions was to reward her family richly, promoting her twenty-two-year-old brother Lev Kirillovich to the rank of boyar, a particularly gross piece of nepotism even by the standards of the day, and, in the circumstances, dreadfully unwise.

In late April the *streltsy* began to turn against their officers, complaining that they taxed them illegally and prevented them from pursuing their proper business as tradesmen, obliging them to work on their estates and even build homes for them. These complaints had already been voiced to the late czar Fedor, and on his death the men became increasingly insistent, unruly and vociferous, demanding justice – which meant the heads of their commanders. Otherwise they threatened to sack the city, and revenge themselves "on all traitors who deceive our rulers" – nominating that favourite Russian target, the enemy within.

Faced with an immediate threat from the only armed force in Moscow the new rulers panicked. No attempt was made to deter-

[9] Tumansky, vol. i, p. 124.

mine the justice of the complaints. Instead sixteen commanders were dismissed and condemned to be flogged for abusing their power, although the patriarch did expressly forbid the men to take justice into their own hands. The men agreed. The commanders were arrested and beaten for two hours a day until they restored to their men the money they were alleged to have taken from them. It was a process in the course of which "many sticks were broken and many thousands of roubles changed hands". The business was conducted in the government's name, but according to the will of the *streltsy* . . . who acted as judges. The beatings only ceased when they called *enough*. Some of the least popular commanders were beaten twice a day.[10] In the meantime the *streltsy* were busy lynching their junior officers, tossing them off high buildings to the chant of *lyubo, lyubo* – "It pleases, it pleases." Discipline had evaporated and the men were quite beyond any kind of government control.

The capital stood poised for days of a violence which would only be equalled twice more in Moscow's history, by Napoleon in 1812 and the Bolsheviks in 1917. The impact of the imminent *streltsy* revolt upon Peter was to be both profound and traumatic. Throughout his adult life he would display a surprising capacity for panic, over-reacting savagely to the slightest threat of mutiny or treason coming from the supporters of old Muscovy, even, or rather especially, if the threat came from his own kith and kin. It is not an exaggeration to suggest that the building of St Petersburg derived ultimately from a deep-seated fear and mistrust of Moscow, a fear which was about to be instilled in the young czar by the events of the next few days. Although we know little of the boy's immediate response to the mutiny, his subsequent behaviour, over the years, suggests that it went very deep indeed; it does not require much imagination to guess at the kind of impression the events that now follow made upon Peter's young mind.

The private apartments of the Kremlin were kept as quiet and secluded as any monastery. Only the patriarch and close relatives of the czarina were admitted; doctors were only summoned in the final resort, and even they were seldom allowed to see the face of their patients. The seclusion of the *terem* was virtually inviolate, and in its atmosphere the young Peter still continued to play. Aged ten he had rosy cheeks, large shining eyes, dark

[10] Ustryalov, vol. i, p. 24.

red hair that curled naturally, and was lively both in movement and in gesture.[11] As revolt and mutiny brewed in the city he continued in blithe ignorance to place daily orders for spears and various kinds of firearm right up to the moment the rebellion exploded.

Matveev made his way back to Moscow as fast as he could. En route he had been warned that the *streltsy* were making trouble, but he hurried on although not exactly popular with them. "Matveev's house is built of *streltsy* bones," they were known to mutter, blaming him for losses incurred in past campaigns. He arrived in Moscow on May 15 and went directly to the Kremlin. It was a date that was marked with blood; the anniversary of Boris Godunov's murder of the czarevich Dmitri in 1598 – and a great deal more would flow before May 15, 1682, was out.

Peter must have been issuing the day's request for yet more military toys just about the time that the *streltsy* regiments heard the ring of the *nabat* or tocsin, as agitators galloped through their quarters crying that the Naryshkins had murdered the czarevich Ivan. They assembled by regiment and advanced in military order with drums, standards and cannon. Before them they bore a vessel with consecrated water and an especially powerful icon, the Virgin of Znamensky, which the Miloslavskys had just had restored and had obligingly made available. They set off in bright sunshine, but as they approached the Kremlin heavy clouds gathered and darkened the sky, a wind got up making their banners wave and sending up flurries of dust.[12]

Immediately after Matveev's arrival a meeting of the czar's council was called. It was only as it broke up that Prince Fedor Urusov came to Matveev with the news that mutinous *streltsy* were on the move and had already passed through the city gate. Matveev called the patriarch, warned Natalya and ordered the duty force of *streltsy*, the Stremyanny regiment, to stand to and shut the Kremlin gate. It was much too late, the mutineers were already streaming in. Discipline had collapsed as they crowded across the Moscow river, and the regiments melted into a violent howling mob. It sealed off the Kremlin, and crowding up to the Faceted Palace called for the heads of the Naryshkins, challenging them to bring out czarevich Ivan. An 18th-century historian subsequently observed that their lawless con-

[11] Ustryalov, vol. i, p. 15.   [12] Tumansky, vol. i, p. 265.

duct was sufficient refutation of the preposterous notion that all men were equal, since persons of birth would never have behaved like that.[13] Indeed 18th-century guards officers would prove themselves infinitely more discreet and circumspect when it came to assassinating czars.

The Naryshkin faction conducted itself with dignity and considerable courage. Natalya, accompanied by the patriarch, Matveev, Prince M. Yu. Dolgoruky, the commander-in-chief of the mutineers, and the Prince of Circassia, led Peter and his brother out to the top of the Red Steps opposite the Cathedral of the Annunciation to show the mob that Ivan was still alive. At first his identity was in doubt; *streltsy* climbed up the steps, some even clambering on ladders, to ask if he really was the czarevich, to which he replied that he was and that he had suffered at no man's hand. The mob was appeased for a moment, but then started to call for the head of Natalya's brother, Ivan Naryshkin, for allegedly trying on the czar's crown. This brought Matveev forward. He tried to calm the rebels, reminding them of their past glories, while the patriarch also preached calm. It might have worked, but at that moment the hot-headed Dolgoruky, misreading the situation completely, came out and began to abuse the men, telling them to go home at once. Without further ado they stormed the steps, snatched him and tossed him down on to the waiting spears below. Matveev went next. They tore the old man from Natalya's arms, while Peter and Ivan stood by in helpless tears. Down in the square drums were beating, the tocsin rang out and the mob chanted its cry of *lyubo* as flying bodies were caught on the spears below. By the time they had done with him Matveev was utterly dismembered, no limb remaining joined to his body.

The *streltsy* then called out that "the time has come, and who shall we take next", and proceeded to invade the czar's private apartments while Natalya took Peter to the Faceted Palace and those with her made for whatever cover they could find.

The mutineers poured through the Kremlin in search of "traitors" and when they found them they carried them out and tossed them to the crowd below, calling "catch" as they threw them. However, they had as yet failed to find the chief traitor, Natalya's brother Ivan, whom she had managed to hide.

The *streltsy* acted with a selective violence. They did not harm

[13] *Ibid.*, vol. iv, p. 242.

Peter or his mother, they did not touch the patriarch, they did not lynch indiscriminately. They were out for specific "traitors", Matveev, Ivan Naryshkin, and in this respect at least they were controlled. There was less control outside the Kremlin, where there was plenty of indiscriminate raping, looting and score-settling; in other words Russian soldiery went on a very stand-ard rampage. Drunken *streltsy* were to be seen staggering about the city dressed in rich boyars' robes, male and female, or selling stolen jewellery for the price of a drink.[14] They displayed occasional flashes of that stupid yet farcical violence which is the hallmark of every Russian army. Some drunken soldiers burst into the house of Prince Dolgoruky's father to apologise for kil-ling his boy in the heat of the moment, and to ask for something to eat and drink. While they were feasting the old man observed quietly to his distraught wife that "the pike may be gone, but its teeth can still bite". The remark was reported by a servant, whereupon they took out the eighty-year-old, cut him to pieces, tossed him on a muck heap and covered his body with a quantity of salt fish removed from his store house, "as if he were given that fish to eat".[15]

Curiously enough as night came the *streltsy* proceeded quietly back to their quarters, leaving the Kremlin under guard. On the night of the 15th and those that followed it the streets of Moscow remained perfectly quiet.[16] But next morning they were back in force, flooding into the Kremlin and calling for Ivan Naryshkin's head. Sophia considered him to be the last serious threat to her position, for the time being, and needed his death at all costs. The *streltsy* searched hard for him all day, but failed to find him hidden, together with Matveev's son, in a store room full of feather bedding, with the door left half open to suggest that it had been searched already.

In the city itself the lynching continued – among the victims were two German doctors suspected of poisoning the late czar with their attentions. The fate of one of the doctors was sealed when the *streltsy* looted his house and discovered pieces of dis-membered cuttle fish in his store room. It was immediately con-cluded that he was a sorcerer who kept snakes.[17] We can get an impression of that day from the account of the Danish resident, a friend of one of the doctors with whom he was confused with

[14] Tumansky, vol. i, pp. 271–2.   [15] *Ibid.*, vol. i. pp. 153–4.
[16] Pogodin, p. 49.   [17] Tumansky, vol. iv, p. 268.

nearly fatal consequences. He was arrested in his house by a body of *streltsy* who decided, for reasons best known to themselves, that he should be taken to see Sophia in the Kremlin:

As I reached the Red Square a colonel of the *streltsy* . . . was killed, and there were many corpses scattered about which had met lamentable ends, this frightened me considerably, but the most terrifying thing was that when various *streltsy* saw me approach they called out that I was Doctor Daniel, the traitor and sorcerer, and was to be handed over to them. My escort had all it could do to keep them back, calling out that I was not Doctor Daniel but an envoy who had to speak with the czar. As I approached the Kremlin gate it was opened for me and shut behind me at once. I met numerous *streltsy* dragging the naked corpse of the doctor's son along . . . . As I came to the great square large numbers of *streltsy* saw me and at once the drums began to beat, and the tocsin rang which was their sign that they were about to kill. Almighty God raised my spirits, and my *streltsy* kept calling on them to be still, since I was an ambassador who had to talk to their majesties. They stepped aside for me and I rode up to the stone steps, went up to another staircase where the Princess Sophia Alekseevna was standing with various gentlemen. I wished to advance but my escort could no longer clear the way for me, since it was so crowded that one could have walked across the heads of the throng. Prince Ivan Khovansky came out and called to the *streltsy*, asking them if it pleased them that Natalya Kirilovna Naryshkina leave the court, and they replied that it did. . . . Khovansky turned round, saw me, and asked me why I had come. I pointed to the *streltsy* and told him that they had brought me here. [He approaches and Sophia, after a short discussion, waves him away in a friendly fashion. Khovansky orders his escort to see him home.] As I went down, the *streltsy* below waited to see me thrown over like the others, but when they saw my escort bring me down they clustered round me asking why I had been up there, and why they had let me go. Many still supposed me to be Doctor Daniel. My *streltsy* shouted to them that I was an ambassador, and had spoken with the princess. They tried to bring me to my horse but were unable to for some time because of the press. I went out through another gate where numerous *streltsy* ran up to attach themselves to my escort. I was warned to proceed slowly and calmly if I wished to get home alive, and when I got there I was greeted as one returned from the dead. I was by then accompanied by some two hundred *streltsy* and I ordered as much wine and vodka for them as they could drink. In the meantime three of their leaders came to me and asked me for money. I agreed and thought I could settle for some twenty roubles, whereupon they laughed most insolently and asked for a thousand, whereupon I got extremely angry. They went on to demand satisfaction or otherwise they would kill everyone in the house, since they were now in power and everyone had to tremble before them and they would go unpunished for any action they might commit. . . . [He informed them that he simply could not raise such a sum and after some bargaining it was agreed that each man present was to receive half a rouble.] When they emerged the other *streltsy* would not agree and demanded a rouble apiece, but the leaders answered that they had agreed on half a rouble with the head of the house and could not go back on their word and they would have to be content with half a rouble a head. They all fell silent: I fetched the money, wrapped each half rouble piece in a separate bit of paper and had it paid to the *streltsy* who numbered 287 persons. They went into my courtyard and sat round in a large circle, and were handed the money by two of their number. When they had all had their share they passed the drink round one more time, thanked me warmly and went away. When they were gone I and my people fell to our knees and thanked God for delivering us and standing by us . . . for I was most fortunate to escape with my life.[18]

On May 17 the *streltsy* returned, calling again for Ivan Naryshkin. They threatened to kill everyone in the Kremlin unless Natalya delivered her brother to them. Sophia approached her and told her that he could not escape whatever might happen, and it would be pointless for them all to die with him, thus disingenuously dissociating herself from the rioters. Sophia's sentiments were fervently echoed by the boyars whose heads were at stake, and Natalya resigned herself. She had her brother brought into church and gave him a sacred icon, telling him that she was obliged to let him go, but hoped that the *streltsy* might still spare

[18] Ustryalov, vol. i, pp. 344–5.

him. A certain Prince Yakob Odoevsky interrupted her farewells with the chivalrous observation that Ivan ought to be getting on his way or else they would *all* perish. She accompanied him to the golden grille that separated them from a mob "where without respect for her Majesty they were waiting like lions for their prey, howling threats; like the iconoclasts they showed no respect for the icon he bore, seized him by the hair, and dragged him down the stairs across the square, carried him through the Kremlin to the torture chamber of Constantine, tortured him, took him to Red Square through the Gates of the Saviour, tossed him on pikes, catching him on their points, dismembered him and stamped the fragments into the ground".[19] They decreed that all bodies were to remain where they lay for several days before burial.

Some 20th-century historians have been tempted to ascribe "social" motives to the actions of the *streltsy*, and they have a case, of sorts. They directed their attentions exclusively towards boyars and foreigners. Moreover they tried to turn the serfs of Moscow against their masters, suggesting to them that they were exploited and oppressed, offering them liberty and protection. They attacked the Slaves Office, a government department, destroying its records and proclaiming the emancipation of the serfs.[20] Whether it was a reflection of that natural servility of temperament which travellers appeared to find in Muscovy, or because the *streltsy* appeared an unreliable support, the serfs were singularly reluctant to be emancipated. Instead they warned the *streltsy* that unless they moderated their behaviour they, the serfs, who outnumbered them two to one, would proceed against them. "Russia is great, you cannot master her," they said.[21]

In fact the riots proper ceased with the dispatch of Naryshkin; however, the *streltsy* continued to run wild for the rest of the summer, settling scores, collecting debts, imaginary or otherwise, and even murdering. They remained beyond effective control and believed themselves to be the masters now.

Sophia appears to have been the only authority they would listen to. She addressed them often enough, trying to persuade them to keep the peace. She ordered a reward of ten roubles to be paid to each man, and used every spare penny in the treasury in her attempt to pacify them. She had a pillar erected in Red Square commemorating their achievements, and further

[19] Tumansky, vol. i, p. 161.   [20] *Ibid.*, vol. i, p. 166.   [21] *Ibid.*, vol. ii, p. 274.

honoured them by giving them the clearly more prestigious title of "The Court Foot". She also gave them a new and popular commander, a secret Old Believer, like so many of their number, and himself a person of considerable ambition; Prince Ivan Andreevich Khovansky.

By and large Sophia had got what she wanted. On May 26 the *streltsy* announced that henceforward there would be two czars, Ivan and Peter, with Ivan as the senior. After a service in the Cathedral of the Assumption the two rulers accepted the congratulations of court and clergy and paid the *streltsy* the particular favour of letting their leaders kiss their hand. The regiments were entertained, two at a time, in the czars' banqueting hall. Sophia's triumph was completed three days later. Her agents rapidly convinced the *streltsy* that Ivan was not fit to rule in his own right, so that a regent had to be appointed, and on May 29 the *streltsy* informed the court that "in the view of the youth of the two rulers the government should be entrusted to their sister".

Khovansky, an Old Believer and fierce traditionalist, cannot have accepted the regency of a woman happily. Besides, a descendant of Lithuanian princes, he had ambitions of his own, and enjoying as he did the support of the *streltsy* had aspirations to the throne. Certainly he felt he held the whip hand: 'The whole kingdom is held together by me, if I were gone the people of Moscow would be up to their knees in blood."[22]

The next invasion of the no longer sacrosanct precincts of the Kremlin was executed by a drunken mob of Old Believers who came to challenge the authority of the orthodox church, carrying heretical books and icons and clamouring for public debate. A monk, Nikita, drew up a petition expressing their point of view, and with this and considerable violence the mob of *streltsy* and other heretics poured into the cathedral of the Assumption where they listened for some hours to a reading of the articles of their faith. Tension mounted and they began to call for the patriarch to debate with them. Khovansky called for him too, warning Sophia not to show herself since he could not guarantee her safety. However, this remarkable woman refused to be governed by Khovansky. She insisted on a public debate in the Faceted Palace itself, and the dissenters were invited to proceed there. Led by the now intoxicated Nikita they crowded into the chief

[22] Sakharov, p. 79.

audience chamber to be met with a remarkable sight. Sitting on the throne, dominating the patriarch and a whole series of churchmen and courtiers, was the regent Sophia; for the first time in the history of Muscovy the supreme authority was being visibly executed by a woman.

A long, violent and inconclusive debate took place. The patriarch and his churchmen were at the mercy of the militant crowd of schismatics and feared for their lives. However, Sophia's moral authority and courage carried the day. Twice she intervened to rebuke Nikita for threatening a bishop and for referring to patriarch Nikon, the architect of the reforms, as a heretic. The debate collapsed into a shouting match and the crowd was eventually called upon to withdraw, which it did, claiming that it had won a great victory.

However, not all the *streltsy* were Old Believers. Sophia quickly rallied orthodox elements, reminding them of her favours and calling on them to stand for their faith. A tense week ensued and there were rumours that they would march again. However, in the event orthodoxy prevailed and the *streltsy* handed the ringleaders over. They were all incarcerated in monasteries except for Nikita, whose head was taken off. A large number of other participants ran away – but the threat of Khovansky remained.

Sophia seems to have understood perfectly the extent of that threat. The *streltsy* controlled Moscow, and Moscow only, so in August she suddenly moved the czars and the court out of the capital to the village of Kolomenskoe. A week later she moved on and settled in Zvenigorod where she summoned the nobility and their retinue to rally to her. Khovansky had missed his chance. Her army would soon outnumber the *streltsy*, while it was unlikely anyway that these would make a formal move against their rulers, since such treason, if unsuccessful, carried only one penalty: death for all concerned.

Khovansky had more or less come out in open opposition to Sophia. It was therefore extraordinary that he and his son should now allow themselves to be lured to a village outside Moscow, virtually unescorted. They were seized, taken to Sophia and executed with some dispatch by an amateur headsman. Sophia was reluctant to wait for the services of a professional, possibly fearing that the longer the Khovanskys were left alive the more likely they were to reveal her complicity in the *streltsy* mutiny.

Khovansky senior was killed first, then the son kissed his dead father's back and took his place on the block.[23]

The *streltsy*'s first reaction to the news was fury. They proceeded to fortify Moscow and get ready for a siege, but as Sophia moved in they thought better of it, and begged the patriarch to intercede on their behalf. With some difficulty he secured their pardon, on condition that the ringleaders be surrendered to Sophia at the Troitse Sergeevsky Monastery.

Accompanied by lamenting wives and children they set out, with ropes round their necks, carrying candles, as was the custom for persons en route for their execution. Others carried their own axes, and even blocks. On arrival they fell to their knees and begged Sophia and the czars for mercy, as the executioners or "speculators", as the contemporary eye-witness mysteriously refers to them, stood over them. However, on this occasion they were pardoned, an uncharacteristic act of mercy which suggests lack of confidence on the part of Sophia. The court returned eventually to a pacified Moscow on November 16, and no more would be heard of mutinous *streltsy* for some seventeen years.

We do not know much about the precise effect of these months of continuous alarm and insecurity upon Peter. Hagiography depicts him facing the Kremlin mob with dauntless gaze; a claim not founded upon evidence. Another source describes Ivan and Peter in tears, which seems an infinitely more probable reaction for a ten-year-old, used to the peace and inviolable security of the Kremlin, who had been playing soldiers only that morning, as he saw the mob snatch relatives and courtiers from his side and dispose of them elaborately at his feet.

When the mob of Old Believers entered the Kremlin to discuss finer points of religion in the Faceted Palace he was described as showing signs of considerable distress. Indeed there is good reason to suppose that these events made a profound impression upon him. The nervous twitch that in later years distorted his face to the point of convulsion may well have had its origins here. More important, he had met an aspect of Old Muscovy which could only reinforce the subsequent aversion he would show for all its traditions, its rituals, its attitudes. He would always dislike the Kremlin itself, and all that it represented, and was to prove quite uncompromising in his hostility towards the *streltsy* and any sign of conservative revolt. He would respond to anything

[23] Tumansky, vol. i, p. 278.

of the sort with a degree of violence and suspicion which usually seemed excessive. An overdeveloped readiness to suspect treason from within is not a characteristic unique to Peter among Russian leaders. However, if, in the future, he was to show himself indiscriminately savage in his treatment of treachery, actual and potential, and impatient with the ancient ways of Old Muscovy, it is perfectly proper to suppose that much of that impatience and suspicion was born between May and November 1682.

CHAPTER THREE

The Regency of Sophia

Tradition would have it that after 1682 Natalya Kirillovna and Peter lived in virtual exile in Preobrazhenskoe, leading a secluded life with a few faithful attendants and denied access to the Kremlin. Like many Russian historical traditions it is not true. Natalya had access to the Kremlin at all times and it remained her base, as it had always been; there was no question of exclusion. However, it is true to say that she and Peter spent more and more time in the czars' country palaces, settling increasingly in Preobrazhenskoe, but without any form of compulsion whatsoever. Peter continued to submit urgent requests for weapons, and now also for wood- and metal-working equipment, indicating that he was already developing what was to become a lifelong passion for the lathe.

He also did his duty as czar: going through the paces of court ritual, acts of public worship, formal reception of ambassadors, although interestingly enough court records show that his half-brother did a great deal more of this kind of thing than did Peter, and also observed the rituals more strictly.[1] The first careful description of Peter that we have comes from a secretary to the Swedish ambassador who was received by both czars in 1683. "In the audience chamber, covered with rugs, the two czars sat beneath icons, on silver chairs, with all their regalia resplendent with precious stones. The elder brother, with his hat over his eyes, stared down seeing no one, and sat motionless; the younger looked at everybody; he had a handsome open face; young blood flowed through him as soon as anyone addressed him. His

[1] Bogoslovsky, vol. i, p. 53.

astounding beauty surprised all present and his liveliness embarrassed the sedate Muscovite dignitaries."[2] When the ambassador presented his credentials the two czars were supposed to rise together to inquire after the health of His Majesty; Peter, the younger did not give the old man time to raise him and his brother as etiquette required, jumped down quickly from his place, took off his hat himself and had to be held back and restrained from inquiring after the health of His Majesty until the elder was also ready and they could ask together.

Liveliness, curiosity, and impatience with the pace of Muscovite protocol, much of the future Peter is already here. In years to come he would make no secret of his dislike of such formal ambassadorial receptions and would go to considerable lengths to avoid them or cut them short.

Some years later a Dutch resident describes him as growing apace and well. "He is tall and carries himself finely, and his understanding and intelligence develop as fast as he grows taller. He is generally active and shows a great love of things military which leads one to expect that in due course the Tartars will be hearing from him, and be brought to heel."[3]

It was not just impatience with court ritual that made Peter spend more and more time in Preobrazhenskoe over these years. He was beginning to play war games on a generous scale and the village provided him with scope. The eleven-year-old Peter had grown out of toy weapons, toy soldiers, and was beginning to play those games with people out of which the new Russian army would be born. For 1683 saw the beginnings in Preobrazhenskoe of Peter's so-called *poteshnye* – the word does not translate easily, it is an adjective from *potekha* meaning fun, amusement, entertainment, but with slightly more concrete undertones than those words, it suggests an activity or undertaking which will amuse. Equally *poteschnye* almost comes to mean "those one has fun with". However, it is not possible to render it with an expression such as playmate or companion, since *poteshnye* used in this sense is a term applied solely to Peter's companions of those years and is thus tantamount to a proper name.

Essentially the *poteshnye* were children largely of Peter's age with whom he played war games. It had always been the custom for young czars or czareviches to have a group of contemporaries, the sons of boyars, as playmates. Peter's group was different,

[2] Posselt, vol. i, p. 408.   [3] *Ibid.*, p. 409.

recruited indiscriminately from the sons of those who had taken Peter's side in 1682 and the sons of court servants and stable lads. From the outset Peter had no respect for rank; he demanded service and anyone who served him well was worthy to serve him.

He seems to have begun with some thirty-five companions, and as early as 1683 he was already indulging in their company one of his enduring passions – playing with fire. He would love fire always, bombs, grenades, fireworks, and already he and his playmates were working with gunpowder, rockets, fireworks, even cannon. On May, 30, 1683, Peter's birthday, there was an artillery display supervised by a foreign gunner which made a considerable impression upon Peter. Immediately afterwards he called for no less than sixteen pieces of ordnance of various kinds to be placed at his disposal. Over the next few years a perpetual stream of cannon, drums, muskets, swords, saddles and bridles were to make their way to Preobrazhenskoe by the waggon load.

The games grew increasingly elaborate, involving the building of a fortified play city, Pressburg, outside the village. As the numbers of *poteshnye* grew they were organised into two groups – the Preobrazhensky and Semenovsky regiments – the founding regiments of the Russian Guard; the first man to join the Preobrazhensky *poteshnye*, Sergey Butkhvostov, was subsequently held to be the first Russian guardsman. By 1687 Peter was filing regular requests for more and more troops to the Kremlin, notably for fife-players and drummers – and Sophia only gave her assent with considerable reluctance,[4] for the *poteshnye* were beginning to be something more than a toytown army.

Peter's way with them was characteristic both of his strengths and his weaknesses. Here as always he displayed no regard for his own rank. It is said, and could well be true, that he served as a common soldier, and it is probably here that he first acquired the skills of a drummer boy which he would proudly display on the slightest pretext over the next thirty-five years. Peter believed that even czars had to come up through the ranks and earn promotion with the sweat of their brow. Indeed one of the characteristics that commonly command admiration in Peter is this blend of total lack of vanity with magnificent pride. Peter as czar was confident enough of his true stature to be able to serve as a common soldier and earn his promotion, in the certain knowledge that because he was czar nothing he might do could ever diminish

[4] Gordon, P., pp. 227-9.

him. Throughout his life he would project real grandeur through his total lack of vanity and petty self-importance. However, one cannot help wondering how useful it was for Peter to be able to beat a drum? The war games were fine as far as they went, but they did not go beyond a purely tactical level. Peter was learning to be a good soldier, NCO, junior officer, when he might have been spending his time more usefully learning how to be a commander. There was no one at Preobrazhenskoe capable of teaching him anything of the sort. Peter preferred tactics and technics to the study of strategy. His practical bent had many virtues, but it prevented him from ever becoming, or wanting to become, a great military leader. Perhaps it was his continual readiness to tackle practical problems in person, and, if need be, in shirt-sleeves, that made him less successful than his father in choosing advisers who would implement his policies efficiently and honestly on his behalf.

Zotov appears to have been appointed Peter's tutor in 1683. He did not do a great deal for his charge. Certainly there are no signs of Peter's receiving any kind of formal education. His education began, to all intents and purposes, at sixteen and at his own instigation, founded on practical and technical considerations and sparked off by a particular incident. Prince Yakob Dolgoruky returned in 1688 from a foreign embassy with an astrolabe which he had acquired at Peter's request. The young czar found himself at a loss to know what to do with it, so a Dutchman, Franz Timmerman, was brought to Preobrazhenskoe to give him instruction. He was immediately engaged to teach Peter arithmetic, ballistics and fortification. This was at a time when the prospective pupil could scarcely write his own name, let alone spell. His handwriting is a hasty ill-formed scrawl, impatient and untidy. In some of his surviving notebooks we may see him wrestling with the most elementary sums, addition, subtraction, multiplication and short division. In order to get what he wanted the young co-ruler had to begin at the beginning.

Sophia was a worthy half-sister to her arch enemy Peter. Her rule also brought its changes to Russia. Far from respecting the values of the *terem* she made no attempt to conceal the fact that the stateman V. V. Golitsyn was her lover. He was a highly cultured person who was a Latin scholar and the possessor of a large library. Under the regency the study of both Greek and Latin was widely encouraged, and Ukrainians – closer to Rome,

better educated and less mulish than their Russian counterparts –
came to play an increasingly important part in ecclesiastical and
hence educational affairs. Golitsyn was in many ways a remarkable man. He was perfectly aware of the need for change in
Russia – radical change extending to eventual emancipation of
the serfs. He was moreover one of the rare Russian grandees to
seek out the inhabitants of the Foreign Quarter, calling on them
frequently and inviting them to his table. Yet curiously enough,
for all his otherwise advanced attitudes, Golitsyn was inordin-
ately superstitious, as indeed was Sophia, and together they both
made strangely ample use of divination, sorcery and other occult
modes of consulting the future.

Prince V. I. Kurakin, later to serve Peter, notably in Holland,
looked back on the Regency as a golden age. Trade prospered,
and, as he put it, there was much *politesse* among the upper
classes.[5] It was also a time which saw the establishment of the
first permanent Russian representatives abroad, other than in
Austria and Spain. The changes instituted by the regent and her
lover were moreover introduced gently and never offered a
head-on challenge to the old ways; besides, the Europe which
Sophia turned to was the Europe of the Mediterranean seaboard,
whereas Peter would prefer the Europe of the North – and drill.
Again in contrast to her half-brother, Sophia had an instinctive
understanding of the power and significance of the old rituals,
seeing them as a way of unifying ruler and ruled. For example
she maintained a tradition which Peter was to abolish whereby
the *terem* supported droves of beggars that came to it for charity,
thus forging a particular and philanthropic link between the
Kremlin and the people. The empirical absolutism of Peter
severed all such ties as it evolved its own patterns of government en route. Certainly Russia would have turned its face to the
West, Peter or no, yet some aspects of Sophia's regency suggest
that it might have done so in a very different and less violent
way.

Sophia's political position was precarious, being dependent on
the age of her protégés. She could not expect to remain regent
for long and once Peter became a major there could be only one
prospect for her – a convent. Her brother whose marriage she had
arranged, could produce nothing but daughters, so that by 1686
Sophia's position was not a happy one. It must have been this

[5] Kurakin, vol. i, p. 50.

that explains her extraordinarily rash bid for personal rule. She began to describe herself in official documents as "autocrat", had a special crown made for herself, struck coins and medallions in her image, and regal portraits appeared depicting her holding a sceptre, while she made frequent appearances playing the most important part in public ceremonies.

In 1686 Russia had signed a perpetual peace with Poland which ceded Kiev in return for 146,000 roubles. This also saw the establishment of a Russo-Polish league against the Turks. The Crimean Tartars, who were more or less under the ultimate control of the Porte, offered a constant threat to the southern borders of Russia. Not only did they take tribute from Moscow, they mounted raid after raid on her territories in search of prisoners to be sold into captivity. Russia was now more or less committed to war against the Turks or their allies, while the prospect of a military victory with her lover as its architect and commander-in-chief appealed to Sophia as a means of consolidating her power. A *levée en masse* was accordingly called in the spring of 1687 and the Muscovite army assembled laboriously. Golitsyn was not universally popular. Many of the regiments were below strength, suggesting a certain reluctance to flock to the standard. Moreover when Golitsyn attempted to re-organise the basis on which lower ranking courtiers were to serve he met with bitter resistance, some of their number coming to the assembly point wearing black in mourning for their lost ways. The superstitious commander, taking this to be a dire sign as well as an act of insubordination, had them arrested and stripped of their estates, much to general disapproval.

The campaign started late, as the Muscovite army, 100,000 strong, moved south towards the Crimea with a baggage train of 20,000 waggons. At Samara they were joined by another 50,000 cossacks under their hetman Samoilovich, and proceeded to advance into the steppe; at which point somebody set it on fire. The Muscovites were greeted with clouds of black smoke and choking dust, but Golitsyn continued to advance – at the rate of four miles a day. They checked on the third day, the men exhausted, the horses dying. There were still 120 miles between them and their objective. They had made no contact whatsoever with the enemy, but notwithstanding, Golitsyn decided to go home. The Scottish commander, General Patrick Gordon, who was on the campaign, believed that it was the cossacks who had set the steppe alight in order to preserve their independence of Moscow by ensuring that the Crimean Tartars remained an active threat.[6] Golitsyn appears to have agreed with him. He arrested and deposed hetman Samoilovich for treachery, sending him into exile and appointing in his place a man who was to prove of less then unshakeable loyalty, Ivan Mazeppa.

When the army returned to Moscow Sophia did her best to present its modest achievement – it had gone, it had come back – as a splendid victory requiring celebration with elaborate parades; a response combining wishful thinking, despair at a deteriorating situation and a very real love or affection for Golitsyn. One qualifies the assessment of her feelings since she also had a second lover in the shape of one Fedor Shaklovity, a stronger, darker and more able man than Golitsyn, though not as well endowed with *politesse*.

Next year Golitsyn tried again. This time he got further, reaching the Crimea itself. He actually made contact with the enemy near the lines of Perekop, a lightly fortified line across the north of the Crimean peninsula. His 100,000 men had no trouble in beating off the Tartars, but it must be said that Golitsyn was not an aggressive commander. He was much too easily discouraged by the prospect of advancing across the large, waterless territory facing him, having made no provisions to deal with this fairly obvious contingency; rather than press on when the Crimea seemed his for the taking, he preferred to come to terms. A considerable degree of incompetence was displayed throughout. When Golitsyn set an ambush of 400 men to take a prisoner for interrogation they could only succeed in capturing a wild cat, which General Gordon observed was as wild as any Tartar.[7] In the meantime Sophia wrote her lover the most passionate love letters. She cannot wait to see him and the light of his eyes, while God has guided him back on the retreat from Perekop as he guided the Israelites out of Egypt.[8]

This second failure did nothing for Golitsyn's popularity. Before he set off he had received anonymous threats warning him that he would be killed were he to fail. His generalship had displeased many officers on his second campaign while back in Moscow Sophia had made a lot of enemies by her obvious desire to reign in her own right. There were many who now wished to see the two czars rule by themselves.

[6] Gordon, P., p. 77.   [7] Ustryalov, vol. i, p. 237.   [8] *Ibid.*, *loc. cit.*

On the return to Moscow various rumours spread to explain Golitsyn's failure to press his advance. It was even suggested that he had been bribed by the Tartar Khan with two barrels of gold coin. It was only when he returned to Moscow that he discovered that these were mere gilded brass.[9]

Throughout this period tension between Peter and Sophia was growing. Yet again she was beginning to stir up the *streltsy*, sensing that there would soon be an open clash. Her agitation took various forms, some of which were extravagant; her supporters had a *streltsy* commander murdered, suggesting that the killing was the work of Natalya's brother Lev Naryshkin. Another no less extravagant agitator disguised himself as a woman and appeared in various *streltsy* quarters complaining bitterly that he had been ill used by the Naryshkins. Sophia herself had asked the *streltsy* leaders to insist that she be declared czarina, a suggestion to which they had responded with little enthusiasm, indeed none of her efforts to rouse them seemed to have much effect.

In January 1689 something happened which, in the long run, would weaken Sophia's position enormously; Peter's mother arranged for her son to marry. His bride, Evdokiya Lopukhina, was the daughter of a courtier, Fedor Abramovich Lopukhin, whose family was close to the Naryshkin clan. The wedding took place very quietly on January 27 in the small court church of Peter and Paul. Although Peter had given his assent to his mother's plan the seventeen-year-old czar displayed little enthusiasm for the arrangement. Indeed Evdokiya was an entirely unsuitable bride. She was a quiet, devout and limited girl of traditional Muscovite cast; gentle, emotional, and – a fatal drawback – clinging; hopelessly ill-equipped for the difficult business of being married to the future Peter the Great. Right from the start her husband neglected her. The few letters from Evdokiya to Peter that have survived are all in the same beseeching cast:

To my most dear lord, my light and joy, czar Peter Alekseevich, I beg you my light for a favour, make me happy, father, write, my light, and tell me how you are to cheer me in my misery. How is it that you depart and do not care to write me a word of your health. Do not spurn my request, my light. In case you might care to know I myself am keeping well.[10]

[9] Sakharov, p. 10. [10] Ustryalov, vol. i, p. 100.

No woman who approached Peter in this supplicant manner could ever hope to do more than provoke his impatience. Yet notwithstanding the fundamentally unsatisfactory nature of a marriage which would bring little but tragedy to Peter's luckless bride, the threat it posed to Sophia was very real, since a son born to Peter would strengthen his position immeasurably.

Peter was beginning to show his hand, and his resentment, at the actions of his half-sister. On July 8, 1689, a religious procession was held, which involved proceeding from the Kremlin cathedrals to the Kazan cathedral and back again. Peter had arrived from Kolomenskoe at eight in the morning to take part. Both czars and their sister proceeded from the Church of the Saviour to the Cathedral of the Assumption. Opposite the corner of the Faceted Palace they were greeted by the patriarch and his retinue who gave them their blessing and joined them on their way to the cathedral. This was the moment Peter picked to clash openly with Sophia. She had taken up an icon to carry it in the procession as if she were the titular ruler; Peter demanded she stand down. She refused, a furious argument took place, and Peter left the procession immediately to return to Kolomenskoe. He was protesting against the public part Sophia played in these rituals, a part reserved for the czars alone; neither now nor later did she pay the slightest heed to his protests and carried on processing as before.

The next clash took place a few days later, and was occasioned by the return of Golitsyn and his less than victorious army. Sophia had arranged a splendid reception, greeting him with banners and icons, and conducting him into the city in person. Peter held the behaviour of the commanders to have been a disgrace, and no less disgraceful were the rewards and promotions which Sophia conferred upon them on their return. He could only be persuaded with the utmost difficulty to authorise these remunerations, and refused to receive the commanders to listen to their thanks.[11] For Gordon, who was in Moscow at the time and keeping a careful eye on the turn of the weather, this was the moment which marked the definitive rift between Peter and Sophia.

Every attempt was made to keep the rift secret, conceal the division from the masses, yet Gordon's diary for the following days makes it clear that the atmosphere was building up: "29th Things are taking a bad turn. . . . 31st Anger and bitterness increasing steadily and it looks as if things will break at any

[11] Gordon, P., p. 266.

moment." His entry for August 6 simply and cautiously records that there were "rumours unfit to be uttered".[12]

Peter had changed considerably since we last saw him, and now seemed marked by his experiences. In 1689 he appeared "very tall, well built, and quite good looking. He has quite large eyes, the gaze wanders and it is not pleasant to look on him. Even though he is only twenty [in fact he was seventeen] he twitches his head without cease."[13]

On the night of August 6 an anonymous letter was found announcing that, on the following day, the *poteshnye* would come in force from Preobrazhenskoe to murder Ivan and his sister. The Kremlin gates were closed and the *streltsy* stood to, while another unit was posted in Lubyanka. There was some doubt as to why they had been mobilised; some thought it was to defend the Kremlin, others that they were to march on Preobrazhenskoe. Certainly a handful of *streltsy* loyal to Peter thought that an attack was planned. Later that night a chamberlain of Peter's arrived in the city, was promptly arrested and taken to Shaklovity in the Kremlin for interrogation. This seemed to convince Peter's supporters that a plot was brewing and they galloped off to Preobrazhenskoe to warn the sleeping czar. They arrived a little after midnight to announce that the *streltsy* were arming in the Kremlin, and were about to march and do away with various people, Naryshkins in particular.

Peter greeted the news with one of his occasional moments of spontaneous panic. Although he would regularly display exemplary courage on the battlefield he remained capable of frenzies of terror, and it was into such a state that he now lapsed. He jumped out of bed and made off to a nearby wood without pausing to draw on his boots.[14] His clothes, boots and all, were brought to him there together with a horse. He and whoever was ready rode as hard as they could to the Troitsa Sergeevsky Monastery which he reached, exhausted, at six the following morning. He fell on to a bed and, in floods of tears, asked the archimandrite for sanctuary. He was in a state of almost total prostration. In the course of the day he was joined by his *poteshnye* who brought up some cannon with them. His mother and a loyal regiment of *streltsy* also joined him that day. Peter may have been terrified, but he had not lost his head. He could have chosen no safer spot than the monastery. Not only was it fortified

[12] *Ibid.*, p. 267.   [13] *Russ. Star.*, 1891, vol. lxxi, p. 258.   [14] *Ibid.*, p. 268.

but it was holy. It was simply not possible either to attack an anointed monarch there or to have him murdered without losing all popular support. It seems likely that in his judicious choice of sanctuary Peter was following the advice of Boris Alekseevich Golitsyn, the cousin of Sophia's lover and one of Peter's most loyal supporters.

Once inside the monastery he was out of immediate danger. He had, as it were, set his standard up, and now it was a question of seeing whether he had the pulling power to deprive Sophia of her authority. Support only came to him gradually. One of the first to rally was a colonel of the *streltsy*, Tsykler, with some fifty men. He had been involved in the revolt of 1682 and now recognised that he had backed a loser. By coming across early he hoped that Peter would recognise and reward his "loyalty".

In Moscow, news of Peter's flight caused, in Gordon's words "great alarm and contention".[15] The initial reaction was to keep it quiet, then to present it as being without significance. In the meantime Peter and Sophia exchanged messages. Peter wanted to know why she had mobilised so many *streltsy* – she replied that they were to escort her on a visit to a monastery, and in her turn sent an envoy to call Peter back to Moscow. On the 16th Peter made a first bid for authority, sending a written order to all *streltsy* and foreign officers to appear before him by the 20th. This placed the officers in a difficult situation, requiring them to commit themselves, and lose their heads should they back the wrong side; a point that Sophia made perfectly clear to them, when she ordered them to remain in the capital on pain of death. For the time being Peter's order was not obeyed.

Sophia then sent the patriarch to see Peter – a serious tactical error, since the patriarch did not come back, and this weakened Sophia's position appreciably.

The turning point came on September 1 when Sophia and her brother received an emissary of Peter's calling for the arrest of Fedor Shaklovity for plotting Peter's death, demanding that he be delivered at once. The move placed her in an intolerable situation – the ironic reversal of her demands for the arrest of Natalya's brother just seven years before. Either she handed over her lover and fellow conspirator or she would be seen to condone possible treason or the intention to commit it, an intention tantamount to the crime itself.

[15] *Russ. Star.*, 1891, vol. lxxi., *loc. cit.*

Having threatened to behead Peter's envoy – Gordon tells us that he only escaped because no headsman was available – Sophia addressed the *streltsy* in defence of Shaklovity and her regency, suggesting that Peter was advised by evil men, and that much more than the life of Shaklovity was at stake; there was her own life and that of her brother too. However, she failed to convince the *streltsy*, who began to go across to Peter in large numbers; Shaklovity took refuge in the Kremlin. On September 2 Peter issued another summons to the *streltsy* and foreign officers. Many now went over to him, but it was vital that he win over the senior foreign commander, General Patrick Gordon. A Scottish soldier of fortune in his mid-fifties, royalist and Catholic, Gordon had left Scotland to serve first the Swedes, then the Poles and, since 1660, the Russians. A careful and somewhat dour man, touchy and money-conscious, he had fought for his foreign masters bravely but with increasing reluctance, for his one ambition was to return home. Now finding himself caught up in the power struggle between Peter and Sophia he proceeded with some caution. As yet uncertain as to which way to jump he contented himself with a message saying that he had not yet presented himself, since he was not certain he would be welcome.

Two days later senior foreign officers received a personal communication from Peter informing them that Shaklovity, together with certain other named persons, was guilty of plotting against his life; they had planned to murder Peter, his mother and the patriarch. He ordered the officers to appear before him fully armed and mounted. The order compelled Gordon and the rest to commit themselves. Gordon went first to see V. V. Golitsyn and showed the order to him. Golitsyn promised to consult Sophia and the elder czar, while Gordon reminded him that failure to obey would endanger their heads. Golitsyn promised to have an answer by the evening while Gordon returned to his quarters and prepared to ride. He told his fellow officers that he had decided to go to the monastery, and they joined him to a man. They left at dark, rode through the night and arrived at 11 o'clock on the morning of the fifth. They were greeted with enthusiasm by Peter, who gave them his hand to kiss, and a glass of spirits each to drink. He had every reason to make them welcome, since now they had come across victory was certain.

As the remaining *streltsy* grew more and more restless Sophia announced to the general excitement that she would go to the monastery in person and talk with Peter. When the news reached him he ordered her to do nothing of the sort. She set off regardless, having no other card left to play, but after receiving and disregarding a series of warnings she finally realised that, unless she was prepared for a battle which she could not possibly win, she would have to return to Moscow.

Sophia emerges as a woman of great energy and stature in these early September days when her power base was crumbling away almost by the hour. There are no visible signs of despair, no loss of energy, no broken apathy. She continues to act as a ruler, trying to rally the *streltsy* to her, flattering them, appealing to their loyalty, and when all else failed threatening them. She ended one address with the sinister reminder that, although they were of course free to go to join Peter, they would do well to remember that their wives and children would remain in Moscow.[16]

None of it worked. On September 6 the *streltsy* moved and arrested Shaklovity. He was delivered to Peter early the next afternoon, and was interrogated immediately. He confessed to plotting to put Sophia on the throne, but denied that there was any plan to murder Peter. He was tortured, strappado and sixteen lashes, but stuck to his original story.

That afternoon V. V. Golitsyn and his son arrived at the monastery, where they were put under house arrest. Gordon found Golitsyn somewhat "thoughtful, and with every reason".[17] Threatened with another session in the torture chamber Shaklovity made a more elaborate confession, implicating Golitsyn, and it was agreed that he would not be tortured again. When he was finally set down after his second strappado and interrogation he astounded everybody by asking at once for food, since he had not had a decent meal for some days. Shortly afterwards he was beheaded, while others were beheaded, flogged or had their tongues wholly or partially cut out.[18]

Golitsyn escaped relatively lightly – with his life. Doubtless thanks to the intervention of his cousin he was merely exiled and stripped of his estates. The initial exile was a relatively harmless affair, although it was commuted almost at once to exile in the far North. Sophia was imprisoned in the Novodevichy monastery in Moscow. Peter's party was in sole command and his personal rule begins, effectively, on September 12, 1689.

[16] Ustryalov, vol. ii, p. 70.   [17] Gordon, P., p. 279.   [18] Tumansky, vol. i, p. 208.

CHAPTER FOUR

Prince Hal at Play

The young czar who bolted to the monastery for sanctuary was little more than a figure-head, a rallying point in those early autumn days. It was the Naryshkin faction that had won, not Peter the young autocrat. He displayed little interest in government and the initial consequence of the change in the balance of power was the re-assertion of Naryshkin conservatism. Natalya's brother – Lev – effectively took over the business of government, while other persons who came to power were also of a distinctly conservative disposition in contrast with the relatively liberal and unorthodox Sophia. Thus one of the men who now attained prominence, Tikhon Nikitich Streshnev, would remain a loyal servant to Peter for some thirty years; but to the end of his life, despite his allegiance to the reforming czar, he would remain a resolute conservative who would always sigh sadly for the ways of old Muscovy.[1]

For the moment the ways of old Muscovy appeared to be in the ascendant. The early months of Peter's rule are marked by strange incidents smacking of superstition and xenophobia. Thus Gordon tells of a peculiar case of witchcraft. The governor of Terki, a town on the Caspian, one Bezobrazov, was taken to Moscow and charged with trying to win the czar's favour through sorcery. As Gordon observed: "Because he was old and sick he was taken to the place of interrogation by sledge."[2] His denouncer was tortured first, and since he stuck to his story, Bezobrazov was flogged in turn. After the fifth stroke he confessed. Supposing himself to be out of favour since he had been

[1] Ustryalov, vol. ii, p. 101.   [2] Gordon, P., p. 288.

given such an unattractive office, he resorted to a sorcerer who declared himself capable of putting matters right. His method was to stand between the person whose favour was being sought and the wind. He would then cause a wind to blow which would waft the desired favour toward his client. This particular client was exiled and stripped of all he possessed.[3]

The case of the would-be Russian Icarus falls somewhere between superstition and technology. A peasant summoned the Kremlin guard saying that he had an important matter to communicate to the czar. He was interrogated and announced that "he would make himself wings and fly like a crane". The czar authorised expenditure of eighteen roubles on the manufacture of a set of mica wings. When all was ready the peasant put them on, crossed himself and started to inflate some wine skins hung about his person, flapping the while: "He did not leave the ground and said he made the wings too heavy" – but when he asked for more money for a second set he was beaten and sent packing.[4]

Hatred of foreigners took a more violent turn. One of the first edicts banned the entry of any foreigner into Russia without express permission of the czar, while it was rumoured that the new régime intended to pull down all foreign churches.[5] These policies were the work of the patriarch Ioakim, an uncompromising supporter of the old ways. He opposed the appointment of foreign, and thus heretical, officers and was highly suspicious of the Protestant churches of the Foreign Quarter. He was particularly alarmed by the presence in the capital of a half-witted Silesian Lutheran, one Kühlmann, who had preached a peculiar and personal form of Protestant mysticism in various European cities before coming to Moscow. He referred to himself as a prince, saint or prophet, son of the Son of God. Thanks to Ioakim's insistence he was arrested and interrogated; he declared he had come to Moscow at the behest of an angel who had appeared to him in white robes in Amsterdam and ordered him to proceed to Moscow immediately to carry out the will of God; should they not listen to him in Moscow he was to return and send out his wife, who was even more skilled in prophecy.[6] He was found guilty of heresy, and he and his books were burnt publicly in Moscow in October 1689.

It may well have been Peter himself who provoked these mani-

[3] Gordon, P., p. 289.   [4] Sakharov, p. 21.   [5] Ustryalov, vol. ii, p. 111.
[6] Ibid., vol. ii, p. 117.

festations of xenophobia. He had met a great many foreigners during his stay at the monastery, and one of them, Gordon, he took to enormously; so much so that he tried to invite him to a banquet celebrating the birth of his son Aleksey. Significantly it was the patriarch who insisted that it was not fitting for a heretic to attend such an occasion, so that Peter felt obliged to turn an indignant Gordon away.

The patriarch, who by now was a dying man, was sufficiently alarmed by the foreign threat to make it the subject of his deathbed testimony. He called on the czars to prevent foreigners from holding command over the orthodox since they "do not share our faith, do not agree with our national traditions and are estranged from our mother the church. How can such accursed heretics help our orthodox armies, they will only attract God's wrath." He went on to blame the failure of Sophia's Crimean campaigns on the presence of foreign officers.[7]

Foreigners were indeed generally unpopular. Their ways and customs were targets for scorn – for example their willingness to eat "grass", i.e. lettuce, like cattle.[8] They were regularly objects of popular abuse and mockery. Their settlement was given the derisive nickname of *kukui*, or "cuckoo", and few Russians of standing ever went there, while foreigners were seldom invited to Russian houses. In ceremonial processions the highest ranking foreigners were preceded even by merchants of various ranks and standing.

Xenophobic conservatism was encouraged by Peter's mother, who still kept some hold over the tastes of her son, as can be seen in the disagreement surrounding the appointment of a new patriarch. Peter wanted the metropolitan of Pskov, Markel, an educated and open-minded scholar who spoke Latin, French and Italian and was well disposed towards foreigners. His mother favoured Adrian, metropolitan of Kazan. On this occasion Peter gave in. Some years later his version was recorded as follows:

He told us a story that when the patriarch of Moscow was dead he designed to fill that place with a learned man, that had been a traveller who spoke Latin, Italian and French. The Russians petitioned him in a tumultuous manner, not to set such a man over them, alleging three reasons: 1. Because he

<hr>

[7] *Ibid., loc. cit.*   [8] *Ibid.*, p. 118.

spoke barbarous languages. 2. Because his beard was not big enough for a patriarch. 3. Because his coachman sat upon the coach seat, not upon the horse as was usual.[9]

The xenophobia of these early years was in part a reaction against the policies and style of the regency, witness Ioakim's comments on foreign ways, but partly also a recognition, on Natalya's part, that Peter was not conducting himself in a manner appropriate to a czar of Muscovy.

The young ruler had stumbled on education – through the agency of the astrolabe, which had led to his acquaintance with Timmerman and his first contact with the West. It was another chance encounter that led to his eventual and enduring love of the sea. Peter had always enjoyed playing with soldiers, fire, bombs and fireworks, but until 1689 he had not displayed the slightest interest in water, let alone the sea. The Russia of his time was virtually landlocked. It possessed a single northern port, Archangel, which was icebound for half the year, while its access to the Caspian was of no great significance since what trade there was with Persia used to travel overland. It is true that the inland waterways, the network of rivers running north–south across Russia, the Volga, the Oka, the Moskva, the Don, were vital thoroughfares, but despite the efforts of Peter's father to build a ship, boats did not loom large in the world of old Muscovy. Nor did they in Peter's world until a certain day when he was going through a storehouse belonging to his cousin Nikita Romanov, in Preobrazhenskoe, when he chanced upon the object which would one day become "the father of the Russian navy".

The object was a boat of unfamiliar design, which had been made for Peter's father by Karsten Brandt, a Dutch shipwright, who had been imported to build boats for the Caspian. Peter asked Timmerman what made it so different from Russian boats, and was told that, unlike them, it could sail into the wind. It was this evidently unusual capability that first fascinated Peter. He was not, it would seem, drawn to boats as such, rather it was the apparently miraculous possibility of tacking, using technology to defy the elements, that attracted him. Whatever form his subsequent passion for the sea might have taken it is worth recalling that the passion had its origins in the possibility of mastering

[9] Posselt, vol. i, pp. 486–7.

72

the elements, and not in any instinctive childhood passion for messing about in boats.

Peter had the boat restored, and sailed first on the Yauza river, then on a small lake at Izmailovo, before moving on to a much larger lake at Pereyaslav' Zalessky – where old Brandt began to build him boats of his own to play with. Although he did not visit his yard between 1689 and 1691, on March 14 of that year Brandt launched him his first yacht. Henceforward he would take an equal delight in both water and fire.

Early contacts with Timmerman and Brandt had opened his mind to the technological West, and the encounter with Gordon and his fellow officers had reinforced a curiosity which developed rapidly through his meeting with the first and perhaps the most influential of all his strangely mediocre favourites, the Swiss adventurer Franz Lefort.

Lefort appears to have come to Moscow in 1686, and was one of the first foreigners to rally to Peter in August 1689. Aged thirty-three, he was an immensely cheerful, forthcoming, easy-going gentleman with considerable zest for life, an eye on the main chance and an almost unlimited capacity for drink supported by an iron constitution. No stretch of the imagination could make him into a person of exceptional intelligence or ability. He was in many ways a mediocrity, but one who understood instinctively how to charm and lead young Peter. The czar would never respond to normal sycophancy; he would look for a brand of loyalty and seeming independence, the ability to stand up to him – to a point. He required those close to him to combine familiarity and a concealed deference. Impatient with the traditional kow-towing veneration with which Moscow treated its czars he was always susceptible to treatment as a kind of pseudo-equal, and could be easily won over by those who dared approach him with a blend of good humour and touches of carefully timed and re-strained irreverence. Lefort understood instinctively how to play Falstaff to Prince Hal.

From 1690 on his influence increased steadily. It was Lefort who encouraged Peter to make unprecedented visits to the Foreign Quarter, actually calling on its inhabitants, in their homes. He encouraged still more outrageous breaks with the old ways. In 1691, for the first time, a Russian czar adopted Western dress. Official records show that in that year Peter had a foreign costume made; a camisole, hose, shoes, swords on a gold embroidered baldric, and "artificial hair".[10] The material was purchased from "General Lefort".

Peter had promoted his friend to the rank of lieutenant general and made him his constant companion. Lefort wrote to his mother in that year apologising for not writing more often, saying that he was so occupied with the czar that he never had a moment to put pen to paper.[11] Another foreigner reported that "His Majesty loves him dearly, above all other foreigners. He is much loved by great lords and foreigners alike. At court the talk is of His Majesty and Lefort alone. They are inseparable. His Majesty visits him often and drinks with him two or three times a week ... Lefort has great influence at court ... No foreigner has ever had as much power in Moscow. He is in the process of winning a great fortune ... His Majesty gives him magnificent presents."[12] Not the least of these was a splendid town house, a palace indeed, to permit Lefort to entertain Peter and his company on an appropriate scale. The building has not survived, although the name – Lefortovo – has, and became the name of one of the grimmest of Stalin's Moscow prison houses.

We can see the influence of Lefort and the Foreign Quarter begin to work on Peter. Although he still observed the patterns of court protocol in 1690 and 1691, he did so half-heartedly. The records show that he often arrived at ceremonies late and left early, in contrast with his punctilious half-brother. Moreover the eighteen-year-old began to supply elements of his own invention. High days were now marked by artillery and musket salvoes, not to mention firework displays attended by the entire court, while Peter even made ceremonial journeys upon the water.[13] Although he still wore traditional dress on such occasions he increasingly went about in foreign clothes at other times, and moreover began to sign his letters with the Latin "Petrus". In 1691 he increased the scope of his foreign visits beyond Lefort and Gordon to include other inhabitants of the Foreign Quarter, including the house of a brewer by the name of Mons.

Lefort, for all his limitations, was acting as Peter's mentor. He introduced him to Western dress and showed him how to wear it. He introduced him to Western manners, and now he even found him a Western mistress.

Peter had been effectively estranged from his wife almost from

[10] Bogoslovsky, vol. i, p. 102. [11] Posselt, vol. ii, p. 63.
[12] Ibid., loc. cit. [13] Bogoslovsky, vol. i, pp. 140–1.

the outset. Although she had borne him a son the most powerful emotion that she inspired in him was impatience. He quickly lost any feelings that he might have had for her. Not only did she represent the old Muscovy that he had already grown to dislike, she was quite unable to accept or understand him and his unceremonious and indeed frequently drunken ways. Lefort now forged yet another link between Peter and the West by encouraging his liaison with Anna, the daughter of the brewer Mons. We know very little about the relationship except that it lasted for over ten years before ending, as we shall eventually see, in strange and somewhat comic circumstances. Certainly over that period Anna Mons was the only woman to feature by name in Peter's life. He never displayed a great capacity for *amour passion*, or indeed for *galanterie*, and apart from his second wife, Catherine, Anna Mons was his only known regular mistress. He was never averse to occasional encounters, but these appear to have been no more than short bouts of physical excess. His sexuality was crude and uncomplicated. On one occasion many years later Peter was dining in Copenhagen with the king of Denmark. The latter observed in his cups that it was said that like him Peter also kept mistresses. "Peter", wrote the Saxon resident Baron Los, "did not find this observation to his taste, answering: "My whores cost me little. Yours cost you thousands that might be more usefully employed elsewhere.' "[14]

Although Anna Mons was a mistress, not an inexpensive whore, the remark tells us something of Peter's attitude to her. His loves never had any real hold over him and there is no evidence to suggest that his relationship with Anna Mons affected him in any significant way, except perhaps to confirm him in his turn to the West. However, regardless of what it might have meant to Peter, for others it had a different importance, particularly since he made no secret of his liaison with her, appearing with her in public and even attending her father's house upon her birthday. To Peter's orthodox and xenophobic subjects he now appeared a czar bewitched. Lefort was a sorcerer who had put a spell on Peter, making him leave the old true ways, visit foreigners in their houses, put on foreign dress and false hair, and now, finally, break with his Muscovite wife and take a foreign girl for his mistress.

In the early years of his reign, the 1690's, Peter remained

[14] Wittram, vol. ii, p. 287.

content to learn and play, and it was not always possible to say where learning ended and play began. When Peter worked side by side with his master shipwright, Karsten Brandt, at Pereyaslavl' Zalesky, a powerful element of pure pleasure was most certainly present. Peter enjoyed the outrageous spectacle of the czar of Muscovy acting as a common labourer. He was proud of his physical strength and skill, of the sense of personal achievement manual labour gave him as a self-made man. "I have tasted bread in the sweat of my brow as God ordered our ancestor Adam," he once wrote in the course of a later bout of shipbuilding.[15] Moreover he understood with great clarity and from the beginning of his adult life that the only way he could gain mastery over the technical skills which he sought from the West was to acquire them in person. He would never be content simply to engage foreign technicians, nor would he rely upon any spontaneous curiosity and eagerness to learn in his subjects – which was probably as well since such qualities were rare among Russians. Whether or not he already had plans to force Russia to take a violent turn to the West we cannot say – he was never obviously the maker of long-term plans. What is certain is that as an individual, if not as a ruler, Peter had an urgent desire to acquire a whole order of practical skills for himself. Throughout his adult life one of his greatest delights was to work at his lathes. He became a skilled turner, working both in wood and more delicate materials such as ivory. It is totally characteristic that here too it is not possible to determine where play ends and work and learning begin.

There was plenty of play as such. The early 1690's see the beginnings of Peter's "company"; a collection of associates with whom he felt he could be himself, drink and indulge in informal, familiar behaviour free of any kind of kow-towing protocol. That he had a clear sense of the existence of such an inner circle emerges, for example, in a letter in which he reproaches a certain Apraksin for writing to him giving him his czarish title, saying that he ought to know better "since you are one of our company".[16] There is an expression in Russian "svoy chelovek", roughly "our man", "one of us", to which the language and attitudes implied by it attach rather greater significance than is found in the equivalent English idiom. Being either for us or against us, with the rigid and absolute division which the phrase implies,

[15] Ustryalov, vol. ii, p. 131.　　　[16] Corr., vol. i, p. 113.

accords with a certain strain of uncompromising orthodoxy in the Russian temperament. It is significant that the Russian for compromise, *kompromis*, is so obviously a borrowed word. Peter cannot easily be accused of uncompromising orthodoxy in any conventional sense, yet he was very conscious of the notion of "one of us". Just as we find members of his *poteshnye* forming the core round which the new Russian army would be built, so now many of the members of the intimate circle of friends of these early years would play prominent parts in the government of Russia in peace and war until his dying day. In so far as Peter consciously or unconsciously sought to break with the old ways it was perfectly understandable that he should choose his most senior advisers from among the intimate circle of friends and companions whom he took with him as he made the break.

The company's most important member, or presence, was a certain Ivashka Khmelnitsky – the popular Russian counterpart to Bacchus, *khmel'*, meaning both hops and intoxication. The company devoted itself to his celebration with an astounding assiduity. Peter himself loved to drink on a Gargantuan, not to say Russian scale, and indeed the love of alcohol and ceremonious excess which he and his companions practised in the early years and would continue to practise until the end has something in it distinctly reminiscent of Rabelais' Gargantua without the latter's Renaissance humanism.

Peter, Lefort and his cronies would indulge in bouts of enforced celebration which might last for days; enforced in the sense that no one was ever allowed to stop drinking before they had had more than enough. Total intoxication was the rule, and anyone seeking to avoid that fate would have drink poured down him until he collapsed. General Gordon, who had neither the capacity nor the constitution to come through such entertainments easily, records a bout which left him seriously ill for many days; he was luckier than some who never recovered at all and literally died of drink. Peter would always, host or guest, display a violent streak of authoritarianism in his entertainments. Everyone was compelled to drink regardless of their inclination. This is a characteristic developed to extremes in Peter, but by no means unique to him. Making one's guests eat, and above all drink, to the point of physical discomfort and beyond remains an enduring feature of Russian hospitality; while for guests to exercise any form of restraint or moderation is taken as a serious breach of etiquette and an insult to the host.

If Peter remained distinctly Russian in his cult of Ivashka Khmelnitsky, he was the same also in one other respect. For all his impatience with traditional patterns of ritual Peter was far from impatient with ritual as such. Simply, he preferred to create his own. Already in the early 1690's his celebrations take on a weirdly formalised pattern, whereby members of the company are given facetious nicknames or titles, and are expected to fulfil particular roles which are comical and yet taken with a peculiar seriousness. The head, indeed the pontiff, of the company was Peter's old tutor, Nikita Zotov, who was given the strange title of *Kynaz' Papa* or Prince Pope. In due course he was to preside over a whole chapter of cardinals, deacons and masters of ceremony, who indulged in the most elaborate rituals of intoxicated and carnivalesque pageantry. Peter treated his pontiff with an owlish solemnity. He took the title and the respect which it commanded altogether seriously – since otherwise the joke would have been pointless. Once a joke of this kind was made Peter would be slow to tire of it, indeed he could and did sustain it for a lifetime. He loved his humorous relationship with Zotov. In a short letter to him signed Bombodir Peter he refers to him as "Our father, the great gentleman, most holy sire, panikrit, archbishop of Pressburg, patriarch of all Yauza and Kukui" – a formal appellation which made up a quarter of the entire letter.[17] Moreover, Peter's sense of humour called for jokes that were elaborate, protracted, at odds with czarish dignity of a conventional kind and which had the outward appearance of incongruous solemnity, while he was seldom in such a hurry that there was not time for joking. Many years later when Peter was nearly fifty he still took his Prince Pope as seriously as ever. A visitor to his court from the Duchy of Holstein saw him hurrying away from an assembly to the launching of a ship; on encountering his Prince Pope he stopped immediately to kiss him and ask him for a blessing which he received at some length before hastening on.[18] His readiness to stop for an informal piece of "ritual" in such circumstances suggests either that Peter took play very seriously indeed, or that to him his rituals were something more than a mere joke.

Another member of the company was the elderly boyar Ivan

[17] *Corr.*, vol. i, p. 31.   [18] Busching, 1786, vol. xxi, p. 228.

Ivanovich Buturlin. Known for his passionate loathing of Poles he was accordingly granted the title of King of Poland – and would feature as such as a military commander in Peter's manœuvres. Tikhon Nikitich Streshnev, another member of the company and a man of some ability, was addressed by Peter in his letters as "Holy Father", or *"Min her heilige Vater"*. However, the strangest of all these early companions and one of the darkest of all Peter's intimates was the redoubtable Prince Fedor Yurevich Romodanovsky. A violent man with close-set eyes and a cruel mouth, subsequently in charge of Peter's office of secret police, the first permanent establishment of its kind in Russia, he was a rich and powerful boyar of the most traditional stamp, but one who was none the less unswervingly loyal to Peter. Yet he would always retain his old Muscovite colouring. Astounded guests arriving at his entertainments would find themselves received in a most unusual manner:

> It was his custom to force his guests to drink a cup full of strong brandy mixed with pepper, which a huge bear was artfully taught to present to them with one of his paws, and even for diversion's sake to pull off their hats and wigs, and take hold of their clothes if they scrupled to pledge.[19]

The entertainments themselves could be violent enough affairs. One of his guests, Peter's postmaster Vinius, once observed that he had come away from an evening chez Romodanovsky with his cheek bitten through. There is no reason to suppose that this was the bear's doing. Peter treated the bear's owner with a peculiar blend of humour and genuine deference. Romodanovsky was known as the *knyaz'-kesar'*, the Prince Caesar, and Peter would play up to him as if he were his subject. He called him "Your Majesty" and the deferential letters he wrote to him would begin with the Dutch words *"Min her kenich"* and were signed "Your vassal Pieter". In similar vein he would refer to Romodanovsky's "royal letters", while in later years he would make formal announcements of his victories to him as if he were a successful general reporting to his ruler.

There is more here than mere humour. Peter would appoint Romodanovsky to govern in his place during his absences on

[19] Weber, vol. i, p. 137.

campaigns or on his great embassy. He clearly felt Romodanovsky to be a person of presence. Unlike the "King of
Poland", which was clearly a joke title, "Prince Caesar" combined humour with an element of genuine authority. Peter's acts
of homage were both the recognition of that authority and also,
and as usual, the affirmation of his sense of his own personal
dignity. It is because nothing could diminish that dignity that he
could address himself to Romodanovsky as a vassal, in that blend
of play, pride and a no less real sense of personal humility which
makes Peter's character unique. Yet Peter also understood perfectly that there were moments when play must stop. On learning
of the death of a suspect Peter writes as follows:

Prince Fedor Yurevich,
    You wrote to me that Ivashka has died. Let God be your
judge, for you seek to suppress that crime. Yet it shall not
happen like that with the shade of Ivashka Ashikhmin. God
avenges innocent blood and will take vengeance on you.[20]

It would appear that Ashikhmin, suspected of robbery, had,
according to Romodanovsky, jumped out of a window while his
guards were busy kow-towing to their chief who had turned up
for the day's interrogation. He broke his leg badly on falling and
confessed he had tried to kill himself to avoid being tortured.
He died shortly afterwards. The tale of a suspect "falling
from a window in police headquarters" seems to have made
Peter suspicious, and the episode shows incidentally that, for
all Peter's own capacity for violence, he had a strong sense of
justice.

Peter's biographers and hagiographers who love to detect
genius informing his every action try hard to perceive a political
purpose in his organised ritual carousings. Certainly they developed forms which parodied ecclesiastical rituals with steadily
increasing degrees of elaboration. The synod's blasphemous
overtones raise the question of Peter's own religious beliefs.
Throughout his life he would continue to attend church services
and take great delight in his own singing in church. He also
believed it important that his subjects should attend church regularly. More important, he believed himself to be directly answerable to God for the condition of his country, following, in this

[20] *Corr.*, vol. i, p. 480.

respect, European conceptions of the obligations of the absolute monarch. However, by the standards of traditional Russian orthodoxy, his was the faith of a rationalist, a deist almost, which had none of that profound piety or *blagochestie* and total commitment to the rituals of fasting and prayer which had marked earlier Russian rulers. It is not improbable that Peter intended the distinctly blasphemous pageants and processions which we shall see him mount partly at least as a shock and a provocation to his conservative subjects, a challenge to the patterns of Muscovite tradition. Moreover even now, in the early days of the company, we find Peter including powerful and influential figures such as Streshnev and Romodanovsky in their number, taking them with him into the Foreign Quarter where they make formal visits to persons such as Gordon and Lefort. If indeed there was any profound political purpose here it must surely have been the wish to create a company of more or less like-minded and influential Russians loyal to Peter, sympathetic to his ways and accustomed to the company of foreigners.

The company was particularly active in the days between Christmas and Twelfth Night. It was a long-standing custom that over those days priests would pay calls upon households where they would be generously entertained. Charactistically Peter distorted the traditional practice to his own ends. The company would set out, preceded by its "cavalry", twenty-four dwarfs mounted on ponies, and descend upon some luckless foreign merchant or Russian grandee, where they would drink themselves into a stupor at their host's expense. Peter took his sense of grotesque pageantry further still, combining traditional Muscovite practices with his own evolved sense of humour to invent new rituals. Earlier czars had frequently enjoyed freaks, dwarfs and jesters. Peter simply enlarged the scope of their entertainments and took them into the streets. Witness the marriage of his own jester Yakov Turgenev, an ancestor of the novelist's. The couple rode to church in Peter's best coach, while behind them processed some of the highest dignitaries in the land, riding oxen, donkeys, pigs and even in some cases large dogs, dressed magnificently, or in sacking, cat skins, straw boots and mouseskin gloves. The pageant, which must have been the subject of as careful planning and organisation as any more ordinary procession, ended in a three-day drinking bout.

In November 1692 Peter fell seriously ill. He had some form

of dysentery possibly aggravated by too much time spent in the company of Lefort and Ivashka Khmelnitsky. By the middle of December his life appeared to be in serious danger and his supporters began to fear for their heads, since were he to die Sophia would most certainly return to power and go for a clean sweep. However, by Christmas he recovered sufficiently to preside at the wedding of a German goldsmith where he obliged everybody to drink beyond their fill, although remaining moderate himself.

Some months earlier Lefort had written to his brother in Geneva asking him to find him a good engineer, i.e. siege engineer – and above all a firework designer, who would come to Russia. The latter would most certainly make his fortune.[21] Indeed Peter's firework displays were becoming ever more elaborate, his delight in fire combining with something not altogether removed from a sense of propaganda; the use of images and emblems to impress certain political values and attitudes upon the eye of their beholder. On February 21, 1693, there was an elaborate display which he had designed himself. After a fifty-six gun salute, fire traced out the intials of Romodanovsky in Latin script. Next came a fiery Hercules mastering a lion, while Peter himself set off rocket after rocket. These displays were not without their hazards. Gordon recalls one in which a five-pound rocket returned to earth unexploded and hit a nobleman on the head, killing him instantly.[22] The display ended with a banquet which went on till three in the morning, in the course of which Peter's mother rewarded her son for his spectacle by granting him a sergeant's uniform, thereby promoting him from the rank of simple bombardier.[23]

That May Peter worked again in his boatyards in Pereyaslavl' Zalessky, but after three weeks he left, not to return for over twenty years. Both as soldier and sailor Peter believed in starting modestly and then moving on; for the sailor the time had come for the next step.

For some years I fulfilled my desires on the Pereyaslavl' lake, when it grew too small I moved to the lake of Kuben. That also was too small. I then decided to see the open sea and asked the permission of my mother to visit Archangel. She urged me

---

[21] Posselt, vol. ii, p. 196.   [22] Gordon, P., p. 267.   [23] Ustryalov, vol. ii, pp. 144–5.

many times not to undertake such a hazardous journey, but seeing how greatly I desired to go reluctantly she granted me permission.[24]

The Archangel trip made a profound impression on Peter. It was the first time that he had travelled beyond the environs of Moscow, his first sight of the sea, his first contact with sea-going ships and foreign sailors. He appears to have been both overwhelmed and delighted, spending days clambering over ships' rigging, drinking and talking his broken Dutch with the crews. When a convoy of merchantmen sailed for Holland he accompanied them in his yacht, returning to Archangel five days later. It was no doubt the impact of this first contact with the sea-going West that made him realise that he could never find the skills and experience that he wanted in the boatyards of Pereyaslavl'. The sheer scale and scope of the foreign merchantmen, of the sea itself, had seen to that.

Natalya Kirillovna was aghast at the news that her son had put to sea. She wrote Peter a series of anguished letters that are strangely moving, full of exclamations and protestations of an alarmed love. They radiate a particular kind of maternal warmth which may threaten to suffocate unwary offspring, but which is the strongest suit of a certain kind of Russian lady; narrow, easily alarmed and worried by trivia, yet utterly devoted to her children with a love both overpowering and completely genuine. Dostoevsky has rendered the type superbly with his affectionate portrait of Raskolknikov's mother in *Crime and Punishment*. Natalya Kirillovna did all she could to make Peter return, relying on the mother's favourite weapon, emotional blackmail. "My light, my joy, my dear one, dearer to me than my own life. Greetings my joy, czar Peter Alekseevich, long may you live. We, my joy, live on. But we are sad, my light, my joy, that we do not behold you, my light. I wrote to you in the hope that I might expect you home, my joy, and you, my light, have saddened me since you wrote nothing of that...."[25] Peter's reply was cool and circumstantial. He would not return until some ships from Amsterdam should arrive. In the meantime he was impatient with her alarms, in other words resented the blackmail. He was in God's hands and could therefore not be safer. Natalya's subsequent efforts to get him back from the sea even include a letter

[24] *Ibid.*, p. 146.　　　　[25] *Ibid.*, p. 152.

purportedly written by his three-year-old son asking him to come home as quickly as possible:

> To my most powerful lord father, my joy, czar Peter Alekseevich, may you live for many years. Your small son Aleksashka entreats you for your blessing. I, my joyous lord, thanks to the loving kindness of my grandmother, czaritsa Natalya Kirillovna, am in good health. Please come to us, my joyful lord, and without delay. I ask you for this grace because I see my grandmother looking sad. Please do not be angry my lord if this letter is poorly written. I have not yet learnt."[26]

Peter replies, telling his mother not to be sad, since this made it difficult for him to be happy. In its brusqueness it reads like an order in comparison to the eloquent and emotional tone of the letters that he received.

Peter was busy acquiring new skills in the shipyards; he arranged for the construction of a wharf, began to lay the keel of a merchantman. He also ordered a ship to be built for him in Holland. He stayed in the north almost to the end of the sailing season, and shortly before he left there was a firework display to celebrate the launching of a ship. Archangel was built almost entirely of resinous wood, and surrounded by forests. In the circumstances the celebration was a little unwise. Peter describes the ship as being "launched in the name of the apostle Peter, smoked in the incense of Mars, whereby there was a liberal sacrifice to Bacchus". He goes on to complain that Vulcan, the god of fire, was as bad at sea as on land, since Peter's drunken antics had nearly set alight every ship in the harbour, and threatened to burn down the town.[27]

On his return Peter announced elaborate plans for a second visit to Archangel the following year, stating that henceforward anyone who had dealings with him of a maritime nature should address him exclusively as "*shkiper*". He worked hard through the winter on a ship that was being built for him, turning tackle blocks on his lathe in Preobrazhenskoe, casting cannon, and making gun carriages. He singled out various persons from his army and informed them that they were henceforth to be sailors, with a cheeful arbitrariness that is altogether characteristic of his style. He also drew up sets of naval signals, and began to appoint

[26] Ustryalov, vol. ii, p. 151.   [27] *Corr.*, vol. i, p. 23.

officers to the as yet non-existent fleet. Romodanovsky was to be its admiral, while Buturlin and Gordon were to be joint vice-admirals; he was the *shkiper*. The appointments were something of a joke; Romodanovsky was no admiral, while Gordon's experience of the sea was limited to a handful of sailings.

This foundation of a Russian navy was little more than a whim. Peter wanted a navy, so he created one at once. A navy required sailors, so he made soldiers into sailors at the stroke of a pen, and by another stroke created the flag officers to command his fleet and a *shkiper* to sail it. The whole business smacks of an impetuous and enthusiastic potentate who wants instant results. One is tempted to draw comparisons with, if not the heads of some more recently emerged states, then at least the ruler of Evelyn Waugh's *Black Mischief*. But along with those similarities there remains one profound difference. Peter never created the most supreme of supreme ranks in order to promote himself to it. He did not drape himself in decorations of his own creation, nor did he dress in resplendent uniforms. It was this capacity for play, together with the complete absence of self-importance and vainglory, which enabled him never to lose sight of essentials, never to be dazzled by pomp. Indeed it is perhaps these qualities before all others that made him a truly proud and great ruler, who may have begun his navy with three joke admirals and a *shkiper* but who ended with a fleet.

The regular pattern of hard work and heavy drinking was interrupted in 1694 by a rapid decline in the health of Peter's mother. He behaved strangely. When he was told that she was dying he spent some hours at her bedside before rushing off to Preobrazhenskoe, where Gordon found him very sad. Hours later she was dead. It looks as if Peter could not bear to stay with her to the end. Instead, as he was known to do when under severe stress, he ran away. His subsequent behaviour is also peculiar. He did not attend the funeral or the series of services that took place later. However, he went alone to the Voznesensky monastery to pray privately at her grave after vespers. It was as if he rejected public ceremonial in favour of private grief. Certainly Peter felt the loss of his mother, but felt it in an unusual way. Rather than go into mourning he feasted two nights running with Lefort in an attempt to dispel his sorrow through drink. He also made every attempt to drown it through work. Writing to Apraksin a little later he talks briefly of his sorrow and sense of loss before giving detailed instructions about clothing for himself and other workers engaged in shipbuilding. "Now like Noah, having rested a little after my misfortune, I will write about the living...."[28]

The second trip to Archangel was a more elaborate affair. Peter insisted that his admirals Gordon and Romodanovsky accompany him. As yet the Russian navy had only one ship, the *Saint Paul*, which had been built that winter and was launched on their arrival. Her maiden voyage was nearly disastrous. Peter planned to sail to Solovetsky monastery at the mouth of the White Sea but met a terrible storm in the course of which he received the sacraments. However, a good pilot got them ashore and Peter erected a cross to commemorate their deliverance. His act of seemingly traditional piety was qualified by the foreign inscription "*Dat Kruys maken kaptin Piter van a Cht.* 1694" (This Cross was made by Captain Peter in the summer of 1694). On their return they found a second ship, the one ordered in Holland, awaiting them, fully armed.

Peter's *poteshnye* had proved themselves invaluable during the crisis of 1689. They had acted as his personal bodyguard and effectively prevented any kind of assault upon him. From that year on he expanded them rapidly, and it was in the course of the early 1690's that the *poteshnye* became the founding units of the Russian guards, the Preobrazhensky and Semenovsky regiments. Peter still found ample time to exercise them. From 1690 onwards we find accounts of increasingly elaborate manoeuvres which involved up to 20,000 men, *poteshnye*, service nobility, *streltsy* and foreign officers. General Gordon, who had seen real action enough in his time, was secretly amused by the war games played by the young czar, who evidently had little understanding of the art of war, although there was plenty of enthusiasm. Gordon referred to the antics of the *poteshnye* as "The field ballet military" and there was clearly a considerable element of "military theatricals" in their training. This emerges in the so-called Kozhukhovsky campaign, the last and most elaborate of Peter's manoeuvres.

A large force of service nobility and *streltsy* under the command of Buturlin, King of Poland, paraded through Moscow with the king bringing up the rear, escorted by sixteen halberdiers and wearing ceremonial "French" dress. Many of his senior

[28] *Corr.*, vol. i, p. 29.

officers were veterans who had seen plenty of service in the wars of Aleksey, but who now assented to playing at soldiers without a murmur. The king occupied the fortified place of Pressburg, and three days later announced to the enemy that he was ready.

The enemy was commanded by generalissimo Romodanovsky, and they too now paraded through Moscow, led by that "famous old warrior and Kievan colonel", Turgenev, the czar's jester. General Lefort led his own regiment, his carriage escorted by cuirassiers. Then came Gordon with his regiment, and he was followed by the *poteshnye*. Both its regiments had foreign colonels but were under the supreme command of Avtamon Mikhailovich Golovin. In front of the Preobrazhensky regiment marched three bombardiers, including a certain Peter Alekseevich.

On September 27, after a large banquet given to Romodanovsky by the senior merchants of Moscow, who entertained him generously if not voluntarily, the generalissimo proceeded to the banks of the Yauza river, while the King of Poland stood on the far side. After a ceremonious exchange of insults, blaming one another for starting the war, and lapsing occasionally into common swearing, the two leaders sent forth champions to engage in single combat. This was not an honourable affair. Each fighter was selected for his prowess and courage, but when Romodanovsky's man squeezed off a quick shot at his opponent the latter turned and ran, to be pursued right to his own camp by his victor, who lashed him across the shoulders the while.

Peter's manœuvres also had their serious side, and were quite dangerous enough. The staple and distinctly unpleasant weapon employed was a kind of grenade, or imitation bomb, made of tarred cardboard filled with gunpowder and fused. There were also earthenware pots similarly charged which weighed up to five pounds. The grenades could be dangerous. Once Peter's face was severely burnt, while another grenade wounded Gordon so badly in the leg that he had to stay in bed for a week. Muskets and cannon were used, firing blanks, which could be quite harmful enough at close quarters. There were also mortars firing clay balls. According to Gordon live rounds were loosed off on occasion and there was severe hand-to-hand fighting. The Kozhukhovsky manœuvres culminated in the storming of Pressburg, which involved filling in ditches beneath showers of hot water and boiling oil, exploding mines and eventually taking the place by storm – albeit with blunted swords and pikes. The manœuvre had to be repeated since Peter pronounced himself dissatisfied with the first attempt. All in all it is no wonder that there were occasional fatalities on these affairs, and that there were numerous casualties, burnt or wounded. In other words the manœuvres went remarkably close, in some ways, to simulating conditions of active service even if they did end with a banquet. The campaign should best be considered as an intermediate stage – between the games of the early *poteshnye* and the genuine shooting war that Peter was to embark upon next.

CHAPTER FIVE

Peter Goes to War

Peter understood that his Kohzhukhovsky campaign was a preparation for the real thing. Looking back, he wrote: "Although that game was no more than a game at the time, yet after it was over we had something very different, and the earlier affair turned out to be its forerunner."[1] The observation is revealing, suggesting that Peter had no long-term strategy, no grand design into which his manœuvres fitted. It was simply that the experience gained there happened to help when it came to that very different something which was war with the Turks. Peter always preferred empirically based responses *ad hoc* to anything smacking of a master plan. Yet in retrospect he could make the link between his clowning manœuvres and the subsequent attack on the Turks; as he wrote to Apraksin, "at Kozhukhovo we joked, and now we go to play in front of Azov".[2]

Peter's reasons for declaring war on the Turks were various, and some of his motives for playing in front of Azov may well have been personal, not to say frivolous. It would be wrong to suppose that Peter entered into wars for reasons of high political expediency alone. He himself always claimed that he was decided to wage war on Sweden – a war that would last over twenty years – by the inhospitable reception he and his great embassy were accorded by the Swedish governor of Riga. It is not impossible that one of the reasons that prompted him to move on Azov was the simple fact that he wanted to fight; he had had his fill of manœuvres and now wished to try his hand at the real thing. Besides he wanted a navy, and a navy needed the sea. The Baltic

[1] *Corr.*, vol. i, p. 22.　　　　[2] Ustryalov, vol. ii, p. 228.

coast was in Swedish hands and Swedes were more formidable enemies than Turks. Accordingly he thought in terms of basing his navy on a Black Sea port. He wanted a navy, a navy needed a port, a northern port was out of the question, QED. Of course there were conventional and traditional political considerations besides. Moscow still paid tribute to the Crimean Tartars, a traditional infidel enemy who remained a threat to its southern border. Moreover Russia was constantly being urged by Poland and Austria to make a more substantial contribution to their war upon the Turk. Then there was the disgraceful memory of V. V. Golitzyn's two Crimean campaigns to be wiped out. There were good reasons also to pick Azov as a target. It had been taken and held in 1637 by cossacks who had withstood massive Turkish counter-attacks – their story is splendidly told in *The Tale of the Don Cossacks in the Siege of Azov*. Unfortunately Turkish diplomatic pressure had required czar Mikhail Fedorovich to hand the fortress back.

It was a combination of these considerations that prompted Peter to start the siege, hostilities beginning on July 8, 1695. Azov itself had once been a Venetian and Genoan trading place, and the arms of Genoa could still be made out on an inner wall. Gordon considered it tolerably but not excessively strong. It was square, with a stone wall and an inner wall of earth, with a deep ditch between them. The river Don flowed close by it into the sea, and this was guarded by two watchtowers and a chain across the river.

Peter had divided his forces among three separate generals, Gordon, Lefort, who knew little enough of war, and Golovin. He remained content to command a unit of bombardiers – "The great bombardier" Gordon calls him in his diaries, a deadpan appellation which was as close as that cautious Scot ever went to irony. The siege opened with an elaborate artillery bombardment, Peter firing the first shot, which went on for a fortnight and was utterly ineffectual. It became obvious that no one present understood the proper application of siege artillery. The whole business was further complicated by the presence of large numbers of Tartar irregulars, some armed with bows, while their officers wore coats of mail. They never pressed home a serious attack, but continued to harass the Russians, making it dangerous for foraging parties and other small units to wander far from camp.

The conduct of the siege did not impress Gordon. Divided command made for long and inconclusive conferences in the presence of the great bombardier; Gordon for one was reluctant to provoke him and kept his opinions very much to himself. There was poor integration of command between the various elements, notably the cossack and Ukrainian irregulars who frequently went into action drunk. Intelligence was poor; there was little or no reconnaissance and the army was vulnerable to surprise sorties.[3] Gordon was frustrated and dissatisfied by the amateur quality of the campaign; 'everything proceeded with great slowness and confusion as if it were not an earnest matter".[4] Officers and men alike were green and proved incapable of complicated tactical manoeuvres under fire.[5] Indeed a prisoner who managed to escape from Azov revealed that its defenders regarded the siege as something of a joke.[6]

For all the shortcomings of his army and its commanders Peter himself displayed great energy and courage as a bombardier. He was often to be found in the front line and on one occasion narrowly escaped a sniper's bullet. He wrote cheerfully home to his sister Natalya, who had warned him to be careful: "As for your letter, I do not go near bullets and cannon balls, it is they that come near me. Order them to desist; though it must be said that, come though they will, they have so far come politely."[7]

The Russians were not completely unsuccessful. After a bloody skirmish, in the course of which some twenty Turks killed or wounded 200 Russians, they took one of the watchtowers, putting its defenders to the sword – an example which persuaded the garrison of the second tower to withdraw at once. With both towers in Russian hands Peter was now able, should he wish, to attack Azov from the river, and more important, he was no longer cut off from the sea. For as matters presently stood his only hope was to take Azov by storm. There could be no question of starving it into submission, since the defenders could get all the supplies and reinforcements they might need by ship.

The taking of the towers, which would in the long run prove an action of considerable importance, was soon followed by a humiliating setback. A Dutchman, and hence a favourite of Peter's Jakob Jansen, for reasons best known to himself, defected to the Turks, and subsequently became a Mohammedan. He revealed

---

[3] Gordon, P., p. 588.   [4] Ibid., p. 578.   [5] Ibid., p. 583.
[6] Ibid., p. 604.   [7] Corr., vol. i, p. 77.

to his new allies certain fundamental weaknesses in the Russian army, not the least of which was their habit of breaking off hostilities around noon in order to take a siesta. The Turks took unsporting advantage of such indolence to make a sortie in force early one afternoon, catching the somnolent besiegers by surprise. They overran Gordon's front lines and butchered some of the *streltsy* they encountered there, while others beat a hasty retreat regardless of a sixteen-gun redoubt which stood in immediate support:

> As I approached and saw our *streltsy* running away I sent them back to effect a rapid rescue. I advanced with the few men I had with me and checked the rout; some more soldiers came up and we sent the Turks flying back across our lines. Paying no heed to my orders to halt and hold the lines, they pursued the Turks up to the ditch where they turned, and were joined by fresh troops, sent up a fearful cry, counter-attacked and put our men to flight again. They could not be persuaded to make a stand in their trenches, running straight over them past the redoubt and out into the open, panicking to a degree I have never seen before. If but a hundred had stood their ground we could have held the redoubt...[8]

Gordon, together with his son and one soldier, attempted to hold the position but was very nearly cut off and had to fight through to safety. He was quite unable to persuade the men or their officers to regroup and counter-attack. The Turks spiked the heavier pieces and took the rest away. It was not until Peter himself came up with his guards that the lines were cleared. Small wonder that Gordon held both officers and men in low esteem.

At a council of war Peter, Lefort and Golovin decided to attempt a storm. Gordon knew perfectly well that the men were not up to such a tactic, although, always too conscious of his situation to commit himself, he did not say as much to the inexperienced and over-eager commanders. The attack was not particularly well conducted. Volunteers had been called for, and there was a severe disproportion between other ranks and officers, not many of whom seemed prepared for death or glory. Moreover, a ditch was to be crossed and a wall scaled without the assistance of fascines or siege ladders. The *streltsy* units,

[8] Gordon, P., p. 575.

reported Gordon, were supposed to move forward at dawn, but displayed no great eagerness to do so, and it was some time before they could be persuaded to advance. Gordon's regiment, on the left, kept up a heavy fire on a certain corner bastion, but the troops supposedly advancing on the right to scale the walls shifted across towards the left wing, "finding it more prudent to linger there than to press home their assault upon the wall".[9] Gordon's men silenced their bastion and actually stormed their section of the wall successfully. However, they met such a fierce counter-attack, the Turks having only that sector to deal with, that they were soon beaten off and forced to retire. Gordon estimates that the Russians lost some 1500 officers and men, while the Turks lost no more than 200.

The siege continued with no greater measure of success. An attempt was next made to mine the city walls; a tunnel was dug and filled with massive explosive charges. Gordon suspected that the mine was too short, and so it turned out. When sprung it proved to be well short of the ditch and did no damage whatsoever to Azov, although the earth and stones caused quite heavy casualties among the besiegers, killing thirty and wounding 200. The engineer responsible, Adam Weide, "was obliged to abscond for a few days".[10] It was growing obvious that the campaign was an expensive failure and in September Peter reluctantly decided to raise the seige. The retreating army was chivvied on its way by Tartar cavalry, which succeeded in cutting off and destroying an entire regiment. Poor fodder and dysentery did not make the retreat any easier, and by the time it reached Moscow Peter's army was not in good shape.

Unlike Golitsyn, whose only answer to an initial failure was to start a second, otherwise identical campaign somewhat earlier in the year, Peter proved able to face his mistakes and learn from them. Failures never crushed him, he regarded them as valuable if sometimes expensive lessons which should provide the foundation of subsequent success. The first Azov campaign had taught him his weaknesses. His command structure had been bad; an understandable reluctance to lead himself had made him adopt a divided command. His army lacked effective gunners and engineers. He was unable to prevent the Turks from supplying Azov by sea.

He responded immediately by sending to Prussia and Austria

[9] *Ibid.*, p. 586.   [10] Gordon, A., p. 101.

for siege experts, mining engineers and gunners, to Holland for shipwrights, and proceeded to turn the town of Voronezh into an enormous shipyard.

It was an excellent site. Some 250 miles north of Azov, it was the southernmost town on the Don – or rather a tributary which joined the main river ten miles downstream, which was still in the afforested part of Russia as opposed to the treeless southern steppe. Peter was determined to make it the cradle of the Russian navy, thinking entirely in terms of a Black Sea fleet at the time.

He quickly mobilised colossal supplies of labour – soldiers, convicts and serfs – and by the end of that year, 1696, some 30,000 men were working in the yards. Timber procurement was entrusted to a certain Grigory Titov, who had to supply and cut up over 7000 trees by February 1, "for galleys, galeases and branders", i.e. transports of various kinds. He also had to provide supplies of pitch, hemp and nails, and have all ready by the time Peter should arrive in the early spring.[11] This alone was a considerable undertaking, particularly since sawmills were unknown in Russia. Although Russians had built boats before, they had fashioned them with axes. Russian peasants were marvellously skilled with the axe, but the process was none the less a slow and wasteful one. However, 1696 saw the first water-driven mills in use, and Peter expressly forbade the use of the axe when a sufficient number of mills became available.[12] There was also the fact that those ordered to procure the supplies were totally ignorant of shipbuilding. The survey team sent to select the timber had no idea what kind of trees were suitable for felling – so they proceeded according to the traditional Russian principles of "*na avos*" – "who knows, it might work" – and felled without discrimination.

In the meantime Peter had his workforce labouring day and night to prepare a flotilla. He came to work, too, as a labourer and supervisor, entering into an extraordinary degree of detail. Thus we find a letter in which he concerns himself to ensure that there is an adequate supply of rules and compasses.[13] He was either constitutionally incapable of delegation, or, more likely, simply understood that there was no one sufficiently reliable to whom to delegate. Inevitably this dramatic and instant mobilisation of resources produced the most mixed results. Many ships proved so ill-proportioned that they were quite unseaworthy.

[11] Ustryalov, vol. ii, p. 260.　　[12] Wittram, vol. ii, p. 285.　　[13] *Corr.*, vol. i, p. 63.

Others were made of frozen or green wood and were equally hopeless. Construction was also hampered by fires, late frosts and snowstorms. Yet for all the ignorance, inefficiency and incompetence, Peter's personal energy and his extravagant use of natural and human resources produced results. It was a characteristically Russian success story, a triumph of quantity rather than quality, and a costly one, but a triumph none the less, the kind of Russian success that recalls the comment of the French engineer who invented the gear box: '*C'est brutal, mais ça marche.*"

By spring Peter's energies – he had lived for months in a two-roomed wooden house with his workmen – had created out of nothing a fleet of two warships, twenty-three galleys, four fire-ships and a quantity of smaller craft, and he was ready for the second Azov campaign to begin.

He announces his success in a characteristically facetious letter to Romodanovsky:

> *Min her koninih,*
> The royal letter that you wrote on the 23rd was given to me on the 29th. In it it pleased you to express your anger at the fact that I, your vassal, had not written to you my lord; and now, my lord, I write yet another letter since the earlier one I sent has gone astray. And here, my lord, thanks to the mercy of God and your good grace everything about the caravan is ready and matters go forward apace; I shall keep you informed of what will happen in the future.
> Your vassal, Kapten Piter.[14]

Peter's flotilla his "caravan" – sailed on May 3 and reached Azov a fortnight later. The army, now under the supreme command of Aleksey Semenovich Shein, was already in position. On arrival it was revealed to Peter's great excitement that two Turkish supply ships were lying off Azov. It was decided that he would attack these with nine galleys, carrying a regiment, together with forty boat-loads of cossacks, a total strength of 800. Peter left Gordon on the evening of 19th but, much to that general's surprise, less than forty-eight hours later the czar and his troops were back, without having fired a shot. Peter explained to the bewildered general that there were twenty and not two Turkish vessels, and that in the circumstances he felt it prudent to withdraw, declaring himself very upset by the whole business. Perhaps

[14] Bogoslovsky, vol. i, p. 297.

it was too much to expect a twenty-four-year-old would-be naval commander to press home his first attack with inexperienced troops acting as marines for the first time in such circumstances. Nevertheless Peter must have had mixed feelings, including an element of confusion, when he learnt, the next day, that the cossacks had gone in alone. Out of a total of forty-two galleys and light craft they had burnt twenty-four while six had got into Azov and the rest had withdrawn. The cossacks captured large quantities of military supplies, bombs, grenades, powder, and also food. The prisoners they took told them that the ships had contained 800 reinforcements which the attackers had driven away. All in all it was a very successful action, and one which discouraged any further attempt to supply Azov by sea. Peter, who would always delight in announcing victories in personal letters, wrote triumphantly to "*Min Her Kernih*" Romodanovsky, though the letter gives no account of the part he played: "When the [Turkish] vessels were opposite the river mouth, we your vassals in small vessels and the cossacks in their boats, praying with God's help, threw ourselves upon the enemy..."[15]

The siege did not make much progress at first. The foreign experts had not arrived and the artillery made little impression on the defences. Curiously enough the strategy that probably turned the tide for the Russians was suggested neither by Peter nor his generals, but by the men. Gordon informs us that they came to their commanders and suggested "the throwing up of a wall of earth and driving it towards the town wall", a suggestion which was immediately accepted.[16]

The idea seems to have been to build up an earth rampart, and then move it forward by filling up the space immediately in front of it. The technique had been employed to some effect in the 10th century, but it is strange that it should have been adopted in the 17th. Perhaps it was Gordon's failure to do any damage to a corner bastion he had been shooting at for a month that made him accept the plan and pursue it so energetically. "There were 12,000 men at work who threw the earth up from hand to hand like so many steps of a stair. The greatest danger was of course at the top where, the earth being so loose, the enemy's small shot killed and wounded several."[17] The rolling rampart gradually approached the city walls, and being higher than the walls themselves, the besiegers were actually able to shoot down

[15] Ustryalov, vol. ii, pp. 332–3.   [16] *Ibid.*, p. 285.   [17] Gordon, A., p. 108.

into the city. Moreover the earthen wall had come so close that, according anyway to Peter, hand-to-hand fighting with the defenders was possible.[18]

The wall was almost finished when the imperial siege experts finally arrived – on July 9 – gunners, miners, engineers. They had taken their time over the journey since no one at the Austrian court associated Russian military operations with any kind of urgency. The Russian ambassador had known nothing of Peter's early start to the campaign for the excellent reason that the head of the Ambassadorial Office, a certain Ukraintsev, had sent him no news of the army in case he should spread it about Vienna. When Peter heard this he observed with feeling that, whatever Ukraintsev henceforth failed to write on paper, he would personally inscribe upon his back.[19] The Imperial experts were amazed by the scale and nature of the Russian operation, though they had their doubts as to its efficiency, preferring more conventional methods such as mines and guns. Indeed, once the Imperial gunners had redirected the Russian batteries they did such severe damage to the corner bastion that the Turks were obliged to abandon it. The siege was virtually over, and the Turks accepted an offer of surrender on July 18. They were permitted to leave with weapons, families and personal effects. Some difficulties were made over the handing over of the traitor Jansen, who had became a Turkish janissary, but Peter was adamant, and the wretch was duly passed across. Peter immediately penned a brief triumphant dispatch to Romodanovsky:

> I beg to tell you Sire, that the Lord God has blessed our arms, since yesterday, thanks to our prayers and good fortune, the defenders of Azov, finding themselves sore pressed, surrendered, I shall tell you what I can about terms and booty. They have handed the traitor Jakob over alive.[20]

When the Russians entered the town they found it in ruins. Gordon noted that the Turks had not even bothered to repair their defences after the siege of the previous year, suggesting either idleness, or the low opinion in which they held the Russian threat.

Azov was indeed Russia's first victory over Turkey, and as such had great symbolic value. It captured the imagination of Europe,

[18] Ustryalov, vol. ii, p. 285.   [19] *Corr.*, vol. i, p. 90.   [20] *Ibid.*, vol. i, p. 95.

and was quite correctly taken as a sign that Russia was at last beginning to emerge from her legendary sleep. Azov was moreover Peter's victory, first and last last – except for that moving wall. He had picked his target, learned from his failures, built a flotilla, secured the services of military experts, taken the town. Now, as he thought, the way lay open to build a Black Sea fleet.

Peter loved pageantry, as long as it was pageantry of his own devising, and he was particularly fond of elaborate victory parades. He had wanted to have a new bridge built over the Moscow river to celebrate his triumph, but it could not be finished in time, so instead he decorated his capital with arches and allegorical figures such as Hercules, Mars and Neptune. It is not known where Peter acquired his smattering of classical mythology, although the probable source was Lefort, nor can we say what impression these alien emblems made upon the people of Moscow, though one imagines very little. They saw a procession headed by the foreigner, Admiral Lefort, and General Shein, both dressed magnificently, riding in gilded sledges, while behind them walked their anointed monarch who had now attained the rank of Captain Peter, in plain foreign dress, marching at the head of his bombardiers, and carrying a pike on his shoulder. The sight must certainly have created an impression – one of profound bewilderment and indignation, for Peter's style, his blend of ironic modesty and sense of the grandiose, was enough to bewilder persons more sophisticated that the common people of Moscow.

After the parade came a winter firework display upon the Moscow river, in which Peter took a prominent and characteristic part:

> His Czarish Majesty took a particular delight to be among the engineers, and had himself a hand in making the greatest machine, which was erected in the very centre of the rest. It was a double spread eagle, who with his left claw darted rockets upon a horizontal line at one of the horns of a half moon ... the whole design being laid out by his Majesty himself, and drawn up with his own hand.[21]

Peter loved such displays for their own sake, and throughout his life would be prodigal in his extravagant consumption of gun-

[21] Bouvet, pp. 34–5.

powder for fireworks and salutes. Yet here too we find a characteristic blending of play and instruction, for Peter believed that even fireworks had their uses:

> I know well enough that when it comes to fireworks I pass for extravagant ... However, I believe them to be necessary since these fiery entertainments can teach my subjects to grow accustomed to the fire of war, and exercise themselves properly. I have discovered from experience that people grow less afraid of gunfire as they grow accustomed to handling fireworks.[22]

After the fireworks Peter continued his celebrations at the house of Lefort. There he learnt that Shein had taken all the captured Turkish standards back to his own residence. Peter immediately sent for them, but Shein was reluctant to give them up. A second messenger met with no more success, and it was only on a third request, couched in the most peremptory language, that the successful commander-in-chief reluctantly passed them across.

Peter now began to make elaborate plans for a Black Sea fleet. At a council meeting in November 1696 he decided that every nobleman owning a thousand serfs was to build one ship while lesser lords were to constitute companies, each of which would be responsible for a vessel. In this way a total of forty-eight ships would be built and were to be ready by April 1, 1698. At the same time work was begun on the restoration of Azov while 20,000 men were sent to Taganrog, a nearby town, which was to be turned into a port. More ambitious still was yet another plan, to join the Don and the Volga by means of a canal – which among other advantages would make it possible to travel from Moscow to Azov by water. Immense numbers of men were mobilised for the various enterprises; up to thirty thousand laboured in unattractive conditions on the canal alone. Work on the canal continued for some years before it was finally abandoned. It was first supervised by a German engineer, Colonel Breckell, but when one of his sluices "blew up" he requested a travel pass for one of his servants to go abroad for essential supplies, and made use of it himself to escape the country. His place was filled by an Englishman, John Perry, who was bemused by the scale of the enterprise and the ruthless yet wasteful deployment of labour.

[22] Dashkov, p. 49.

The work "went on at vast profusion of treasure and expense of the lives of men".[23] There were other difficulties such as the local governor, who had been less than helpful, being opposed to the whole enterprise as "a thing impossible to be done by the hands of men ... declaring it was his opinion that God had made the rivers to go one way and that it was presumption in man to turn them another".[24]

The labour forces deployed, on the Don and in the Voronezh area, eventually extended to under-age children sent to help their fathers in the woods. It embraced both peasants and the lower levels of the service classes, and was the first example of that subsequent institution of the Soviet labour camps, which co-opted anyone and everyone without regard for rank, age, sex or professional qualification, making murderous use of forced labour for timber felling, the *lesopoval*. Yet Peter's régime could not match the efficiency of modern Russia. The desertion rate was tremendous, tantamount sometimes to mass emigration, and records show that some labour contingents were reduced to half strength within six weeks. Yet typically, despite colossal waste and inefficiency, the work went forward, and results were achieved.

Peter was no less direct in his solution to the problem of finding officers to sail the ships that were about to be built. Just as foreign travel had hitherto been prohibited by decree, so Peter now ordered that fifty young noblemen were to travel; to go to Holland and England to study seamanship at their own expense, on pain of dispossession of their lands. They were not to return without a certificate of competence.[25]

That Peter's style of leadership should have inspired bewilderment, mistrust and downright hostility in a nation so profoundly conservative that noblemen of the highest rank were reluctant to disturb rivers in their course is scarcely surprising. Peter would always have to struggle against a conservative opposition which ranged from mulish inertia through more or less orthodox criticism to high treason. Very early on he had established the Preobrazhensky Office to deal with actual or intended crimes against the state. It was run by the redoubtable Romodanovsky, who enjoyed his work. On one occasion he wrote to Peter defending himself against accusations of drunkenness: "I have no time to consort with Ivashka Khmelnitsky; I am perpetually awash with

[23] Perry, p. 7.   [24] *Ibid., loc. cit.*   [25] Bogoslovsky, vol. iv, p. 306.

blood."[26] He was answering the complaint of a Scotsman, Jacob Bruce, who had informed Peter that he had been tortured "by mistake", by an intoxicated Romodanovsky. The latter replied indignantly that it was he, Bruce, who was drunk and had inadvertently burnt his own hand or tortured himself. This magnificent reply recalls the classic line in Gogol's *Inspector General* in which an apprehensive mayor informs the person he presumes to be the inspector that a certain NCO's wife had not in fact been flogged, but that "she had flogged herself". The first permanent institution of its kind, the Office was the father of the Russian secret police. It made extensive use of severe methods of interrogation, and judicial torture was automatically applied to anyone suspected of the shadow of a criminal intent against Peter. The czar justified this practice ingeniously. His secret office relied very largely upon the time-honoured Russian habit of denunciation. Commenting on his extensive use of torture Peter once observed that he "did not want an unclean conscience before God, so would never rely upon a denunciation that had not been thoroughly tested by torture".[27]

One of the most interesting of the Office's early cases concerned a group of junior civil servants and peasants, one of whom, Ivan Pososhkov, was to write a fascinating treatise on the Russian economy, *The Book about Poverty and Wealth*. They used to gather in a monastery cell belonging to a monk, Avramy, in order to discuss their discontent with the state of the nation. They complained that the civil service was being expanded excessively, recruiting proceeding according to corrupt and nepotic principles. Judges too were corrupt, and should perhaps be paid salaries in order to discourage them from taking bribes. They were disappointed in Peter for failing to improve matters. They criticised him for abandoning the Kremlin, for forsaking his wife and failing to have a large family. They complained of the often blasphemous antics of the company, of the cost, inconvenience and dangers of his manœuvres. They were profoundly shocked by the part Peter had played in the Azov victory parade, walking behind Lefort's sledge. They also suggested that Peter played too active a part in the proceedings of the Peobrazhensky Office, interrogating and torturing in person. Avramy was extremely distressed; ready to risk martyrdom, or else, even by the standards of his age and nation, simple-minded to a degree, he composed a

[26] Soloviev, vol. ii, p. 584.　　　　　[27] Dashkov, p. 111.

kind of open letter to Peter informing him of the people's disappointment in their czar, "who indulged in play, abandoned the path of righteousness and had begun to bring misery and tears to all".[28] Not surprisingly the critics were all arrested; what is surprising is that the ringleaders were merely exiled while Pososhkov succeeded in establishing his innocence. It is impossible to account for the leniency of the sentences or for Pososhkov's escape in an age in which nobles were frequently flogged for voicing the faintest criticism of Peter, and another would-be critic, a certain Talitsky, a clerk, would be roasted, smoked and quartered for *intending* to publish a work criticising Peter – although he did admittedly advance therein the thesis that Peter was Anti-Christ.

Criticism also came from Peter's relations by marriage; witness the case of his wife's uncle, Peter Abramovich Lopukhin, who was tortured and exiled for allegedly conspiring against the czar. It was easy enough to be executed for wishing him ill, all too easy to be severely punished, witness the case of a monk who reported Peter's half-brother to have said: "My brother does not live like a czar, he visits the Foreign Quarter and keeps company with foreigners." He was flogged, lost his tongue, and was sent to Siberia for life.[29] Indeed, by a kind of lunatic logic, Peter had the tongues cut out of persons convicted of accusing him of cruelty. As much was done to a lady subsequently exiled for life who observed: "On days that his Majesty and Prince Romodanovsky drink blood they are merry, and when they do not their bread seems tasteless."

In view of the widespread opposition to Peter it is curious that we should know of only one actual plot against his life. The chief plotter was the *strelets* colonel, Tsykler, who had rallied early to Peter in 1689. An ambitious man, he had been disappointed by Peter's failure to reward him adequately. He plotted with two friends, Fedor Pushkin, an ancestor of the poet, and Andrey Sokovin, to start a fire somewhere in Moscow, knowing that Peter always attended and fought fires in person. He was never heavily escorted on such occasions and could easily be cut down. Tsykler's part in the plot was revealed by two *streltsy* informers and after intensive interrogation he revealed the names of his associates. Their intentions emerged in part in the protocol of their interrogation. They hoped to restore Sophia and V. V.

[28] Bogoslovsky, vol. iv, p. 387. [29] Golikova, p. 43.

Golitsyn, who would act as regents to Peter's son. They wished to see the *streltsy* regain their authority. Peter would be the ruin of them all, and moreover they could never gain his favour since he associated them with Ivan Miloslavsky, who had died some twelve years ago, and who had once suggested to Tsykler that he assassinate Peter. There were other reasons besides; Tsykler resented working on the construction of Taganrog, while Sokovin, an arch-conservative and Old Believer, was distressed at the order to send two of his sons abroad.

Peter responded to anything recalling Sophia's plotting and the *streltsy* rebellion with extreme brutality, and, on this occasion, with a particularly vile piece of ceremony. Tsykler and Sokovin were sentenced to lose their hands and feet and to be beheaded. Pushkin was simply to lose his head. The body of Miloslavsky was disinterred. An eye-witness says that his head had shrunk to the size of a fist, his black beard had grown to his navel, but his body, swollen tight as a drum, was entire.[30] It was taken to the place of execution on a sledge drawn by pigs, and the blood of the victims poured over it before it was quartered and hung on a gibbet.

One cannot help feeling that Peter brought a particular, calculating barbarism to the execution. It even shocked contemporary observers, although one at least made a valiant attempt to justify it. Writing some twenty-six years later Daniel Defoe observed: "The severity of the executions in this case are excused by their being at Muscovy, where experience has taught that such executions are needful; and where if such a severe course had not been taken it might have been hard to persuade the people to believe that the conspiracy had been real, the government in earnest."[31]

[30] Tumansky, vol. iv, p. 218.   [31] Defoe, p. 43.

CHAPTER SIX

A Grand Tour

His journey is an epoch in the
history not of his own country
but of ours and the world.
Macaulay

The Tsykler conspiracy had come to light on the eve of what
must surely be the most elaborate grand tour in history, Peter's
eighteen-month embassy. When considering the unusual nature
of his enterprise we should recall that it was anything but the
custom for the czar of Muscovy to travel abroad, that Peter had
reason to believe that there was considerable unrest and discontent at home, and that moreover his country was still at war
with the Turks.

The formal intention of the embassy was indeed to negotiate
a great European alliance against Turkey, and to strengthen
Moscow's diplomatic links with the nations of Europe. However,
beyond such relatively conventional motives lay Peter's curiosity
about the West, more particularly about shipbuilding. It was in
order to extend his own knowledge and skills, to recruit foreign
experts, to buy foreign ships and naval supplies, that he planned
to visit Holland, England and Venice. It was quite consistent with
Peter's habit of starting from small beginnings and later to expand
that he should now pay an extensive visit to the West in person,
in order to develop the first modest contacts with Western ways
which he had made through Timmerman, Gordon and Lefort.

The wisdom of his leaving his country did not impress itself
upon all observers. The Count d'Avaux, French ambassador in

Stockholm, described the embassy as "quite bizarre, and indeed quite against *le bon sens*".[1] For another contemporary, however, "the motive which could induce so great a prince to leave for some time his native country cannot be attributed to any other cause than his most ardent desire of improving his own knowledge and of his subjects, quite contrary to what has been practised by his predecessors, who looked upon the ignorance of their subjects as the main foundation stone of their absolute power".[2] Peter's aims are best rendered by the seal he used on his travels, portraying a young carpenter surrounded by shipwright's tools and military equipment, bearing an inscription in Old Church Slavonic: "I am in the ranks of the pupils and require instruction".

Typically, Peter did not lead his own embassy. There were three ambassadors, Golovin, Voznitsyn and, inevitably, Lefort. Numbering about 200 persons in all, the most important element consisted of some thirty volunteers, *poteshnye*, bombardiers and nobles from Peter's immediate entourage and including a certain "Peter Mikhailovich". Peter took this incognito very seriously – to the extent of having all outgoing mail censored to prevent the news of his presence escaping,[3] although it rapidly became common knowledge that one of the volunteers was indeed the young czar. Peter was not difficult to pick out. He appeared at this time:

> a very tall and lusty person, well set, with very good features in his face, and there is a great deal of vivacity in his eyes, which are black and sprightly; he has certain marks of a sweet disposition in his physiognomy.[4]

Published just two years after the embassy set out, the description has to be read between the lines. The "vivacity of his eyes" is a tactful way of suggesting that, as other observers found, even from an early age his somewhat bulging stare could inspire real terror,[5] whereas the certain marks of a sweet disposition suggest that this terror could be tempered by good nature.

Peter elected to travel incognito partly for the sake of freedom from those ambassadorial ceremonials which would always provoke his impatience, partly because informality of this kind appealed to him. Yet there is another reason. Peter seems to have had a profound aversion, a terror almost, of crowds. He hated

[1] Wittram, vol. i, p. 132.   [2] Crull, p. 206.   [3] Ustryalov, vol. iii, p. 16.
[4] Bouvet, p. 51.   [5] Soloviev, vol. vii, p. 552.

being singled out and treated as a public spectacle. This of course fits in with his love of informal modes of behaviour. It would be preposterous to try to determine whether love of the informal created fear of crowds or *vice versa*, yet instinct, a legitimate guide for a biographer if not a historian, suggests that Peter's dislike of crowds, ceremonies, the old rituals, all have a link with his feelings on that morning in 1682 when the *streltsy* streamed into the Kremlin.

Among Peter's volunteers was a certain Alexander Menshikov, a protégé of Lefort, who would soon become, after Peter, the most powerful and quite possibly the wealthiest man in Russia. A person of great intelligence and an unmitigated scoundrel, his origins are obscure. It used to be rumoured that he had once sold pies in the streets of Moscow a rumour he did not discourage. On one of the many occasions that his corrupt practices earned him Peter's rage, the czar threatened to put him back to pie selling. He allegedly collected a trayful and brought them to Peter, shouting his wares, and winning back the czar's favour by judicious clowning and self-abasement. However, his father appears to have served in Peter's guards, which would not be consistent with his son vending pies. We do know that he was an employee and favourite of Lefort, and it is through him that he first grew close to Peter.

Menshikov was a person of striking appearance: "tall, well-shaped, very handsome in his person and of great penetration".[6] He impressed foreigners by exceptional cleanliness and tidiness of dress, which distinguished him from the rest of his countrymen. Over the years Peter's affections for him would develop into a passion, which to some observers went well beyond the limits of normal friendship. He would heap favours and honours upon him, and raise him above the highest in the land; moreover Menshikov would be the one exception to Peter's rule never to continue to trust anyone who had once betrayed him or let him down.

Like Lefort, only more so perhaps, Menshikov understood how to please Peter. He addressed him with a blend of servility, familiarity and impertinence, while being a past master at mocking or humiliating others for Peter's pleasure. He would pimp for him or appear to share his enthusiasm for building ships with equal ease. Vain, greedy, ambitious, with an insatiable appetite

[6] Bruce, p. 91.

for money and for pomp, he was also a person of considerable ability. Although practically illiterate he seems to have been able to fulfil the various responsibilities, military and civil, conferred upon him by Peter, and, more to the point perhaps, proved able, for all his massive corruption, to survive. The impression Menshikov leaves as a character is conveyed by two Russian words, both pejoratives, *naglost'* and *nakhal' stvo* – "effrontery" and a "coarse and cocky insolence" – along with considerable intelligence and understanding of Peter. A final characteristic, Menshikov was expert at a certain kind of kick employed in a form of Muscovite wrestling, which he used quickly and deftly to sweep his opponent's legs from under him.

The embassy left Moscow on March 9, 1697, taking with it enormous quantities of food, especially honey and dried fruit. It took the northern route out of Russia, through Swedish Livonia, and the first major foreign city it arrived at was Riga. This was the embassy's first contact with the West, Peter's first sight of a modern city, and clearly a critical moment for the young man so aware of his own ignorance that he was prepared to travel abroad to learn, for all his overpowering sense of his dignity as the absolute ruler of the largest land in Europe. It requires little imagination to suppose in him a blend of excitement, apprehension and insecurity as his embassy entered the strange new world of Baltic Europe.

Peter was anything but delighted by the way in which the Swedish governor, Dahlberg, received the embassy. Perhaps not realising that Livonia was suffering from grave shortages of food and fodder that year, and that the embassy placed a great strain upon its resources, Peter was enraged at what he felt to be a cold and mean reception. His official incognito was perhaps respected rather more completely than he had anticipated, although he resented the way that crowds of townsfolk stared at him, and he felt that his retinue had been thoroughly swindled by the local merchants. A complaining letter which he wrote has a strange, almost Gogolian ring to it, when protesting about what he felt to be the dishonesty of the traders; since they *looked* like persons of distinction they ought to have behaved better. "The tradespeople here all wear cloaks and appear to be very decent people, however...."[7] He went on to complain bitterly of their sharp practice. When his Russian drivers attempted to sell the sledges

[7] *Corr.*, vol. i, p. 145.

upon which the embassy had arrived they were offered prices which he felt to be preposterous, forgetting perhaps that by no means everybody would be anxious to buy up large quantities of sledges towards the beginning of spring. Peter then proceeded to fall foul of the Swedish army. He was most eager to conduct a thorough inspection of the defences of Riga, it being the first town he had seen "completely fortified after the French manner",[8] i.e. according to the principles of military architects such as Vauban. In the course of his inspection he started to take measurements, only to be aggressively challenged by a sentry who pointed his musket at him, acting perfectly properly, particularly since, in view of Peter's incognito, there could be no question of *lèse majesté* or offence to the person of the czar. Although the matter was cleared up Peter left in a bitter rage. In a letter he observed that "In Riga it was only with looking that we had our fill".[9]

Peter and the embassy left Riga with a strong sense of humiliation, so much so that the account of their journey which they gave to J. Bouvet some months later in Holland omits any mention of the visit. As he heard the story from members of the embassy, they stopped first at Königsberg and then at Berlin; of Riga there is not a word. Indeed, Peter took such personal affront at his reception that he actually made it the declared reason for going to war with Sweden three years later.

His indignation was doubtless increased by the very different reception accorded him by his next host, Duke Frederick Casimir of Courland, who entertained the party lavishly in his capital, Mitau, although the duchy was far from rich. On May 2 Peter sailed to Pilau, the port of Königsberg, where he met the Elector of Brandenburg, Frederick III, soon to become the first king of Prussia. Once again Peter was lavishly entertained, and found time, between banquets, to study gunnery and obtain a certificate of proficiency.

Peter reveals another aspect of his character when writing to Romodanovsky from Mitau. He had found nothing of interest for "His Majesty" unless it be the object he was sending which His Majesty might care to make use of when avenging himself on his enemies.[10] To judge from Romodanovsky's reply the object in question was a headsman's axe! Romodanovsky observed that he had already made use of it to remove the heads

---

[8] Defoe, p. 51.   [9] *Corr.*, vol. i, p. 137.   [10] Bogoslovsky, vol ii, p. 40.

of a brace of criminals. It is not enough, when considering this episode, to observe that people in those days were rather different. There is no denying that Peter and his Prince Caesar shared a streak of black and violent humour, the sort of humour that went into the ceremony of Tsykler's execution, and which made them both appreciate Peter's present from abroad.

Although Peter had to date enjoyed his stay in Prussia he did not leave happily. He had come to like the elector and was hurt by the latter's failure to call on him on his name day, for which Peter had prepared a firework display. He sent apologies through his representatives; he was unable to bid Peter farewell in person since he had pressing business elsewhere. Peter wrote to the elector complaining of his envoys' behaviour, and a certain von Kreisen was sent to look into the matter, only to be treated by Peter with remarkable boorishness. First von Kreisen was made to cut short an already abbreviated "compliment" by the impatient gesturing of Lefort. Peter himself paid no attention to him, and walked away as soon as he was finished. Von Kreisen then sat down at table with the ambassadors, who ostentatiously drank toasts without proposing the health of his master, while Peter, ignoring the Prussians, talked solely to his retinue, kissing Lefort openly and repeatedly while Lefort continued to address him with a pipe in his mouth. He also kissed the sweaty dark head of his jester. Later Peter interrupted a conversation to observe in Dutch that, "The elector is good but his councillors are devils", frowning darkly at one of the same as he spoke; the councillor backed away from his rage, but Peter seized and shook him, telling him to leave at once.[11] Von Kreisen found the whole experience both alarming and almost beyond belief, for as usual Peter had acted without the least regard for protocol or *politesse*, making not the slightest effort to hide his rage. Perhaps as in Riga, his readiness to take offence stemmed from the insecurity and uncertainty which he still felt abroad. Peter's last word on the subject took the form of an indignant letter to the Prussian king, which sought at the same time to be conciliatory:

In view of the fact that your envoys, bringing your compliments, did not behave well, but actually angered me, and since I have never heard any unfriendly words from you, a true friend, and since, even worse, they left without finishing their

[1] *Ibid.*, p. 101.

compliment or awaiting a reply, I feel obliged to write to you as a true and undoubted friend, in order to prevent a vain quarrel from arising between us, occasioned by your useless servants. Never doubt my good will. Piter.[12]

He had stayed longer than intended in Prussia, for political reasons. The Polish throne had become vacant, and there were essentially two contenders, Frederick Augustus, Elector of Saxony, and Prince Conti, the French candidate. France was an ally of Turkey, and it was thus in the Russian interest to favour Frederick Augustus. Although, as was sometimes the way of Polish politics, both candidates were elected to the throne, it was largely thanks to the pressure Peter put upon the Polish diet – and the troops he moved to the frontier – that the elector of Saxony was duly proclaimed Augustus II, King of Poland.

One of the most interesting accounts we have of Peter abroad was occasioned by his meeting Sophie, Electress of Hanover, and her daughter, Sophie Charlotte of Brandenburg. Peter and his retinue had put up in an inn near the castle of Koppenbrugge where the ladies were staying. Curious to observe the Muscovite at close quarters they sent him an invitation to join them. Peter at first refused point blank, displaying great and undisguised reluctance, and it was only when their envoy grew most pressing that Peter accepted an invitation to dine. Sophie Charlotte has left us a most animated account of the evening, and of Peter. At first he was so shy when faced by the ladies that he held his hand in front of his face, saying: "I cannot speak." However, they broke down his reserve and soon he answered their questions quickly and intelligently. Sophie Charlotte found the twitch which marred his face less difiguring than she had expected, but was amazed at his indelicate table manners, and the mess he got into as he ate. After the meal Sophie Charlotte brought on a troupe of Italian singers and musicians. Peter listened patiently but then confessed that he had little love of music. The electress went on to ask whether he enjoyed hunting, to which he replied that his father loved to hunt, but he best loved sailing the seas, letting off fireworks and building ships. However, she was most impressed by his altogether natural manner. He soon, she wrote, "began to behave as if he were at home". He grew very merry, pulling the ears of Sophie Dorothea, a ten-year-old princess and

[12] *Corr.*, vol. i, p. 178.

future wife of Frederick the Great, and lavishing kisses upon her brother George, the future King of England. Later the ladies showed him how they danced and tried to make him join them, but, having previously proudly shown them his calloused hands, he now refused to dance since he was unable to find any gloves. Instead he taught them how to drink "Moscow style".

The electress' mother Sophie also reported on the czar. She found him good-looking and very intelligent, but wished he were not so coarse. He needed a jug of water to clean up after the meal. However, to her surprise Peter did not drink himself into a stupor. She found him and the other Russians short of *politesse*, however; when dancing with the German ladies they mistook their whalebone corsets for bones and commented on the massive nature of their partners' frames. Both mother and daughter were a little hurt to find that Peter showed scant interest in the opposite sex; that is to say that he declined to flirt with them. They ascribed this failure to the fact that he was accustomed to Muscovite women who wore a lot of powder and rouge. Nevertheless Peter made a profound and on the whole favourable impression on both women. Their accounts suggest that he was very obviously a remarkable man, whom it was necessary to meet face to face if one were to hope to understand the electrifying presence which radiated from him. Certainly they found him fascinating enough to spend a whole night in his company without retiring, setting off from the castle the next morning at dawn.

Peter was in a hurry to get to Holland, his first and most eagerly awaited destination. He had, after all, chosen Dutch for his second language, a preposterous choice were it not for his fascination with the sea. He had acquired the rudiments from Brandt and Timmerman, and practised in the company of those Dutch seamen whom he used to seek out with such assiduity at home. He was able to communicate with Dutchmen, and indeed with Germans, fairly adequately, although he would have an interpreter to back him up when necessary. Now he looked forward to his stay in Holland to fulfil many of the objectives of his embassy. On the diplomatic level he hoped that the Dutch would help him in his war with Turkey by providing both ships and men – a Dutch-built man-of-war was the flagship of his modest fleet. He also hoped to purchase large quantities of the naval stores which made up the bulk of the embassy's shopping list. Above all he expected to learn, with his own hands, how to build ships and, as usual, he put his pleasure and instruction first. Since he was not leading the embassy he was not governed by its itinerary. As they approached the Netherlands he broke away with a handful of volunteers, including Menshikov who was now part of the inner circle, travelling straight to his first training ground, Zaandam, where he arrived in early August.

He had heard so much about Zaandam from Dutch shipwrights in Moscow, Archangel and Voronezh, that he expected to find all he wanted there. In his impetuous way he had not ascertained that Zaandam specialised in building merchantmen and whalers; men-of-war were built in Amsterdam.

Peter arrived by boat early one morning dressed as a Dutch seaman in "a Monmouth cap, short jacket and wide white breeches".[13] He immediately saw a familiar face, one Gerit Kist, a smith, whom he had known in Moscow, and who was now sailing along with a boatload of eels. Kist was surprised to be hailed by the czar of Muscovy, more so when the latter announced his intention of lodging with him. In the meantime Peter stopped at an inn. When his followers' strange clothes and manners drew a large crowd about the place he tried to dispel their curiosity by telling them that they were carpenters in search of work – and set off for Kist's home.

As soon as he could he purchased a set of tools and found work in a local yard. Like any other worker he appeared at dawn and put in a full day. A whole body of local legend has been handed down to the effect that "Peter Mikhailov" worked here, took a glass of gin there, dined at so and so's house, and made love to such and such a girl. On one occasion it appears he was followed and teased by some urchins who found his size and appearance comic. Peter, never at his best in such circumstances, appears to have responded with a relatively moderate rage and no actual violence. But all too soon it became common knowledge that the czar was working in a local shipyard, and Peter found himself hounded by growing crowds of onlookers – which he found intolerable. It was moreover becoming clear that he would not learn how to build his navy in Zaandam. The time had come to move on:

He bought a small yacht about 25 or 30 foot long, which he would take a particular pleasure to steer himself, and to sail

[13] Defoe, p. 61.

in the company of one of those gentlemen that attended him up and down the river of Amsterdam, where his great delight was, to make his own observations, and to feed his eyes with that most beautiful prospect of that vast number of ships, which not unlike a forest, lie close together in the road of that city.[14]

The striking impression that Amsterdam made upon Peter and his embassy comes out clearly in its official journal. It was obviously the first place they had come to which evoked real wonder in them. Earlier towns had been given at the most a perfunctory mention, scarcely more than a naming of names. Amsterdam is given a lengthy description, with great emphasis on the scope and quality of its public buildings and institutions: workhouses, hospitals, asylums and houses of correction. Peter's subsequent determination to build hospitals and workhouses in the city of his own creation must have had its origins in what he was now discovering in Amsterdam.

The embassy had made a magnificent entry into the city. Once again Peter presented himself in modest contrast with his ambassadors. Lefort was splendid:

He was clad after the Muscovite fashion, in a long robe of cloth of gold, lined with the most precious sables that ever were seen. This robe, as well as the vest which he wore under it, was covered before with diamonds of an inestimable value, and upon his bonnet there appeared a large jewel of diamonds in the shape of a heron's feather with such a lustre as dazzled the eyes of the beholders.[15]

Behind walked Peter, modest and explicitly European in contrast with this Muscovite display. He wore "a plain blue coat, a large white perriwig and a white feather".[16] They were warmly received by the mayor, Nicholas Witsen, who had already had dealings with Peter, having sold him his man-of-war. He was sympathetic to Peter's urgent request for work in the East India docks, and in the meantime saw to it that the czar and his retinue were properly received and entertained. Peter was shown the docks, and the admiralty. He paid a visit to the theatre, where he saw a play entitled "L'avocat imaginaire". The city of Amsterdam gave a banquet in his honour, followed by an elaborate

[14] Bouvet, p. 47.   [15] Ibid., p. 54.   [16] Defoe, p. 68.

display of fireworks and firepower both on land and on water. The crowd was so great that the support of a bridge on the Burgwal canal gave way and several spectators fell into the water and were drowned.

In the middle of the banquet Peter was told that the East India Company would not only take him on, they would begin building a new frigate so that he might go through the whole process of construction, starting with the laying of the keel. Peter displayed remarkable patience on hearing the news; he sat through both the banquet and the fireworks before announcing that he had to get back to Zaandam for his tools. He resisted all warnings of the hazards of travelling by night and set off immediately. It was necessary to send for the keys to unlock the port barriers before he sailed, at 11 p.m. He reached Zaandam at one, fetched his things and paid Gerit Kist what he owed him. It appears that he was less than munificent; not having lived like a czar, Peter had no intention of paying like one.

The next day Peter went to work in the docks where he was to spend four months. His volunteers worked beside him, specialising in sail-making, rigging, gunnery and seamanship. However, he did not spend all his time there. We find him observing a public execution in Amsterdam: "The czar or Grand Prince of Muscovy Peter Alekseyevich attended throughout this sad ceremony, on a platform in the town hall. He stayed to the end of the proceedings and observed the execution attentively. He was some 26 years old and very tall."[17] The occasion does not seem to have inspired Peter to send any more axes home.

He also took time off for other entertainments. He spent some hours with an astronomer, made a study of the network of canals and locks, visited military factories, workshops and schools. He was particularly interested in medicine and dentistry – and as always was ready to take a hand himself, remaining till the end of his day an inveterate and dangerously indiscriminate puller of teeth. At the university of Utrecht he was especially taken with the anatomical laboratory. He became acquainted with its professor, attended his lectures and visited the hospital with him, where he kissed the face of a dead child being prepared for dissection, that smiled almost as if it were alive.[18] In Leyden, in another anatomical theatre, noticing that some of his Russian companions were disgusted by the corpses, he used bullying coer-

[17] Scheltema, *Rusland en de Nederlanden*, vol. ii, p. 37.   [18] Soloviev, vol. vii, p. 554.

cion to dispel prejudice, obliging them to tear at the dead muscles with their teeth.[19]

Holland gave Peter his introduction to European civilisation, with the emphasis on the practical and technical. However, in some respects it was beginning to disappoint. The Dutch were not prepared to commit themselves to Peter's anti-Turkish crusade, since they were in the process of negotiating peace with France. They continued to stall Peter's requests for aid, making him complain in his letters that he was being fended off with a positively Muscovite "We'll get it done at once".[20] Moreover, he was beginning to discover that Dutch shipbuilding techniques could not be easily translated to his own country. They were based on models, rule of thumb, traditional skills and techniques: craftsmanship as opposed to plans drawn up according to mathematical principles of design.

It was on just such plans and principles that English naval architecture was founded, so that Peter was delighted when the King of England, William of Orange, whom he and Lefort had met at Utrecht, invited him to continue his education in the naval yards of Greenwich.

Leaving the bulk of the embassy behind in The Hague, Peter sailed to England on the *Yorke*, arriving on January 11. He had travelled dressed as a Dutch seaman and spent the voyage discussing nautical matters with Vice-admiral Sir David Mitchell who had been sent to escort him. Indeed he went further – clambering up the rigging on one occasion, from where, when quite aloft, he called down to the admiral to join him. Sir David wisely replied that he was grown too fat to climb.

On arrival at Gravesend he transferred to a baggage boat to escape attention. This took him upstream to the modest accommodation he had asked for near the river, a row of houses in Norfolk Street. On the 13th "the Earl of Macclesfield went to see him and he chanced to be at dinner; but suddenly rose from table and went upstairs, locked himself in his chamber and said 'twas strange he could not eat without being stared at".[21] It was a typical flash of angry irritation, and one cannot help wondering whether Peter was not beginning to have doubts about the acceptability of his eating habits. Next day he received the visit of the king, who found Peter in shirtsleeves, in a bedroom he had shared

[19] *Ibid., loc. cit.* [20] *Corr.*, vol. i, p. 239.
[21] L. Lowenson, *Slav & E. European Rev.*, 1959, no. xxxvii, p. 432.

with three or four others. Although there was a heavy January frost King William, who stayed for half an hour, was obliged to ask for the window to be opened.[22] There was nothing unusual about this crowd in Peter's bedroom. He could not sleep alone and would quite literally use one of his orderlies as a pillow. He was "very angry if they awakened him and in his sleep he often grasped them very hard".[23] The royal visit was further disturbed by Peter's pet monkey. "As soon as the king was sat down the monkey jumped upon him in some wrath, which discomforted the whole ceremonial; and most of the time was afterwards spent in apologies for the monkey's misbehaviour."[24]

Peter and William went on to exchange several visits. Peter took to the king and frequently observed that they were the only two monarchs of their day who had the courage to travel beyond their own frontiers. William appears to have been impressed by Peter's single-minded interest in the sea. He found Peter indifferent to the beauties of nature, to architecture and to gardens – he was particularly right on that score – while the czar's command of Dutch was limited to maritime matters.[25] Nevertheless Peter saw more of London than its dockyards. He visited the mint on four occasions. We do not know whether he met its master, Sir Isaac Newton, but he certainly made the acquaintance of Flamsteed, the Astronomer Royal, at the Greenwich Observatory. He visited the opera in Drury Lane, and also went to the theatre, which seems to have provided him with a mistress, a certain Mrs Cross, found for him by Menshikov. When Peter gave her a purse of 500 guineas on leaving, she complained to Menshikov that his master was less than generous, a complaint which Menshikov relayed. Peter is alleged to have replied: "Do you suppose, Menshikov, that I am as great a fool as you are? I have grey beards working for me for 500 guineas, diligently using their brains, while this wretch worked with her..."[26]

Peter also visited Parliament, although he showed little interest in the principles of parliamentary democracy. In his desire to avoid being stared at he made himself a laughing stock:

He had a great dislike to being looked at, but had a mind to see the king in Parliament, in order to do which he was placed in a gutter upon the house-top, to peep in at the window, where

[22] Gray, p. 227.   [23] Gordon, A., p. 319.   [24] Burnet, pp. 406–7.
[25] Bogoslovsky, vol. ii, p. 300.   [26] Maikov, p. 9.

he made so ridiculous a figure, that neither king nor people could forbear laughing; which obliged him to retire sooner than he intended.[27]

Peter called upon the author of those lines, Bishop Burnet, and apparently held a long theological discussion with him, impressing the bishop with his knowledge. Subsequently, and perhaps in the light of later events, the bishop painted an unflattering picture, but one which rings true enough for all that:

He is a man of a very hot temper, soon inflamed, and very brutal in his passion; he raises his natural heat by drinking much brandy, which he rectified himself with great application [i.e. added his own flavourings]; he is subject to convulsive motions all over his body, and his head seems to be affected with these; he wants not capacity and has a larger measure of knowledge than might be expected from his education which was very indifferent; a want of judgement with an instability of temper, appear in him too often and too evidently; he is mechanically turned and seems designed by nature rather to be a ship-carpenter than a great prince.... There was a mixture of both passion and severity in his temper ... After I had seen him often and had conversed with him, I could not but adore the depth of the providence of God, that had raised up such a furious man to be so absolute an authority over so great a part of the world.[28]

Peter's pursuit of knowledge took him further afield – as far, for example, as Oxford, which he visited on April 9. The Russian record describes the founding of the university, the existence of a bishop, the Bodleian Library, eighteen colleges and seven other houses known as halls, where students lived under a cruel discipline; besides them there were a thousand other scholars who were fed and clothed from certain sources of revenue, and who had excellent walks and gardens for their delectation.[29] Peter did not make a good impression in Oxford. In the words of the assistant keeper of the Ashmolean he was "an uncouth figure in a long black wig with dirty scratched hands, accompanied by a gentleman who spoke Latin and the Innkeeper of the Golden Cross Inn, who the czar had brought with him in his coach ... He visited

[27] Burnet, p. 407.   [28] Ibid., loc. cit.   [29] Tumansky, vol. iii, p. 66.

the bookshop, Convocation and the theatre and having spent a little over a quarter of an hour at the museum he then went to Trinity Chapel, but when he saw he had been recognized and that students and townspeople were crowding to look at him he turned back immediately and left town."[30]

Such occasional bouts of tourism were mere distractions. Above all Peter was anxious to learn. As Captain Perry, one of the experts he recruited, put it:

> He spent most of his time in what related to war and shipping and upon the water. He often took the carpenter's tools in his hands, and often worked himself in Deptford Yard, as he had done in Holland. He would sometimes be found at the smiths' and sometimes at the gun founders and there was scarce any art or mechanic trade whatsoever from the watchmaker to the coffinmaker but he more or less inspected it, and even caused a model of an English coffin to be sent into Russia.[31]

Peter also completed a highly successful trade agreement. For many years the use of tobacco had been banned in Muscovy. It was regarded as the devil's weed, another of the corrupt practices of the West, and there had even been decrees declaring that anyone found using the substance was to have their nostrils slit. However, travellers to 17th-century Russia record the passionate craving which the natives displayed for tobacco. Looking suspiciously as if all accounts draw upon a single source, they describe the Russian smoker – who would fill a horn with tobacco, ignite it, draw deeply upon it and then fall to the ground in delighted convulsions. Peter, as a Westerner, was also a great smoker of Dutch clay pipes, and had no regard for these traditional prohibitions. He now negotiated a contract with Lord Carmarthen, who for £20,000 was granted the exclusive right to import tobacco into Russia.

In order to be close to Deptford Yard, Sayes Court, the house of John Evelyn, currently let to Admiral Benbow, was placed at Peter's disposal. Its location enabled him to enter the docks directly through a private door, avoiding any contact with possible crowds. Peter's stay at Sayes Court confirmed King William's impression that the czar had no love of gardens and no other episode shows so clearly the difference in domestic manners that

[30] Lowenson, *op. cit.*, p. 442.   [31] Perry, p. 166.

separated East and West. Peter left Sayes Court looking as if it had been occupied by the Red Army. Christopher Wren was sent to make an estimate of the damage he and his company had executed, and left a remarkable report. The garden, which John Evelyn had laid out with a particular love, was devastated. The bowling green was ruined, espaliers had their branches snapped off, and the czar had broken "my close hedge of glittering holly" by sitting in a wheelbarrow and having himself sent through it at speed. The flower beds had gone unattended and were a mass of weeds, and the sanded walks were full of craters. A hundred feet of iron railing had been broken away. The gardener, who found Peter and his companions "right nastie", estimated that it would cost at least £55 to get the garden right, while some of the damage was irreparable.

The house was worse. Room after room had its wall coverings ruined or torn away. Expensive furniture and wooden floors had been broken up for firewood. Every bed and bed cover in the house had been damaged. Pictures had been ruined and their frames smashed. A grand total of some six tables and a staggering seventy-five chairs had been damaged. Wren estimated the total cost of Peter's stay at £162. 7 shillings to the house and ground, while damage to the furnishings came to £158.2.6. Moreover, Wren pointed out that the small house set aside for a watchman was completely ruined.

Understandably Peter's ravages passed without comment. King William was intent on receiving Peter well and this was not the time for a diplomatic incident. It is less hard to understand Peter's monstrous abuse of hospitality. The actions suggest great bouts of drunken wrecking which are, in their way, comprehensible enough, and must have given great pleasure at the time. However, the total disregard for offence given and, much more, for its potentially quite serious repercussions can only be explained by drunken ignorance, indifference and a lack of sophistication amounting to brutish stupidity. Yet Peter had every reason to be pleased by his stay in England. Not only had he succeeded in recruiting sixty English experts to come to Russia, the king had made him a present of a twenty-gun yacht, *Royal Transport*, in which he returned to Amsterdam.

Before turning for home Peter arranged to send on his various acquisitions and recruits. Besides the Englishmen there were 150 Greeks, Slavs and Italians who travelled to Russia overland. Four ships carried Peter's purchases to Archangel; these included 260 crates of muskets, pistols, canvas, woollen cloth, compasses, files, pulleys, cork, anchors and some cannon.[32] The *Royal Transport* also sailed to Archangel, where Timmerman was ordered to take it, by river and overland, to Yaroslav on the Volga. Peter intended her for use on the Sea of Azov upon completion of the Don-Volga Canal, but the commission proved impossible and she remained at Archangel. However, the order shows that Peter, in April 1698, was still thinking entirely in terms of a Black Sea navy.

Despite its practical achievements the embassy was proving a failure diplomatically. To his consternation Peter discovered that the Austrian emperor was concluding a separate peace with Turkey, and that both Holland and England were giving him every encouragement. Peter got no satisfaction from his indignant questioning of the Dutch States General and, disregarding their tentative offers of a trading agreement, he pressed on to Vienna.

In the meantime he began to receive reports of domestic unrest. The *streltsy* regiments which had been posted to the Lithuanian frontier, in order to assist in the election of Augustus to the Polish throne, were getting restive, and the reinforcements sent up from Azov to join them were equally unhappy. In March 1698 a large group of deserters had gone to Moscow to complain that they were starving. They arrived drunk and insubordinate and disregarded orders to return to their regiments. Romodanovsky grew nervous and told Gordon and his men to restore order. He was moreover alarmed at the lack of news from Peter. The latter wrote in due course, rebuking him for worrying like an old woman, and scorning the notion that rumours of his death might be causing unrest. He went on to reproach him for not investigating the case of the mutinous *streltsy* with greater thoroughness, and also greater severity.

On his way to Vienna Peter passed through Dresden, where for the first time he showed some interest in the arts. He paid two protracted visits to the Kunstkammer, and its magnificent royal collections, although it is true that Peter's official journal concentrates on its collections of weapons, armour and harness, also on the cannon.

Peter was entertained by Prince von Fürstenberg, to whom he had said that he would like female company. Five ladies were provided, together with a military orchestra. Peter, overjoyed,

[32] Ustryalov, vol. iii, p. 110.

gave the company a drumming demonstration. Orders had been issued for an artillery salute to accompany every toast, and several hundred shots were fired in the course of the five-hour entertainment. Peter was so delighted that he embraced his host frequently and the affair finished at three in the morning. Next day Peter visited the foundry and the Kunstkammer yet again and drummed his way through a similar entertainment. It was noted that he detested an elaborate retinue at table, preferring no more than two or at the most three attendants.

Since Peter was trying to form an alliance against Turkey, while the Emperor Leopold was completing separate peace negotiations, the Russian embassy could not have been particularly welcome in Vienna. On the other hand the empire, threatened on three fronts, by Turkey, France and its own Hungarian rebels, could not afford to antagonise the czar. He was received with a blend of caution and condescension. The condescension was the consequence of the relative prestige of the two rulers; the Holy Roman Emperor still ranked as the highest secular power upon earth, in Moscow his ambassadors took precedence over all others, and were treated with particular regard. This may explain the patience with which Peter accepted a reception that was very much *de haut en bas*. The embassy was made to wait several days before being allowed to enter the capital, and upon entry their path was crossed by some marching soldiers. Peter was only granted an audience with the emperor upon his third request, and even then it was to be restricted to an exchange of compliments. Peter accepted the conditions without murmur. Indeed, throughout his stay in Vienna, the young czar behaved himself to the point of being subdued, showing none of the boisterousness, lack of restraint or even boorish bad humour which he had displayed elsewhere. Yet Peter's impatience with protocol and a certain enthusiastic generosity of spirit emerges in his meeting with the fifty-nine-year-old emperor. It had been arranged that the two rulers would enter a gallery from opposing ends and proceed slowly forward to meet in front of the centre window; thus dignity, imperial and czarish, would be preserved. But Peter's impatience proved too much for his dignity; crossing the gallery much too fast he spoilt the careful protocol by greeting the emperor enthusiastically and many windows too soon. Moreover, and again contrary to arrangement, he insisted on remaining bare-headed through the interview, and the emperor graciously responded in kind. The subject of their discussion has remained private. When it ended Peter went down into the palace garden where, to his delight, he found a rowing boat and made a few circuits round the lake before asking how much it cost to provide water for the fountains.[33]

Peter was exposed, in Vienna, to the elaborate ceremonials of the Hapsburg court. On one occasion he attended an opera performed in the Imperial Palace. He sat behind the ambassadors in their box, but we hear that "an intolerable heat obliged him to withdraw frequently into the gallery where he was brought Hungarian and other wines".[34] He felt more at home at an informal masquerade or *Gesellschaft*, which required guests to wear some form of national dress. Unsurprisingly enough Peter appeared as a Dutch fisherman.

He seems to have made a favourable impression on his observers, who were expecting a drunken barbarian. He did not seem like that at all to the Papal Nuncio:

> The czar is a tall young man with a dark complexion, a proud and serious carriage, and a lively expression ... although his eyes resemble those of a blind man, being in constant movement, as are his arms and legs. In order to disguise this he gestures a great deal and is very lively ... He has an alert and quick intelligence, and his manners are closer to those of a civilised man than a savage, and he has doubtless benefited greatly from his travels, for there is a deal of difference between him as he was when he set out and as he is now, although his natural coarseness does emerge, particularly in his dealings with his own people, whom he keeps on a tight rein and treats with severity. He possesses a knowledge of history and geography which he likes to display, but his chief interest is the sea ... However, there is nothing about the person, carriage or manners which might distinguish him or declare him to be a ruler.[35]

For all its reservations the passage is essentially complimentary. It suggests that Peter had acquired a measure of *politesse* in the course of his travels, and could no longer be considered a drunken Muscovite barbarian. Early in the *Gargantua* of Rabelais, the young giant who has not as yet enjoyed the benefits of Renais-

[33] Bogoslovsky, vol. ii, p. 474.   [34] Ustryalov, vol. iii, p. 128.
[35] Bogoslovsky, vol. ii, pp. 464–5.

sance humanist education is required to make a speech; in a manner reminiscent of Peter's hopeless shyness in front of Electress Sophie and her daughter he "began to weep like a cow and covered his head with his bonnet". Once he has been properly educated, he of course becomes capable of sophisticated oratory. Peter never exactly assimilated the precepts of Renaissance humanism, but somewhere between Kopenbrugge and Vienna he had learnt enough to know what to say on most occasions and no longer felt inclined to cover his head. In other words, in the course of the preceding eighteen-odd months the Muscovite Gargantua had come of age.

CHAPTER SEVEN

Mutiny and Reform

Although his sojourn in Vienna might have completed Peter's education in *politesse* the embassy, diplomatically speaking, was not a great success. Predictably enough he failed to discourage the Austrians from negotiating with Turkey, and so, with nothing more to keep him in Vienna, now proposed to travel south to Venice, to seek the support of the Venetians against the Turks and learn what he could about galleys, a form of shipbuilding in which they excelled.

He was compelled to change his plans. Romodanovsky wrote him a letter which plucked at his most deeply rooted anxieties, telling him that the Miloslavskys were flourishing once more and the *streltsy* had mutinied. Peter replied at once, urging Romodanovsky to be merciless, since extreme severity was the only way "to put out this fire".[1] Fire for Peter was never simply a source of delight and display, it was also the enemy which could burn down the whole of Moscow, and which had to be dealt with, if necessary, with astounding ruthlessness. Peter hurried homewards as fast as possible, only to be met with the news, a day or so later, that the immediate danger was over and the mutiny suppressed.

As we have seen, discontent had been growing among the *streltsy* posted on the Lithuanian frontier. Peter had been making ever-increasing demands upon them as a force. They had been used to re-fortify Azov and had also worked on the new port of Taganrog. Now they were experiencing the unaccustomed hardships of winter service away from home. They were more-

[1] *Corr.*, vol. i, p. 226.

over fundamentally hostile to Peter and his breaks with tradition and disliked his *poteshnye*, whom, they considered, he favoured at their expense – they felt they had been used as cannon fodder at Azov. More generally many of them held that under Peter Russia was taking the wrong path, that he had betrayed its values, and that "Orthodoxy had grown crooked".[2] They were immensely suspicious of his embassy, supposing that he intended to collect as many foreigners as possible and definitely dislodge the old nobility.[3] It was accordingly their declared intention to burn down the Foreign Quarter and kill all foreigners. They were determined to move before Peter's return, since they believed that after travelling to so many heretical countries he would most certainly introduce changes that would deprive them of their ancient rights and ancestral traditions, which they knew to be superior to any others.[4]

The *streltsy* had a specific political objective. Romodanovsky could not have known how accurate he was being when he told Peter that the Miloslavkys were conspiring once more. The mutineers had actually been in touch with Sophia in her monastery, via an old beggar woman acting as go-between. She had sent them a letter urging them to march on Moscow, release Sophia and prevent Peter from returning to his capital. In the meantime the strangest rumours circulated round the *streltsy* camp. It was said that Peter was dead, that his son the czarevich had been taken away and a changeling substituted, and that the boyars had beaten Peter's wife when she discovered the substitution.[5]

On June 16 the *streltsy* were told of some additional new postings and on this news they mutinied, drove out their officers, appointed their own in their place and began their move on Moscow.

On hearing the news Romodanovsky ordered generals Shein and Gordon to move out to check them, with an army of some 3700 troops. Their first concern was to deny the mutineers the Voskresensky monastery, a stronghold well supplied with powder, cannon and shot which lay directly in their path. Although the *streltsy* were pressing on to seize it, government troops arrived in the nick of time, getting there an hour before the *streltsy* advance parties came up.

---

[2] Golikova, p. 107.
[3] Bouvet, p. 87.
[4] Tumansky, vol. iii, pp. 109–10.
[5] Golikova, p. 104.

From Gordon's account of the business it is clear that the mutiny was taken very seriously indeed. He deployed his men with the utmost care and caution. Attempts were then made by both Shein and Gordon to persuade the mutineers to return to their posts. These failed, and failed understandably since they were already guilty of high treason. They informed Gordon that nothing could make them turn back, they would no longer tolerate service on the frontier and were determined to spend at least five days in Moscow, even if it should cost them their lives.

When it became clear that talking would get them nowhere Gordon and Shein withdrew and prepared for battle. The *streltsy* crossed themselves and did likewise. Shein then made the mistake of ordering Gordon to fire on the mutineers with blanks. Napoleon once observed that it was fatal to fire blanks at a mob since it made them suppose themselves invulnerable and you had to kill many more in the end. Something of the kind happened now. After the first harmless salvo the *streltsy*'s priests informed them that God must be on their side since a miracle had occurred. They brandished their banners, threw their hats in the air, wrote Gordon, and continued to make ready for battle. Gordon now began to fire in earnest, and as their casualties grew the *streltsy* rapidly lost any desire to fight. Many of them just lay down on the ground, while others tried to run. The shooting went on for an hour, at the end of which they had lost some fifty-two dead and wounded, while the government troops had one man killed.

The entire force was rounded up, and on the next day interrogation began. The ringleaders were quickly identified and tortured. They revealed that on reaching Moscow, they had intended to murder a number of the leading boyars and then, in Gordon's words, "obtain a regulation of their services" – no more winter campaigns. There was no mention of Sophia's letter. In the aftermath of this preliminary questioning Romodanovsky ordered the ringleaders, and others with a bad record for desertion, 150 in all, to be hanged, while the rest of the mutineers were imprisoned in various monasteries to await their czar's return.

Peter reached Moscow sooner than expected, on the afternoon of August 25. He did not go to the Kremlin or visit his wife. Instead he paid several visits in the Foreign Quarter, calling on Gordon, who was away, and on Anna Mons, before going to Preobrazhenskoe.

Peter's mother, Natalya: "She was a stupid and extremely limited woman who would never have any understanding of her son's bewildering and unorthodox energies." *(Novosti Press Agency)*

Peter as a child: "Peter was born into a soft, indolent and magnificent old Russia, utterly foreign to his temperament." *(V.A.A.P., Moscow)*

Peter's half sister, Sophia: "She rejected out of hand the passive and secluded role that Russian traditions reserved for her sex." *(Novosti Press Agency)*

Franz Lefort: "Lefort understood instinctively how to play Falstaff to Prince Hal." *(British Museum)*

Peter's first wife, Eudoxia: "Eudoxia was an entirely unsuitable bride." *(Novosti Press Agency)*

Peter at the time of his visit to England: "He had a great dislike to being looked at, but had a mind to see the king in Parliament, in order to do which he was placed in a gutter upon the house-top, to peep in at the window, where he made so ridiculous a figure, that neither king nor people could forbear laughing; which obliged him to retire sooner than he intended." *(British Museum)*

Alexander Menshikov: "Although practically illiterate, he seems to have been able to fulfill the various responsibilities, military and civil, conferred upon him by Peter, and, more to the point perhaps, proved able, for all his massive corruption, to survive." *(Novosti Press Agency)*

Peter in 1720: "Peter had discovered the way to bring Sweden to her knees—to sack the countryside." *(Novosti Press Agency)*

Peter in 1723: "These years were darkened for Peter by the deterioration of his health." *(Novosti Press Agency)*

ΛΕУѢ II ПЕШРОВИЧЬ
ЦАРЕ ВИЧЪ ЯСЕ РОССІИСКІИ
Alexius Petri Filius
Princeps haereditarius totius Rusiae

The Czarevich Alexis, Peter's son: "Aleksey was by taste and temperament different from Peter in almost every way, although he did have his father's love of drink, and something of his sense of humor." (*British Museum*)

Charles XII of Sweden: "Charles was apparently alarmed at the ruthlessness with which the Russians had scorched their earth." (*Kungl. Armémuseum, Stockholm*)

Catherine I, Peter's second wife: "Catherine was far from hostile to magnificence, and her coronation as empress was a truly splendid affair." *(Novosti Press Agency)*

A life-size wax model of Peter, 1725: "Peter's death could not have been more timely for his wife and ex-favorite, so timely that it might appear suspect." *(V.A.A.P., Moscow)*

The visit to his mistress was a calculated insult to his wife. Peter had long since rejected her as he rejected everything that she stood for, the clinging world of old Muscovy. Moreover he appears to have found her family suspect politically, since her father and two uncles had been exiled by him in the wake of the Tsykler conspiracy, although the reason for their banishment remains obscure. When in London he had written to L. K. Naryshkin, T. N. Streshnev and Evdokiya's confessor urging them to persuade her to take the veil voluntarily. She had refused, understandably since among other things this would entail permanent separation from her only child, the eight-year-old Aleksey, and indeed a lifelong imprisonment. Peter was now prepared to resort to force. It would seem that he made one final effort to persuade her to go willingly, but even the five hours spent *tête à tête* with her could not break her will. Consequently, within a month of his homecoming Peter simply took his son away and gave him into the charge of his favourite sister, Natalya. Evdokiya was sent in a modest carriage under military escort to the Suzdal Pokrovsky convent, where she took the veil under the name of Elena. There is little direct evidence of the reaction of either son or mother to this traumatic separation, for the excellent reason that Peter discouraged such talk. A *streltsy* wife who was heard to say that Aleksey said he missed his mother and Peter ordered him to desist, was severely beaten. The only other direct evidence we possess is the case of a member of the kitchen staff who brought Aleksey his food. She was foolish enough to ask one of his female attendants whether he missed his mother. She replied that sometimes he did, and then he cried, while sometimes he did not. Both women were flogged and sent to convents for being parties to this indiscretion.

Peter seems to have been prompted by a combination of political and personal motives. He was clearly suspicious of his wife's relations and he could not, by any stretch of the imagination, be considered a family man. He wanted kindred spirits, companions, not emotional dependants, he wanted successors not sons. He had now effectively dismembered his family at a stroke. A wife who was an unworthy consort had been put away in a nunnery, while his son would be more or less neglected until such a time as Peter could determine whether or not he was indeed worthy to succeed him. Acting cruelly, by any standards, he had sentenced his wife to life imprisonment, and by separating

Aleksey from his mother he had sowed the seeds of the darkest of all the chapters in his own life, and indeed that of his son.

The day after his return nobles and notables flocked to welcome Peter home. It was a tense occasion, for there was no knowing whom Peter might suspect of being party to the mutiny, so that there was every need to demonstrate loyalty and affection. Peter in fact gave the friendliest reception to all comers, embracing and kissing many of them and talking of his journey. But then he committed outrage. Approaching generalissimo Shein with a pair of shears in his hand he calmly proceeded to trim that distinguished boyar's beard, and having completed his task moved on to do as much to Romodanovsky. He carried on snipping at one beard after another, sparing only the patriarch and the elderly Streshnev. With this crude piece of humour Peter demonstrated that he had learnt from his eighteen months of travel – learnt that beards were signs of backwardness, ignorance and lack of refinement – and showed also that he was determined to impose Western manners. As usual he took a personal hand, combining enforced education with his own mocking and sadistic brand of play, proceeding with callous indifference to the fact that many of the persons whose beards he was now shearing seriously believed that he might thereby be endangering their chances of entering paradise. Peter then tried to show his soldiers a new kind of drill, did not succeed, and went off to dine with Lefort.

Peter was very disturbed by the mutiny, and over the next few weeks displayed a series of sudden and violent fits of rage. Thus, on learning that Shein had been selling promotions, he lost his temper altogether and brandished a drawn sword in the faces of Shein and Romodanovsky, wounding the latter in head and hand. He might have killed Shein had Lefort not seized him from behind. Peter pulled away and hit Lefort hard on the back, but allowed himself to be calmed by Menshikov, and cheered up completely at the sound of a twenty-five gun salute.[6] Peter appears to have become dangerously violent at virtually every entertainment he attended over this period. When he saw Menshikov display his ignorance of Western manners by dancing with a sword he hit him violently in the face. On another occasion we find him hurling Lefort to the ground and kicking him savagely.[7] He was also capable of more trivial cruelties. At a dinner given by the Austrian ambassador, Peter learnt that one of

[6] Cht., 1866, vol. iv, p. 92.   [7] Ibid., p. 105.

the guests, the boyar Golovin, had an aversion to lettuce and vinegar. Peter promptly ordered one of his foreign officers to hold Golovin's mouth open, while Peter filled it, and his nostrils, with vinegar and lettuce, making the poor wretch cough till the blood poured from his nose.[8] Romodanovsky also displayed considerable agitation; in the course of a quarrel with F. M. Apraksin he first lost his temper and then waved a stick at him, causing Apraksin to draw his sword. This made Romodanovsky fall to his knees and beg for mercy, declaring that he was not an enemy but a brother. It was not an edifying spectacle.[9]

That Peter and Romodanovsky should have behaved a trifle oddly over these weeks is not surprising, for they were almost literally bathing in blood every day. Peter had been less than satisfied by the first interrogation of the *streltsy*. His object now was not so much to establish guilt as to squeeze the full story from the unfortunate survivors. He suspected conspiracy and needed to find out just how far the conspiracy ranged. To this effect he had the 1750 odd prisoners assembled at Preobrazhenskoe divided into lots of 50–100, each lot being assigned to one of fourteen torture chambers prepared by Romodanovsky, who would be personally responsible for questioning the ringleader.

The secretary to the Austrian resident, J. Korb, kept a diary that describes the *streltsy* interrogation. Its subsequent publication caused the greatest indignation in Russia and every attempt was made to have it suppressed. It was alleged to be the slanderous account of a malicious foreigner and totally untrue in most respects. Peter's 19th-century biographers tended to use Korb with discretion – since the picture he paints of Peter the torturer was not exactly flattering to the monarchy. However, there is no reason to suppose Korb to be wildly inaccurate. Certainly when he writes as an eye-witness his accounts stand up to crosschecking against other sources. Although the picture he paints is one of violence and vileness on a generous scale, nothing we know of the protagonists or the theatre of action makes it in any way implausible.

Every day more than twenty fires were lit in the torture chambers, since the knout and strappado were accompanied by the judicious use of roasting and burning with red-hot timbers. "The *Streltsy*", wrote Korb, "remained stubbornly silent and were subjected to unheard-of tortures; cruelly flogged, roasted,

[8] *Ibid.*, pp. 106–7.   [9] *Ibid.*, p. 133.

flogged again and taken once more to the flames."[10] Peter had drawn up the interrogators' protocols himself. He was uncertain of the loyalties of his boyars and did not permit them to play any part in the questioning. Korb suggests that Peter did much of the interrogating and roasting himself, and there is no reason to disbelieve him. Certainly the czar was present, and was never one to stand to one side when there was physical work to be done.

It would seem that Peter was profoundly distressed by the obstinacy and defiance of the prisoners. On one occasion he lost his temper and began to beat a man about the face with his stick, shouting "Confess, Confess!" Whatever their shortcomings as fighting men the *streltsy* displayed astounding courage and fortitude as prisoners. They were all doomed, and knew it, and could gain nothing for themselves through silence but further pain. Yet it was only with the greatest difficulty that Peter was able to extract indications of his sister Sophia's involvement. Romodanovsy was, characteristically, the first to break his man and get an inkling of the letters Sophia had written to the regiments. Peter immediately ordered the arrest and interrogation of her ladies in waiting. One of them was stripped and only escaped a flogging when it was noticed that she was pregnant.[11] Others received the strappado and the knout. Peter also questioned Sophia and her sister Martha Alekseevna. They both admitted that they knew that there was unrest among the *streltsy* but denied having any hand in the mutiny. Peter interrogated both sisters in person and at some length. He was convinced of their guilt, and indeed Martha eventually admitted that she had told Sophia that the *streltsy* were marching on Moscow and that she wished her to reign in Peter's stead. However, neither sister admitted anything further. Peter did not resort to torturing them, whether for political reasons or from some vestigial fraternal feeling we cannot say. They were both placed under house arrest during the course of their interrogation, and were then sent to permanent confinement in remote convents, and from that moment on effectively leave the stage of history.

The *streltsy* were all to die with the exception of the very young, sixteen to twenty-year-olds, who were branded, flogged, had their noses slit and ears cut off before being sent into exile. The rest were executed variously, and in batches. Some were sent to Moscow in little carts, each carrying the condemned man's

[10] cht., 1866, vol. iv, p. 100.   [11] Ibid., p. 104.

candle, with ropes around their necks. "Wishing to show that the walls of the city which the *streltsy* wished to take by force were sacred and impenetrable, the czar ordered beams to be set out from the battlements and two mutineers to be hanged from each beam."[12] The *streltsy* priests were executed in front of the Church of the Holy Trinity. Since, Korb tells us, priests could not be handed over to an executioner, it was Peter's jester, dressed as a priest, who placed the noose around their necks.[13] Peter obliged boyars to execute *streltsy* in person. Romodanovsky, who had commanded four *streltsy* regiments, had to execute four of the mutineers. B. A. Golitsyn was especially clumsy, and gave his victims a bad time. Peter, watching dry-eyed from his horse, was displeased by his unsteady hand. Menshikov was later to boast with a vile and vulgar extravagance that he had cut off at least twenty heads in person.

Deciding to experiment a little, Peter invited Gordon to attend the executions of the following day. He would find them interesting since they would attempt the European method of cutting the head off with a sword as opposed to an axe. The idea excited Menshikov so much that that afternoon he drove round Moscow in his carriage, brandishing a drawn sword, "using it to indicate with what impatience he awaited the bloody tragedy of the morrow".[14] The same author goes on to suggest, although he himself did not see it, that Peter conducted the experiment in person, while a boyar held the victim's head by its hair to make sure that the blow was a true one. He doubtless exaggerates when suggesting that Peter accounted for over eighty *streltsy* in this manner; however, there is nothing intrinsically implausible in the notion of Peter playing executioner and venting upon their very persons the savage rage which the *streltsy* inspired in him. Besides the Moscow executions 190 mutineers were hanged in front of the cell occupied by Sophia in the Novodevichy monastery, where they were left to dangle.

Peter ordered all corpses to go unburied throughout the winter. It was only early in the following March that they were collected: "It was a fearful sight for more enlightened races, expressive and full of horror: quantities of corpses lay in carts, tossed there haphazardly, many half naked; like slaughtered cattle being taken to market they took their bodies to their graves."[15]

[12] *Ibid.*, 1867, vol. iii, p. 228. [13] *Ibid.*, p. 230.
[14] *Ibid.*, 1867, vol. i, p. 143. [15] *Ibid.*, p. 152.

Virtually all that Peter had to show from this wretched business was his discovery of the involvement of Sophia and her sister. He had also learned that his boyars were not plotting against him, and that his soldiers were loyal – although the *streltsy* had tried to involve them with fake accusations. The mutiny also provided him with an excuse to break the *streltsy* for ever; their sixteen regiments were disbanded and forbidden to reside in Moscow or serve in the army. Peter had issued a dreadful warning to potential opponents that he settled his accounts fully, and in blood.

Yet none of this can explain or excuse Peter's personal cruelty, his reluctance to concede that there might have been degrees of guilt, or the terrible glimpses of sadistic clowning – Menshikov and his sword, Peter the amateur headsman, his jester hanging the priests. As with the execution of Tsykler one can simply observe that Peter reacted to the threat of the *streltsy* with a violence that even by his standards was remarkable. On that bloody day back in 1682 he had learnt real fear at the hands of the *streltsy* and now sixteen years later he showed them that the lesson had not been forgotten.

* * *

Peter returned from the West with a heightened awareness of the inertia, backwardness and stupidity of old Russia. The *streltsy* mutiny had done nothing to modify his views. His actions in the eighteen months following his homecoming suggest that he wished to attack the old ways on various fronts – the savage elimination of the *streltsy* being one such attack. This is not to say that Peter had a coordinated master plan. His mind did not work like that, he did not have that capacity for abstract thought which shapes grand designs. Instead he applied his energy fiercely to particular targets, an approach that could sometimes prove wasteful of resources. Yet so great was Peter's energy, so effective his personal authority, and indeed so extensive the resources, that the sheer power he could bring to bear was enough to effect the transformations that he wanted.

His first target, as we have seen, was beards. Beard-shaving continued at all Peter's receptions and entertainments. A few days after the first occasion it is his jester we find going round with a pair of shears trimming the beards of high-ranking noblemen who had not yet taken the hint to shave themselves. Beards were something much more than articles of fashion. They were considered an essential attribute of male godliness, so that shaving was held seriously to compromise one's chance of salvation. For Peter the love of beards was not simply a symbol of old Russia, it was also the emblem of barbaric superstition and sheer ignorance, and such as considered an obstacle to enlightenment:

> I wish to transform secular goats, that is to say citizens, ... in order to make them resemble decent beardless Europeans, for our old men are ignorant enough to believe that they will not enter the kingdom of heaven without beards, though God has opened it to all, whatever their faith, bearded or beardless, bewigged or bald, in long or short garments.[16]

He was accused in anonymous letters left in public places – the usual form of protest – of tyranny and heathenism directed against his people in forcing them to part with their beards. In fact some of those obliged to shave did nothing of the sort, still contriving to retain them. Captain Perry met one of his workmen who had just gone through the ordeal:

> I jested with him a little on the occasion, telling him that he was become a young man and asked him what he had done with his beard? Upon which he put his hand in his bosom and pulled it out and showed it to me; further telling me that when he came home he would lay it up and have it put in his coffin and buried along with him, that he might be able to give an account of it to St. Nicholas, when he came to the other world; and that all his brothers had taken the same care.[17]

Yet Peter was by no means a voice crying in the wilderness, not the only man in Russia to be against beards. Shaving was far from unheard of among younger Russians, as we can infer from the patriarch Ioakim's violent preachings against the practice some years earlier. Indeed it is possible that had Peter acted with more moderation, less cruel buffoonery and public humiliation, he would have achieved his ends, at least among the nobility, more or less unopposed. Instead he proceeded in an oppressive

[16] Markov, p. 22.   [17] Perry, p. 197.

and unpleasant manner; by 1699 beards were made into a source
of revenue, being taxed at various rates. In some cases the tax
was paid annually, whereas peasants had to pay a small sum
whenever they entered city gates. They were provided with a
brass token showing a moustache and a beard on one side, while
the other bore the words "Money taken". There are no figures
for the early years, but in 1720 a staff of thirty-seven manned
the gates of Moscow to fine beard-wearers, wearers of Russian
dress and users of Russian saddlery. They raised about 250
roubles a year, which suggested, at an average rate of a rouble
a fine, approximately a dozen arrests per gate per year.[18] Lord
Byron gives us the last word upon the matter, writing to a
publisher about a forthcoming book:

> Then you've General Gordon
> Who girded his sword on
> To serve with a Muscovite master
> And help him to polish
> A nation so owlish
> They thought shaving their beards a disaster.[19]

Next Peter turned his attention to traditional Russian dress,
the long, heavy, fur-trimmed robes with their high collars and
trailing, voluminous sleeves, that were favoured by the nobility.
At the reception Lefort gave in February 1699 to celebrate the
opening of the magnificent palace Peter had given him, the czar
had his shears out again, this time to trim his boyars' attire. He
subsequently commanded that a pattern of clothes "of the
English fashion should be hung at all the gates of the City of
Moscow, and that publication should be made that all persons
except peasants should make their clothes according to the said
patterns".[20] The alternative was a fine. Hems were to be no lower
than knee length.

Peter objected to traditional dress for a number of reasons,
sheer conservatism apart. The massive overgarments and abundant sleeves were not conducive to rapid and energetic movement;
they frequently led to accidents such as broken glasses or else,
he once observed, they trailed in the soup. Moreover Peter, who
detested luxury and conspicuous consumption, resented the idle
magnificence of Russian noble dress, both ornate and heavy. In

[18] Cht., 1899, vol. ii, p. 4.   [19] Gordon, P., p. xi.   [20] Perry, pp. 198–9.

the same spirit he sought to discourage boyars from the practice of taking with them extravagant retinues of outriders and servants which turned their every journey through the city into a procession. He made other more obviously benign changes in custom, beginning his liberation of Russian women from the confinement of the *terem* by altering the way in which marriages were arranged. No longer did bride and groom first see one another at the altar. He insisted that marriage must be based upon mutual assent, and that the couple should visit one another for at least six weeks before their union.

He mounted another assault upon conservative dignity and tradition which proved a source of indignant bewilderment to contemporaries and has never been accounted for since by any single satisfactory explanation. However, it is strangely revealing of that peculiar blend of sport, truculent challenge to received beliefs, humour, pageantry and an elusive and tongue-in-cheek seriousness that come together to form a complex whole that lies very near the centre of Peter's character.

Peter's drunken company had long had its Prince Caesar and Prince Pope in the shape of Romodanovsky and Zotov. They were now made the secular and religious heads of a formal body, the "All drunken, maddest and all joking synod". Its most prominent members bore the ecclesiastical title of "*vladyko*" or bishop, of various cities. At its plenary sessions, held only on high days and holidays, Romodanovsky wore the vestments of a czar, Zotov those of a patriarch. The assembly had carefully composed statutes, all of which emphasised the joys of wine, and stressed the desirability of stupefying intoxication, merriment and the loss of reason.

Korb saw the synod processing on various occasions. On Christmas Day 1698 Zotov, dressed as a patriarch with a retinue of 200 persons, drove through Moscow on sledges. He was wearing a mitre and holding a crosier. They alternately sang praises to the new-born Christ and to Bacchus, and ended up at an entertainment given by Lefort. On another occasion, soon after, his mitre was decorated with a naked Bacchus, with Venus and Cupid on the crosier, while his retinue were dressed as bacchantes carrying mugs of beer and vodka. Others had vessels full of smouldering tobacco leaves, while one member of the company carried two pipes tied together in the form of a cross.[21]

[21] Cht., 1867, vol. i, pp. 145–6.

The activities of the synod were not confined to ritual public appearances. The joke was sustained in private too, for members kept up a lively and prolonged exchange of letters with one another and above all with Peter, using the high style of Old Church Slavonic, parodying the form of official ecclesiastical documents with an elaborate and facetious seriousness. Although the correspondence waned over the years the synod itself was anything but a short-lived joke. It would survive as long as the czar himself. On Romodanovsky's death in 1717 his office passed to his son, and one of Peter's last public acts, when already near death and in continual pain, was to assist at the election of a new Prince Pope. With time the assemblies grew more elaborate, but no less barbaric. A Dane, Just Juel, who attended one some years later, describes Zotov wearing a piece of headgear consisting of a silver Bacchus astride a barrel; every time he leant forward the Bacchus pissed brandy over him. When Zotov wished to follow suit he turned aside and performed on the floor while Peter solicitously held a candle for him. In the meantime his drunken companions bellowed at the tops of their voices, and spat in one another's faces. One of them was known as the Knight of the Order of Judas and wore a silver medal bearing Judas' face hung on a massive silver chain.[22]

The election of a new Prince Pope was turned into an elaborate and disgusting parody of a Vatican election. It took place in a house known as the Vatican. The conclave of intoxicated cardinals were given nothing to eat except the sexual organs of cattle, cats and dogs of both sexes, in highly peppered preparations, and nothing to drink but beer and vodka. Peter visited and drank with them regularly until an election was announced.[23]

Peter took his synod seriously. Romodanovsky would always remain *Min Her Kernich*, and we have seen Peter pause to seek Zotov's blessing. Stranger still, when his son was about to get married, Peter wrote to his second wife urging her to "get the all-joking Prince Pope and the others to bless the young couple, wearing all their robes, together with those attending you".[24]

What then can one make of this extraordinary institution? There is no doubt that it was intended to shock with its unconcealed blasphemy. Peter was not irreligious and believed himself answerable to God both as a man and as Russia's ruler. This did not prevent him from being impatient with the orthodox

[22] Cht., 1892, vol. ii, p. 93. [23] Ibid., 1874, vol. ii, pp. 18–19. [24] Corr., vol. xi, p. 170.

church as a conservative institution and the ultimate basis for
the slow rituals of old Muscovy. By the end of his life he had
largely succeeded in making the church a mere instrument of the
state: the first step being taken with his refusal to appoint a new
patriarch on the death of Adrian – the office would remain vacant
until the 20th century. These blasphemous processions were yet
another example of Peter's cruel teasing of Russian tradition.
Whether or not such mockery was intended to be educational,
there can be no doubt that it gave Peter great private satisfaction.
To Western eyes Peter appeared to be mocking the Catholic
church too, and this is not altogether implausible. He always derived great satisfaction from mock ceremony; witness the strange
parody of his Viennese embassy which he mounted shortly after
his return. Lefort and Golovin reproduced their ambassadorial
entry into Vienna, using every coach and sleigh available. With
Peter in their train they presented Romadanovsky with their
mock credentials, and a monkey in lieu of an ambassadorial gift.
All those attending had to wear foreign dress. The joke was partly
levelled against Romodanovsky, who on hearing that Golovin
had worn Western clothes in Vienna was heard to observe that
he had never supposed him to be such a fool.[25] At all events we
can see Peter here using pageantry of his own brand to purge
the memory of his lukewarm reception in Vienna.

But it is not possible to provide any purely rational justification
for the synod. Ultimately it was Peter's love of grotesque and carnivalesque entertainment, his perverse sense of humour and
drunken ceremonial, that created and sustained it. Whether sober
or drunk himself he always relished the spectacle of hopeless and
if necessary enforced drunkenness in others, while nothing
appealed to him so much as elaborate and sustained comic
pageantry, which, to be effective, had to be conducted with great
seriousness. The final justification and explanation for the synod
was quite simply that Peter enjoyed it. For better or for worse
it took pride of place among the patterns and ceremonies of
Peter's court, but where court life at, say, Versailles was founded
in high seriousness, Peter preferred to found his own patterns
on something that must reluctantly be described as a sense of
humour.

It is not easy to determine the effect of Peter's actions upon
his people. Certainly he was not the only person to consider that

[25] Cht., 1866, vol. iv, pp. 109–10.

the *streltsy* symbolised the values of old Muscovy. Critics of Peter interrogated by the Preobrazhensky Office were known to observe under torture that "the *streltsy* had stood for the faith", traditional orthodoxy and the good old ways. There is no record of any widespread and articulate criticism of the executions themselves – any more than there was any widespread and out-spoken criticism at the time of Stalin's purges. Indeed that kind of criticism has seldom been practicable in Russia. However, foreign residents in Moscow sensed a climate of great tension and hostility. There was a notable increase in acts of violence in the winter of 1698–9, especially violence against foreigners, and Korb at least had the feeling that the atmosphere was so explosive that a serious flare-up could occur at any moment.[26] Flare-ups did indeed occur, in a literal sense. There were many more fires than usual that winter, and it was rumoured that surviving *streltsy* and their sympathisers wished to burn down the city.[27] There was also a proliferation of anonymous and frequently false denunciations.[28] Anonymous letters were found directed at Lefort and now, and for the first time, Menshikov, who were held responsible for the corruption of Peter.

For many people Peter was no longer a proper and orthodox czar; he had become a renegade. One anonymous letter lists his wrongs: his treatment of the *streltsy*, his preference for foreigners, his all-drunken synod "the devil's swarm", and his love of tobacco. He is also condemned for wearing "Hungarian dress", failing to observe fasts and the destruction of the beard;[29] influenced by foreigners and his journey to the West, he had for-saken Russia and the orthodox faith, and put away his orthodox wife and sisters. Indeed Peter now became enveloped in a strange body of popular superstition and myth. Since it was not possible that an orthodox czar could behave as he did, it became apparent to many that their ruler was not the czar at all. Some said that the real czar had been spirited away and that Lefort's son had taken his place. "He orders us to wear foreign dress, he must be the son of a foreigner."[30] It was also suggested that the real Peter had disappeared during the embassy. "When the czar was across the sea and went to 'Glassland' [i.e. Stockholm, Russian *steklo* = glass] a maiden kept him in the kingdom of glass, roasted him on an iron pan and cast him into a dungeon. She put him

[26] cht., 1866, vol. iv, pp. 128–9.   [27] Wittram, vol. i, p. 180.
[28] Soloviev, vol. vii, p. 99.   [29] Golikova, p. 133.   [30] Soloviev, vol. vii, p. 99.

in a nail-studded cask and he who reigns now is a foreigner sent by foreigners to make us into heretics."[31]

However, the most extreme and widely held belief was simply that Peter was none other than Antichrist. A certain Grigory Talitsky wrote a book proving that the world was about to end and that Antichrist, in the shape of Peter, was already ruling. Many shared his belief throughout Peter's reign and well beyond. Even in this century there can be found schismatic tracts that claim Peter was Antichrist and that all his descendants carried his taint.[32]

Despite the undoubted mistrust, hostility and downright hate which Peter and his new ways inspired there was little or no concerted resistance to him in the heart of Russia. Among the upper classes resistance took the form of obstinate sloth rather than overt protest. The *streltsy* revolt was the last act of rebellion in central Russia. The traditional Muscovite response to intolerable oppression, political or religious, was not resistance but flight; flight north or east into the forests, or south to the steppe. For generations there had been a constant stream of fugitives, runaway serfs and, recently, schismatics, who escaped the authority of Moscow by running away. Southern Russia, the huge expanse of steppe between Astrakhan and the Polish frontier, had always been held loosely by Moscow. The cossacks who peopled it were free men, committed to serving the czar but loose in their allegiance, and the south had always been a source of potential rebellion. It was there that we find the first overt acts of resistance to Peter's new ways.

In 1700 a boyar was sent to Kamyshin, a town on the Volga, to instruct the governor and town officials to shave off their beards and dress in the new style. They obeyed and the boyar returned to the capital. Their compliance enraged a nearby settlement of cossack Old Believers who promptly attacked the town and sacked it. The governor escaped and hid on a nearby island while the cossacks cut the heads off of anyone who had been so imprudent as to shave. Persons found wearing Western dress had their pockets filled with stones and were dropped into the Volga. Others were tied to tree trunks and similarly cast into the river to be used for target practice. The cossacks stayed on the rampage for six weeks – until the governor was eventually handed over. Despite the fact that his beard had grown the cossacks still

[31] Golikova, p. 146.　　　　[32] Knyaz'kov, pp. 516–7.

expressed a desire to kill him. They only spared his life when the entire population of Kamyshin interceded on his behalf. They finally withdrew under the threat of an advancing punitive force, having extracted from the townspeople an oath never to shave again.[33] Although this first act of resistance to the new ways was isolated and without consequence, within five years rebellion in the south would flare again, on a much more general and more dangerous scale.

*　　*　　*

Before leaving on his embassy Peter had planned to develop a Black Sea fleet to be built at Voronezh, but the plans themselves had scarcely been taken further than the instruction that such a fleet should be built. He left the details, all of them, to the council of boyars to work out, having stipulated how the construction was to be financed. Peter was not dismayed by the knowledge that none of the Russians engaged in organising the construction of his fleet knew the first thing about shipbuilding. He seems to have been a firm believer in the principle that "you pay to learn", and was as yet in no position himself to do any teaching. Everyone was to learn the hard way, regardless of the waste of resources. The constructors had various Western designs to work on, describing the type of ship to be built, together with its equipment. However, the designs required considerable modifications and the specifications were incomplete. For example, it was planned to equip some ships with "naval mortars", although no one actually knew what a naval mortar was.[34] Peter, abroad, conducted a regular and detailed correspondence on that subject with his builders, including translations of Italian specifications, in the course of which it became clear that no one, least of all Peter, knew what they were talking about.[35] There was no careful and concerted plan, simply Peter's programme: so many ships to be built by such and such a date. All the emphasis was on speed, the fulfilment of the plan, and the ships were built regardless. They were built of unseasoned timber, since there was not time to season it, built in uncovered yards, since there was no time to build covered ones. The designs themselves were frequently faulty, since there was no time to determine correct proportions. The only criterion appears to have

[33] Sokolov, p. 18.　　　[34] Bogoslovsky, vol. iv, p. 170.　　　[35] Ibid., loc. cit.

been the deadline, and ships were built without any thought to whether or not they would prove seaworthy.

The business of the *streltsy* kept Peter in Moscow for a whole two months on his return. He was unable to visit the Voronezh yards until late October, but on arrival declared himself excited by what he found. Some twenty ships were ready to sail, and among other stores were 300 cannon obligingly provided by the young Charles XII of Sweden to assist Peter in his war against the Turks. However, on a closer inspection in the company of foreign experts, it became clear that the fleet was less than perfect. Many ships were so ill-constructed that they were useless, either too frail or of eccentric proportions,[36] and the vast majority required, at the very least, important modification and additions to their inadequate equipment. In the words of an impartial English observer, "little is to be said in favour of the ships built before the czar's return from his travel; to pass them by in silence is the highest compliment".[37]

Yet Peter was never discouraged by setbacks and disappointments. He responded to them by working harder, not by distributing blame and looking for scapegoats. He set to work in the yards in person – writing to Romodanovsky he signs himself "Your most humble servant Peter Schiptimmerman"[38] – and began work on a new ship. The foreign experts he had engaged were beginning to gather at Voronezh and soon a second generation of vessels was under construction. Peter's love of fire is revealed in some their names; among the list of ships launched in 1700 we find *Vulcan* and *Salamander*.

Peter knew that he was making a start, and a modest one; there could be no question of acquiring a model navy overnight. For all his enthusiasm he remained a realist, and the Voronezh fleet occasioned one of the rare times that Peter expressed anything approximating a doubt. In a letter written shortly after his arrival we read: "Praise God we found our fleet and stores in excellent order. And yet a cloud of doubt persists over our thoughts, in case this seed of ours should resemble that of the date palm whose fruit is never seen by those who plant it."[39] Whatever his shortcomings Peter never allowed enthusiasm and wishful thinking to lead to self-deception. Even its founder could see that the Russian navy still had a long way to go.

---

[36] *Ibid.*, p. 172.　　　　　[37] Barrow, p. 4.
[38] *Corr.*, vol. i, p. 324.　　　[39] Ustryalov, vol. iii, p. 249.

The first Russian attempt to build a canal by forced labour, and join the Don to the Volga, proved even less successful than subsequent efforts at canal building over the ages.[40] Despite repeated attempts up to 1810 the canal was never completed. The chief problem was lack of water, since the canal only filled properly when the Don was in spring flood. Peter mobilised a workforce of over 20,000 for the project, recruiting from both near and far. Particular areas had to supply one labourer for every five households, one carpenter for every seven. Needless to say labour conditions were not benign; workers stood up to their waists in water for much of the year. They were inadequately housed and fed, while dysentry and typhus were by no means unknown. However, the scale of construction was remarkable. An engineer inspecting some of the canal locks in 1892 found oak beams of 2 × 4 metres, over 8 metres long, and stones requiring ten horses to shift them. A single lock would, he estimated, have cost a quarter of a million roubles in his day, and Peter had built some thirty-three before the project was abandoned.

The navy, the canals, Azov, Taganrog and the new standing army after the European fashion that Peter now planned to raise and supply, all required a massive increase in revenue, and this occupied much of his attention on his return. In 1699 he attempted to simplify the pattern of urban administration which had been complex, partly conducted by local governors and partly by a series of administrative offices in Moscow, rendering the citizens victims of a combination of inefficiency, malpractice and exploitation. Peter sought to improve the condition of the tradespeople and hence their ability to pay taxes by instituting elements of self-government. He released them from the authority of the governor and the offices, ordering them to choose their own administrative bodies, to be led by a president, which would be under the authority of a supreme chamber in Moscow. In return for their release from other authorities they would be taxed at double the preceding rate. The innovation was not an outstanding success. Self-government was considered a burdensome duty and not the dawn of some brave new era, and what elections there were were conducted according to time-honoured principles such as bribery and corruption.

Peter had drawn on his experience of Dutch and German pat-

---

[40] For other later examples of unsuccessful canal building see A. Solzhenitsyn, *Gulag Archipelago*, vol. i, ch. iii, *passim*.

terns of administration for his urban reforms; now Western Europe provided him with another and more fundamental departure from tradition. The Russian calendar was based upon the Byzantine model, which counted its years from the beginning of the world, and began the New Year on September 1. Peter now proceeded to alter that traditional sense of time by issuing an edict decreeing that a new calendar would come into use on January 1, 1700, which day would start the New Year. New Year's Day was to be celebrated by all persons of rank, who should decorate their houses with branches of evergreen that must be removed a week later. On New Year's Day itself people were to congratulate one another in the street. Those possessing fire-arms should discharge a salvo of three shots or let off rockets as soon as the fireworks started in Red Square.

CHAPTER EIGHT

The Great Northern War

It is altogether appropriate that Russia should have celebrated its entry into "European time", and by implication history, at the dawn of the 18th century. Peter had worked hard for that entry, particularly in the year 1699, which saw the first phase of his reforms and also his preparations for what was to be a long and gruelling war. Consequently it came as a particularly heavy blow to Peter when in March of that year he lost Lefort. He died most unexpectedly after a short illness while Peter was at Voronezh. The czar was very upset by the news and hurried back to Moscow. In Lefort he had lost a close friend, and, perhaps more important, both a mentor and a man he felt he could trust. "Who do I place my trust in now?" he is alleged to have observed on hearing the news of his death.[1] It was a good question. As far as we know, for all his limitations Lefort was not a grossly dishonest man, and was apparently contented by the great generosity with which Peter treated him – in this respect quite unlike his protégé and eventual successor Menshikov.

Lefort's lavish funeral was a characteristic affair. Despite a carefully established order of precedence which gave foreign diplomats a prominent position Russian grandees simply elbowed their way to the front on leaving the church. The diplomats submitted, but Peter noticed the change in order, and when it was explained, observed: "They are dogs not boyars!" The salute did not go off without incident. One of the loaders remained standing in front of his piece and the discharge blew his head off.[2]

[1] Cht., 1866, vol. iv, p. 155.   [2] Ibid., p. 158.

Peter's loss was the more acute since he now stood in particular need of good advice, and not simply because of his plans to modernise Russia. He had plans of a different kind; war with Sweden, the most powerful nation of the north.

Although we cannot say when Peter first conceived of a northern war it is certain that he was persuaded to join an anti-Swedish alliance by meeting Augustus II, Augustus the Strong, the Elector of Saxony, whom he had helped on to the throne of Poland. Peter met him at Rawa in August 1698 on his way back from Vienna. Augustus was two years Peter's senior and superficially not unlike him. Immensely strong, and proud of it, he was no less fond of drunken entertainment. He had great charm and *joie de vivre*, but lacked all distinction, both as a monarch and a military commander. However, at their first meeting Peter found him greatly to his liking and spent a week in his company, a period in which both rulers drank a great deal and Peter gave regular demonstrations of his prowess on the drum. The two rulers exchanged frequent marks of mutual affection, and there was a great deal of kissing and embracing.[3] It would seem that it was Peter who first suggested to Augustus the possibility of an aggressive alliance against the Swedes. The time was ripe to attack them, since Charles XI had died just a year before and a sixteen-year-old, Charles XII, had succeeded him. Peter's official account of the war states that he asked Augustus to help him have his revenge for the insulting reception he was given at Riga – and he would always maintain that this was the principal cause of the war. However, there is no mention of Riga in the diplomatic papers of the time. It is much more likely that Peter's travels had turned his thoughts towards the Baltic, and given him the idea of reconquering Ingria and East Karelia which had been held by earlier czars. It would be wrong to describe Peter's suggestion to Augustus as simply the product of personal caprice or of outrage, but certainly the idea of a Northern War was partly born of an act of will on Peter's part, and the consequences of that particular act were to change history.

Augustus was in no position to agree to an immediate offensive alliance – there was too much unrest in Poland, while before he could contemplate a war with Sweden Peter had to end the one he was supposed to be fighting against the Turks. They were eager enough for peace themselves, and in April 1699 two Russian

[3] Bogoslovsky, vol. v, p. 577.

envoys were sent to Istanbul to open negotiations. The manner of their travelling made it clear to the world that Peter's efforts were begininning to bear fruit. They went by ship, a Russian man-of-war sailed by a Dutch captain, and were escorted for some of the way by a fleet of nine warships and two galleys. Despite Turkish attempts to make them travel overland the ambassadors sailed to Istanbul, a salute announcing their arrival and Russia's beginning as a maritime power.

Peter had been fortunate in his choice of a successor to Lefort. His place had been taken by Fedor Alekseevich Golovin, who was both admiral general and in charge of foreign affairs. He was a person of considerable experience and ability, who was to serve Peter well over the years. He now expected to negotiate a favourable peace treaty with the Turks without any difficulty, little realising that the Western Powers, faced for the first time by the possibility of Russia becoming a naval and mercantile force, would apply all the diplomatic pressure they could upon Turkey to prevent any kind of settlement which might favour Russia too greatly.

In the meantime a secret alliance was being formed against Sweden. One of its architects was a Livonian, Johann Reinhold Patkul. Combining the qualities of intriguer, diplomat and what would now be termed entrepreneur, and immensely proud of his position as a Livonian aristocrat, Patkul was a forceful and energetic figure who devoted great energy to his attempts to restore the Livonian barons, descendants of the Teutonic knights, to their ancient prestigious situation. He had served Charles XI of Sweden, only to be dismissed and condemned to death in his absence for pressing the Livonian cause with too much enthusiasm. He now helped to shape an alliance between Denmark, Saxony and Russia, against the Swedes, his own aim being to free Livonia from Swedish domination. Patkul and a Saxon general, Karlowitz, arrived in Moscow in September 1699. Together with the Danes they were to set up the anti-Swedish alliance. Their task was somewhat complicated by the presence in Moscow of a Swedish embassy that had arrived to re-affirm the treaty of Kardis which pledged Sweden and Russia to an eternal peace! Some rockets set off to celebrate the ambassador's entry had caused a great fire, and this was taken by some as a portent of future hostilities;[4] indeed it was a portent of the longest war ever

[4] Tumansky, vol. iii, p. 117.

to be fought in Europe since 1648. While the Muscovites renegoti-
ated the peace treaty with the Swedes, Peter, Karlowitz, Patkul
and the Danish resident Heins prepared for war. Peter was complete in his duplicity; he superstitiously declined to ratify the new
Swedish treaty in the traditional Russian manner by kissing a
cross, advancing the specious reason that he had done so once
already, and that his assurance was as good as his oath. The
Swedish embassy had to content itself with that assurance.

Since Peter was in no position to commit himself to immediate
war, Denmark and Saxony were eventually obliged to move without him. A Saxon army attempted and failed to take Riga by surprise, setting siege to the city, much to the dismay of Peter who
felt that the Saxon general was more interested in his new bride
than in the war, while Augustus should have been with the army,
as opposed to enjoying himself in Dresden. This failure of
Augustus to take Riga in fact set the pattern for all his subsequent
military enterprises. As Defoe was to write: "The Saxons were
so shamefully beaten in every action and even without action,
that there could nothing be said for them."[5]

Despite the fact that his allies had shown their hand, Peter continued to make every effort to persuade the Swedes that he
wanted peace, going so far as to send an ambassador to Stockholm in the spring of 1700 to renew his protestations of goodwill.
Although it may be that Peter was keeping his options open, in
case the alliance with Saxony and Denmark should break down,
and in case he should fail to secure a peace with Turkey – and
that treaty was indeed slow in coming – he seems to have been
inspired largely by shameful duplicity. He displayed as much to
the daughter of a Swedish diplomat, who was disturbed by news
of Russian troop movements on her north-west frontier, and had
heard it rumoured that Peter intended war. He assured her that
there could be no question of his starting what he referred to as
an unjust war, which would break the eternal peace treaty that
he had just ratified.[6] The Swedish diplomat and his companions
were moved to tears by Peter's honesty. Moreover, he observed
that Augustus was doubtless determined to take Riga, but that
he, Peter, would then take it from him and hand it back to
Sweden.

Despite his preparations for a war in the north, preparations
which were becoming increasingly obvious, Peter continued to

[5] Ibid., p. 111.　　　　　[6] Wittram, vol. i, p. 226.

go to great lengths to convince foreign observers that he wanted nothing better than eternal peace with his northern neighbour, and that he was "most vexed by the business of Riga".[7] On August 8 Peter learned that his envoys had signed a thirty-year treaty with Turkey. Peter was to keep Azov, cease to pay tribute to the Crimean Tartars and would in return demolish certain other forts which he had had constructed. The next day Russia entered the Northern War.

Peter could not hope to fight the Swedes with a traditional Muscovite army based on the annual *levée en masse*. Even against Tartar irregulars it had proved less than effective. A contemporary critic described it as being equipped with inferior guns. It was only any use with cold steel, the *arme blanche* – which was all too often blunt – and its casualty rate was four times as high as that of its enemies. Three Tartars killed constituted a victory, whatever the Russian losses.[8] The cavalry was severely under-horsed and ill-trained, indeed it would remain inferior for years. The distances it had to cover required the use of small, tough horses rather than chargers which had less stamina and were anyway unobtainable in Russia. Even in Peter's military heyday his cavalry would essentially be mounted infantry, dragoons, their horses too light to withstand a proper charge.[9]

Peter needed to raise a whole modern army. He was not helped by the death, in September 1699, of his senior foreign general, Gordon. However, he started an intensive campaign of conscription and also welcomed volunteers. The total number so recruited over the course of the war was to amount to nearly 300,000. His first batches impressed foreign observers with their training and equipment, although they were unable to say as much for their officers. Many of the Russian ones turned out to be unenthusiastic and incompetent to a degree. Indeed the level of native incompetence was such that at this stage of the war nearly a third of Peter's officers were foreign. This did not in itself make for excellence. Foreigners had to pledge themselves to service for life if they were to hope for fair treatment in promotion, and most of them were of inferior quality in the first place; "necessarily regarding Russia no otherwise than as an unavoidable prison".[10]

Recruiting was in general conducted throughout the war according to principles of a peculiarly Petrine kind, principles

---

[7] Wittram, vol. i, p. 227.
[9] Cht., 1874, vol. ii, p. 45.
[8] *Russ. Star.*, 1881, vol. iii, p. 241.
[10] Bridges, p. 108.

that combined absolutism with a taste for a perversely rational regularity. At a somewhat later date Peter refers in a letter to a "regiment of marines recruited from Moscow sleigh drivers",[11] – he was never frightened of changing lives wholesale at the stroke of a pen. Thus it is hardly surprising that there was a high desertion rate; a steady ten per cent per annum, throughout the war, among all ranks, even though deserters received short and often ingenious shrift. Peter once wrote as follows to one of his majors: "When the two deserters Vyalov and Plyakov are brought to you from Kiev have them shot in front of the regiment when you reach Lithuania. If they are in poor shape and you don't think they will survive the journey, do it when it suits. Vyalov should be shot at long range so that he dies more slowly since he is the ringleader."[12] Peter had a marvellous eye for detail.

However, as would prove the case with his fleet, Peter's extraordinary drive, energy and, it must be said, a vivid understanding of what was required enabled him to create, in a matter of months, an army of 40,000 foot soldiers which amazed the Saxon general Baron Langen by its quality, appearance and ability to shoot straight.[13] Not for the first or the last time Peter showed that he could use his talents, authority and the resources of his country to effect overnight transformations that would prove surprisingly enduring.

Peter had already chosen Narva as his first target. Some five months before declaring war he had sent a sergeant of the Preobrazhenskys there, ostensibly to purchase cannon from the Swedes, actually to spy out the fortifications. Now having declared war, Peter set siege to the town. He embarked on this in an unusual manner, by writing to English merchants within the city announcing that he was somewhat short of wine, and wondering whether, if the Swedish commander agreed, they might supply him with some. He was prepared to pay a decent price, and they would have his enduring gratitude in return. At the same time he wrote to the commander, disingenuously suggesting he release the merchants as neutrals. History does not relate whether he had his wine or not, but on the whole it seems improbable. The siege was not a successful one, although Peter, as captain of bombardiers, was congratulated upon his energies by one of his commanders, Carl Eugène de Croy. "He who does not work does not eat," replied Peter proudly, in Dutch, thereby

[11] *Corr.*, vol. ix, p. 130.   [12] *Ibid.*, vol. v, p. 334.   [13] Ustryalov, vol. iii, p. 318.

anticipating an observation of Lenin's by some 200 years. However, energy alone was not enough to take the town. The bombardment was not particularly effective since the Russian gun carriages and axles tended to break after three or four shots, their powder was bad and there was not enough shot. Besides, it would seem that it was Peter's eagerness to join the fight that had dictated the timing of the siege – the roads were so bad in autumn that it was dreadfully difficult to bring up supplies.

Charles XII of Sweden was eighteen at the outbreak of war with Russia. An inexperienced leader, he commanded an army in which only the older officers had seen active service – twenty years before. Yet very soon he and his men were to win the admiration of Europe, especially his personal crack unit, the corps of Drabants, some of the finest cavalry ever seen. At their last parade in 1716 there would be only thirteen men left of those who now rode out to war with Charles, as he left his capital; a city which he would never see again, though he was to live another eighteen years.

Charles landed at Pernau in the Gulf of Riga, and on learning the news Peter sent Boris Sheremetev with 6000 men to reconnoitre. Sheremetev succeeded in occupying a key pass, as Charles and his tiny army of 8000 came up. However, they attacked with such vigour that Sheremetev was dislodged at once, beating a hasty retreat to Narva to announce that the Swedes were coming with an army 30,000 strong.

Peter's courage was unequal to the occasion. He displayed his occasional capacity for panic and decided that it was imperative that he be in Moscow as soon as possible. His official history observed that this was in order to accelerate supplies to the army, and there was also some talk of receiving a Turkish embassy. Be that as it may, on the eve of his army's first battle against Europeans Peter insisted on handing over command to a dismayed General de Croy, who had only just joined the army. At first de Croy refused, then insisted on a written order which he expected to receive from Peter in person, only to discover that the czar had left his army at dead of night and on the eve of battle, leaving no written instruction behind him.

The Russian army was between 35,000 and 45,000 strong, in well-fortified lines. However, these were so long that it would have required an army twice its size to hold them properly. The Swedes made contact with their enemy on the morning of

November 19. On seeing them emerge from a wood de Croy assumed that they could only be a vanguard, having made no attempt whatsoever to confirm Sheremetev's precipitate assessment of their strength. Indeed there had been no reconnaissance of any kind. After a two-hour bombardment Charles realised that he would not draw the Russians from their lines, and so he decided upon a two-pronged frontal assault. The Swedes went in under cover of a fierce and sudden snowstorm that reduced visibility to a few paces. "We charged directly, sword in hand and so entered, and we slew all who came at us so that it was a terrible massacre."[14]

Under the shock of the Swedish attack the Russians panicked, began to shoot their foreign officers, turned and ran, Sheremetev in the lead, crossing the Narva river and losing some thousand men by drowning in the process. The foot soldiers followed and still more died when the only bridge gave way. However, not all the Russians broke; the two guards regiments stood behind their pikes—the Swedes had bayonets for the first time—and against all comers. In the meantime Peter's foreign commander, de Croy, observing "let the devil himself try to fight with such troops", surrendered to the Swedes together with other senior foreign officers. He was to die in captivity some years later, in Revel, where he remained on show in a church in a glass-lidded coffin, in wig and uniform, until 1848.[15] Peter afterwards admitted that had he given him command a fortnight earlier he would never have been beaten.

The guards held out till nightfall, but then their generals decided to surrender. They were allowed to retreat with their weapons but were obliged to abandon their baggage train and guns. Meanwhile the Russian left wing, under General Weide, which had virtually no part in the battle, deciding that it too should surrender, declared itself ready if need be to fight to the last drop of blood and inquired after terms. Weide was told that he could count upon the generosity of the king and promptly laid down his arms. A Swedish observer remarked that with his 6000 fresh troops Weide, even then, could have annihilated Charles's soldiers, who were exhausted, unfed and in a great many cases drunk.[16]

The next morning the guards marched out under the command of Golovin. They were followed by Weide's men. At the last

[14] Bengtsson, p. 87. [15] Ustryalov, vol. iv, pt i, p. 59. [16] Ibid., p. 49.

moment it was decided that the Russian generals, ten in all, were to remain prisoners of war, on the pretext that the Russians had spirited away their war chest of 300,000 roubles. (There had been no mention of the chest in the negotiations.) Weide's men were not well treated. The Swedes stripped them of their weapons, and in some cases their uniforms too, sending them naked on their way.

It has been suggested that Charles failed to make full use of his victory. Eighteen thousand Russians had surrendered unconditionally, and could all have been kept prisoner. Moreover he made no attempt at pursuit or advance into Russia, thereby ignoring the practice of his predecessors who would never embark on a long war with Russia, "but as soon as they were ready for a new war would always cut them to pieces and then slapped up a new peace".[17] Perhaps one of the reasons for his failure to press his advantage home was the extraordinarily low regard in which the Swedes held their enemy. In the early years of the war in particular they appeared to them to be less than human, which is why they preferred killing them to taking them prisoner since they seemed "something between incendiaries and vermin, and their enemies preferred to do away with them quickly when they had the chance, rather than burden themselves with so wretched and profitless a catch".[18] They were also known to send Russian prisoners back – after cutting two fingers off their right hands.[19] At all events Charles was perfectly happy to let 18,000 Russians out of the bag, and was in no hurry to follow up his victory. He had beaten Peter's ridiculous force with such ease that for the time being there was nothing to be gained by pursuing it. There was much more glory and advantage to be had from defeating a real European army; so Charles now turned his attention on the Saxons.

Peter's losses at Narva were severe, 177 guns and many thousands of men, although as Defoe observed, "his infantry was indeed ruined and gone, but everybody knows foot soldiers are pretty cheap in Muscovy".[20] But despite the virtual annihilation of his army and his guns, despite the fact that he and his men had become the laughing stock of Europe, Peter was singularly undismayed. Once again he had paid to learn, and now he set about rebuilding and profiting from his lesson. That the army

[17] Gordon, A., p. 156.
[19] Coll., 1884, vol. xxxix, p. 80.
[18] Bengtsson, p. 116.
[20] Defoe, p. 113.

was indeed rebuilt was due largely to the part he played himself, and the sense of urgency he imparted to others. His letters in these years devote much less space to playful formulae and titles. They radiate pace and energy and are filled with "now", "immediately" and "at once". He used the 27,000 men who escaped from Narva as the basis of his next army, and swiftly raised ten more regiments of conscripts. However, the loss of his guns was more serious. Andrey Vinius, his postmaster, was placed in charge of Peter's foundries, and became the principal recipient of Peter's calls for speed. In order to finance his renewed efforts Peter, doubtless encouraged by the recent death of patriarch Adrian, turned to the church. He confiscated monastery property, reduced the number of monks and regulated monastery revenues. More immediately to the point, in order to get the metal he needed to cast new guns he took bells from every church and monastery in the land. Despite the fact that Vinius complained that his workers were all too frequently drunk, he got results. Within a year of Narva the 177 guns lost were replaced by 243 cannon, mortars and howitzers, all cast from church bells.

In the meantime Peter was most anxious to ensure that Augustus should continue to fight Charles with enthusiasm, and in order to heighten the latter he promised him men, powder and a three-year subsidy which Peter raised by forced loans. His policy succeeded in that for the next few years Charles was content to ignore Peter and remain in Poland. In fact he left his own Finnish Baltic provinces severely undermanned, even forbidding the dispatch of reinforcements.

Fighting against an enemy which it invariably outnumbered, Peter's army began to find its confidence. On December 29, 1701, Sheremetev beat the Swedes under Schlippenbach at Erestfer, killing some 3000 men and taking over 300 prisoners. Peter made him a field-marshal, gave him his portrait set with diamonds and celebrated his victory with a firework display. In the following summer at Hummelshof, Sheremetev beat his adversary again, destroying over half his army of 8000 men – Sheremetev had 30,000.

Acting as Peter told him, the field-marshal proceeded to lay the Swedish provinces waste. He boasted to Peter that the whole county with the exception of Pernau, Reval and Riga had been "utterly obliterated".[21] Peter seems to have given contradictory

[21] Soloviev, vol. xiv, p. 4.

orders, for we find him that year writing to another commander, Apraksin, reproaching him for sacking villages; towns as centres of genuine resistance were legitimate objects of devastation, but villages were to be left alone.[22]

The summer of 1702 saw another significant success. The Swedes had an important fortress on Lake Ladoga where the Neva flows out of it, called Nöteborg. It was manned by some 400 men who, in spite of being assailed by 10,000 Russians, stubbornly resisted a whole series of attacks before surrendering. The terms of surrender were a trifle bizarre: the garrison was to emerge with banners lowered, with their band playing, cannon, arms and bullets in their mouths – presumably to ensure that they stayed silent and did not call insults at their conquerors![23] After this victory Peter hanged twelve men for cowardice and took possession of the fort, which he renamed Schlüsselberg – and it would indeed be the key to the most ambitious of Peter's undertakings. Peter made Menshikov governor of the new place; it was his first office and the beginning of an astounding rise.

The victory was elaborately celebrated in Moscow, by means of a lavish firework display in Red Square. It had a clumsy pageantry of Peter's own devising that makes it an early anticipation of propaganda. Among its emblematic figures was Father Time with an hour glass and a palm frond, a beaver gnawing at a tree with the inscription "Through persistence will he uproot it". There was also a tree with a new branch growing from it, standing by the sea with a rising sun and the inscription "Hope is born". Orthodox priests played an active part in the ceremony which set the fireworks going, as if Peter were anticipating Rousseau's idea of placing the church at the service of the state, or the elaborate quasi-religious parades of Robespierre as a means of rallying his people's hearts and minds. For the victory parade itself Peter had 800 "German" uniforms made – but there were not enough to go round; half the leading regiment wore foreign dress while the rest were in Russian clothes. After the parade Swedish prisoners of war and their families were put up for sale, some being bought by Russians, the less fortunate by Tartar dealers who sold them on as slaves.[24]

Peter followed up his victory with a second one the next year that actually involved a modest naval success. On April 30, 1703, Sheremetev began the bombardment of the fortress of Nyenskans

[22] *Corr.*, vol. ii, p. 78.　　[23] Ustryalov, vol. iv, pt i, p. 203.　　[24] Le Bruyn, p. 50.

on an island at the mouth of the Neva. The Russians had used the preceding winter to invest all the territory between Schlüsselberg and the Neva estuary. The fortress quickly capitulated. Some days later a small Swedish flotilla of four boats sailed up river, not realising that the fortress had changed hands. Captain Peter and Lieutenant Alexander Menshikov filled thirty boats with guardsmen and boarded the Swedes by night. After some fierce fighting two ships were taken, two escaped severely damaged. There were not many prisoners since, as Peter put it, they tended to "ask for mercy too late". Not only was Peter proud to have won a naval victory, he had also and at last won access to the sea. For the flat, swampy unhealthy and unlovely territory he now held would rapidly be transformed into St Petersburg.

CHAPTER NINE

A Favourite, a Mistress and a Victory

It is during these years of the early 18th century that Menshikov takes on an increasingly prominent role in Peter's life. The czar's feelings for him as reflected in his letters are extraordinarily warm, even granted the extravagant manner in which Peter expressed his affections. Peter would address him with a tenderness that was almost deferential and which he reserved for Menshikov alone:

Mein Herz,
We sailed from here three days ago and were on the water until to-day but could get no further owing to contrary winds and so we turned back. Please send twenty good horses and a litter; and come yourself to-morrow around noon. I really need to see you, and you need to have a look around here, and to-morrow we need not work. I ask you again to be sure to come to-morrow. One more thing, for God's sake don't think I am asking you to come because I am ill. I am perfectly well, just need to see you.[1]

Menshikov addressed Peter as "Mr Captain" and signed himself Alexander Menshikov – in contrast, say, to Sheremetev who would write to "The most merciful of monarchs", signing himself "Your most humble of slaves Borisko [self-deprecating diminutive] Sheremetev bows his head".

To foreign observers Peter's affection was hard to understand. The English resident Whitworth found Menshikov "of very base

[1] *Corr.*, vol. ii, p. 220–1.

extraction, extremely vicious in his inclinations, violent and obstinate in his temper".[2] He does not seem to have been alone in his opinion. Yet the hold Menshikov enjoyed over Peter was extraordinary. The czar showered him with honours. They became knights of Peter's newly established order of St Andrew together – in recognition of their victory at Nyenskans. Menshikov would go on to become governor general of Ingria, Karelia and Estonia, first a count and then a prince of the Roman Empire all within a span of five years. Foreigners found it impossible to account for Menshikov's success in terms of his achievements, and some, including the Prussian resident Keyserling, who as we shall see had his reasons for disliking him, felt that Peter's feelings for his favourite went beyond "honourable affection".

Whatever the truth of this, and in itself it is of little importance, the role Menshikov played in Peter's life will never quite be determined. Yet there is no doubt that it was considerable and largely hidden. Throughout Peter's life we can observe Menshikov surreptitiously trying to improve or protect his situation *vis-à-vis* the czar, and as Peter lay dying Menshikov was busy at work ensuring that he would survive him. We can see him jockeying for position from the start. He soon acquired the enmity of Peter's first wife, who felt that he had a corrupting influence upon her husband, sensing that he was trying to weaken any hold she might have over him to his own advantage. It was said that Menshikov hated both her and her son, the czarevich Aleksey, Peter's heir.[3] Certainly Menshikov would always be savagely jealous of any "stranger" who shared Peter's affections, and ruthless in his attempts to bring about their downfall. There is no evidence to suggest that Menshikov had encouraged Peter to divorce his first wife, but he would not have put him off such a step, and would certainly never show much affection for Peter's unfortunate son.

Menshikov's special capacity for vileness and double-dealing comes through in his treatment of the luckless Vinius. One of the most powerful men in the land, in charge of posts, artillery production and the administration of Siberia, Vinius had long made use of his position to "warm his hands" as the Russian idiom goes, and was hopelessly corrupt. Peter came to suspect that all was not well with Vinius' affairs and ordered first Romodanovosky and then Menshikov to conduct investigations. Vinius

---

[2] Coll., 1884, vol. xxxix, p. 124.   [3] Bruce, p. 106.

approached Menshikov with a massive bribe, which he
accepted, and together they composed a letter of exoneration
which Vinius took to Peter. Menshikov then went to the czar and
told him the whole story. Vinius was disgraced, stripped of office
and severely fined; Menshikov kept the bribe. In his letter to
Vinius Peter was curiously kind. Far from losing his temper he
appeared quite genuinely surprised and pained at Vinius' stupidity, short-sightedness and dishonesty. Peter was always prepared to assume that others were driven by the same on the whole
disinterested and generous motives that inspired him. The eventual and gradual discovery that of all those at the head of affairs
he was probably the only person to be so driven was to to cast
a dark shadow over his latter years.

The essential Menshikov comes through with even greater
clarity in the so called Mons-Keyserling affair. In his jealousy of
those close to Peter he now turned his attention to Anna Mons.
She had been the czar's mistress for ten years and had borne him
two children, Peter and Paul, but had now fallen in love with
the Prussian ambassador, who asked her to marry him. In order
to gauge Peter's reaction the couple sought the advice of Menshikov. He listened to them carefully, then told them that he was
certain Peter would not object, suggesting to Anna Mons that
she tell the czar in writing that she wished to marry. He then
promptly took her letter to Peter, and ensured the dismissal of
the royal mistress. Peter treated her generously, incidentally,
merely taking back a diamond-set portrait of himself, but allow-
ing her to keep the rest of her jewels, and to marry. We do not
know whether she did so or not, but it seems unlikely, since Keyserling returned to Prussia without her. She lived on, in total
obscurity, until her death in August 1714. On a later occasion,
when asked to intercede with Peter on behalf of Anna's brother,
Menshikov surpassed himself. He observed to Peter that Anna
was *canaille* and a whore, and that he, Menshikov, had played
his own part in debauching her![4] No other action of his reveals
with such clarity how well he understood how to please Peter,
employing ways that might have seemed calculated to cost him
his head. He reached the czar with a kind of insolent and frequently familiar frankness that placed him in the most unflattering of lights, while displaying a seeming lack of respect for Peter.
Instead of removing the skin from his back for *lèse-majesté* Peter

[4] *Russ. Star.*, 1872, vol. v, pp. 806–7.

would react with warmth, telling him what an unspeakable scoundrel he was.

The scoundrel may well have been instrumental in finding Anna Mons's successor, and if this is so it was the best day's work he ever did, a rare instance of a pander supplying his master with an empress. The empress's antecedents are obscure. We first find Catherine Skovronskaya as an orphan, working in the house of a Swedish Protestant pastor in the Livonian town of Marienburg. In 1702 she appears to have married a Swedish dragoon, living with him for a matter of days before the Russians attacked the town. When Sheremetev took it, the pastor allegedly entrusted Catherine to his care; she was aged seventeen at the time. It would seem that she became Sheremetev's mistress, only to have been claimed soon afterwards by Menshikov, much to Sheremetev's disgust. At some time in 1703 Menshikov passed Catherine on to Peter. However, she would always remain very close to Alexander and his family. In later years, as the evidence of Menshikov's extraordinary corruption grew so overwhelming that he ran the risk of losing his head, it would always be Catherine who interceded with Peter on his behalf. Theirs was a partnership that lasted for Peter's lifetime and beyond.

Catherine was a large, good-looking woman of coarse and jovial good nature, who gave Peter genuine and unaffected warmth, and would always prove able to calm and to comfort him, to soothe his rages. Peter felt that he could be his full and natural self with her, since like Menshikov, and doubtless advised by him, she was free of the sort of deferential servility that exasperated Peter. Early on, she assumed the orthodox faith, with Peter's son acting godfather to his father's mistress! By 1705 she already had two children by the czar, and was to bear him five sons and six daughters, of whom only two girls would survive. Peter married her secretly in 1706, making it public in 1712. In 1724 she was crowned Catherine I, Empress of All the Russias, and on Peter's death the Swedish peasant girl took his place upon the throne.

*   *   *

1704 was a good year for Peter, who extended his Baltic gains considerably, taking two key towns, Dorpat and, at last, Narva. He played a considerable part in both affairs. Sheremetev had laid siege to Dorpat in a somewhat leisurely manner, or so Peter felt on his arrival. Everything was wrong. "The engineer is good but very placid, I wonder if this is quite the place for him," he wrote.[5] Peter altered the Russian dispositions, and within a fortnight an attack was mounted. The Swedes fought hard but discovered a new temper in the Russian troops. For the first time they did not break if repulsed, but retired, reformed, and came again. After fighting through the night the Swedes surrendered and the city fell. It was the taking of Dorpat, according to Defoe, that first convinced Europe of the new quality of Peter's army, which, ever since Narva (1700), had been regarded as something of a joke.

Peter now turned his attentions to the siege of that very city. In the course of the business an incident occurred which shows us something of Peter's qualities as a leader of men. Lack of vigilance on the part of a certain Peter Matveevich Apraksin allowed 700 Swedish reinforcements to slip into the city, much to Peter's fury. Apraksin's brother learned of his potential disgrace, and Peter wrote to him as follows:

> I have heard nothing from you personally about the misdeeds of your brother, but to-day a captain and good comrade told me that you had implored him to intercede, weeping bitterly. I don't know what to say, since your brother is obstinate and even claims that he was in the right and that I am being young and hotheaded. But let me tell you as a friend that if he will admit to his incompetence in public it will not take a lot for me to forgive him; if he does not you can see for yourself that I cannot have mercy on someone who does not acknowledge that he is in the wrong.
>
> PS. I ask you of course not to show this letter to the guilty party.[6]

A month later the Russians took Narva by storm. The Swedish commander, Horn, had rejected all calls to surrender, and paid the price for that rejection. The Russians were so enraged at the Swedish resistance that they got out of hand as they went in, killing soldiers and civilians alike. In fact the ultimate failure to capitulate was the result of an error. Horn, who did not believe that the Russians would attack by day, had half his garrison stood

[5] *Corr.*, vol. iii, p. 94.   [6] *Corr.*, vol. iii, p. 91.

down. He did not even have a drummer available to beat a surrender or parley, so the killing went on needlessly and too long. Peter is said to have done all he could to check his men, even running one through with his own sword. He wrote of the action, "had our soldiers not been restrained from the bloodshed not a soul would have been left alive". He was enraged by Horn's obstinate stupidity, and when the latter finally surrendered struck him, pointed to his own bloody sword and informed him that it was Russian not Swedish blood, and blood for which he held Horn personally responsible.

The Russians sacked Narva, even digging up corpses in churches on the pretext that their faith did not permit burial in church, but in fact in order to loot.[7] Moreover the civilian population of both Narva and Dorpat was harshly treated. Despite the terms of the capitulation of Dorpat which Peter had signed himself, all Swedish inhabitants save two from each trade were to be moved to the centre of Russia. They were given forty-eight hours in which to sell their effects, and only allowed two horses per family. "The circumstances of their removal are lamentable to say no worse", wrote the English resident.[8]

With his military fortunes on the upturn Peter now attempted to forge a grand anti-Sweden alliance with a view to securing peace. Patkul had negotiated an alliance between Russia and Poland – Peter was to subsidise a Polish army and supply Augustus with further Russian troops. Peter also made fruitless attempts to win support from Prussia, Austria, Holland, France and England, each of which rejected all overtures. He was more successful with the Turks. One of the ablest of all his diplomats, Peter Tolstoy, represented him in Constantinople, and he succeeded, by dint of a wide range of tactics, from bribery to the elimination of hostile councillors by poison, in discouraging the Porte from declaring war on Russia.

Broadening commitments such as the Polish subsidy steadily increased Peter's financial burdens. In 1705 war took up 95·9 per cent of his total budget,[9] and he was in urgent need of more funds. To this end he employed a series of ingenious and intelligent ex-serfs as "profit-makers", whose job it was to find additional sources of revenue for Peter. This was achieved in part through a series of monopolies on basic commodities such as salt. In addition various new taxes were levied, on funerals, weddings and

[7] Cht., 1892, vol. ii, p. 55.   [8] Coll., 1886, vol. i, p. 3.   [9] Wittram, vol. ii, p. 48.

baths, on beards and traditional dress, and on belief; the schismatics were allowed to worship as they pleased so long as they paid double rates of taxation.

Resistance came, as usual, not from the centre but the south. In 1705 in Astrakhan, where there were large numbers of ex-*streltsy*, sons of *streltsy* and schismatics, a rumour broke out that Peter was going to ban all marriages for seven years, or, alternatively, to make all girls marry foreigners. The inhabitants grew greatly alarmed and married in the utmost haste to avoid the ban – as many as a hundred weddings were celebrated on one particular day. The wedding celebrations turned into a riot. It was rumoured that the czar was no more, that the local governor and his colleagues had forsaken the faith, put on foreign clothes and shaved. Moreover, they had been observed worshipping idols in their houses – the idols in question being none other than their wig stands! The riot developed quickly into a rebellion, the governor and some thirty Russians and foreigners were lynched, the garrison mutinied and swore to uphold the old ways. Letters were sent to the cossacks of the Don and the Volga calling on them to join. Had they done so there was every chance that the whole of southern Russia would have come alight, the Tartars included, forcing Peter to fight a desperate war on two flanks. However, the cossacks refused to move and the rebellion remained isolated. Peter was in no doubt that the *streltsy* were behind the rising, which he described as the culmination of twenty-five years of work by the "destructive dogs", and ordered it to be repressed with appropriate severity – some hundreds of mutineers being broken on the wheel, or hanged from gallows set in rafts and floated down the Volga.

In the meantime Peter and Charles were slowly beginning to turn to face one another. Since Narva, Peter had been all too happy to confine his actions to the Baltic provinces, while Charles had grown over-involved with the intricate and preposterous business of Polish politics. Peter was perfectly aware of the poor quality of his own army, especially when compared to the Swedes who had, under the leadership of Charles, proved themselves invincible. His standing instruction to all commanders was to avoid major battles at all costs. But now, in 1705, the pace of the war quickened a little as Peter turned towards Poland.

In May Peter joined his army of 50,000 commanded by Sheremetev and Ogilvie, a cautious Scotsman, and detached

Sheremetev to conquer Courland. But the Swedish general Lewenhaupt beat him badly at the battle of Gemauerthof in July. Peter had to come up with reinforcements, obliging the Swedes to fall back on Riga, while Peter captured Mitau and occupied the rest of Courland before moving his army to Grodno for the winter, where Augustus was to join him.

It was in that selfsame summer that Peter, in Menshikov's company, underwent the most curious and savage of all his fits of rage. It would seem that he and Menshikov had visited a Uniate church[10] and quarreled violently with some monks in the course of a religious dispute; so violently indeed that he and his party put four of them to the sword and hanged a fifth.[11] Peter subsequently put his burst of savagery down to drink and had all mention of the episode struck out of his official history of the Northern War.

The following January, 1706, Charles appeared outside Grodno, but failed to induce Ogilvie to leave the city and engage him. He had to content himself with laying the surrounding country waste. Ogilvie found himself in a situation of peculiar isolation. Although Peter was able to get regular instructions through to him, these were in code, and Ogilvie did not have the key. Despite numerous requests to communicate *en clair* the coded messages continued to arrive in quantity for quite some time.[12] Augustus was now determined to finish the Swedes, but in the event it was the Swedes, under General Rehnskjold, who finished him, at the battle of Fraustadt, in February 1706. Of his army of 20,000 Saxons, Russians and Poles only 5000 escaped. Peter, considering that the annihilation of Augustus' army made Grodno untenable, ordered Ogilvie to bury his heavy artillery under the ice and withdraw. He was to proceed as secretly as possible and above all never to commit his entire army to any engagement. Ogilvie protested at the order, and was promptly relieved of his command, which was given to Menshikov. There had long been an unhappy atmosphere among Peter's senior commanders; Sheremetev detested Menshikov, and Ogilvie too had complained bitterly to Peter of his irresponsible and insubordinate behaviour. However, it must be said that Menshikov distinguished himself in the withdrawal from Grodno. He prepared

[10] Orthodox sect founded by Jesuits, 1596, retaining orthodox rituals and liturgy but acknowledging supremacy of Pope.
[11] Ustryalov, vol. iv, pt i, p. 371.   [12] *Ibid.*, p. 463.

a bridge across the river Niemen and got his army away as the ice was breaking up. The Russians secured a three-day lead over Charles and that was enough to escape his pursuit. After resting his army for several weeks Charles turned his attention to Saxony. In the autumn of 1706 Augustus was obliged to sign a separate peace with Charles, the peace of Altranstadt. By its terms he renounced the Polish throne, abandoned anti-Swedish alliances and handed over Patkul, whom he had imprisoned a year before when he tried to transfer some Russian troops from Saxon to Austrian control. Despite Peter's violent protests Augustus had declined to release him, and now, disgracefully, delivered his servant to his enemies to be broken on the wheel and beheaded.

For all the physical prowess of Augustus the Strong he had no strength of character. Five days after the treaty was signed Menshikov, with Augustus in his company, routed a Swedish army near Kalisch. Augustus had tried to avoid the battle, but failed. He at least managed to ensure that the Swedish prisoners, of whom there were many, passed into Saxon hands, soon to be released. In the meantime he had to join the Russians in a victory celebration. Even after news of his desertion of Peter became known he tried to keep the favour of both sides. Not a strong king.

Peter now stood alone against Charles. He desparately wanted peace, and in December 1706 called a conference to discuss ways of seeking it. Golovin had died that summer, and the new admiral general, Apraksin, had been a friend since childhood, having spent the early years of the war at Azov and Taganrog. Golovkin, Peter's minister of foreign affairs, had accompanied the czar on his embassy and had worked with him in the docks. He was supported by a Jewish convert, Peter Shafirov, a man whose considerable intelligence and talent outstripped his integrity. Peter's only chance of peace, it was decided, was to have one of the Great Powers mediate for him. Yet none was prepared to assist the rise of Russia, while Charles remained unwilling to consider terms. He had already put a puppet on the throne of Poland and now he had similar plans for Russia. The Swedish commanders believed, as indeed did Peter, that a single decisive battle would finish the Russians for good.

Peter had every reason to feel alarmed at the prospect of a Swedish invasion. Alarm is reflected in his correspondence, which grows increasingly sombre over these years. There is less and less time for play and jocularity, and a growing sense of urgency that borders sometimes upon panic. Yet even now he retains a capacity to enjoy himself. In mid-war he interrupts a whole series of vital military instructions to Apraksin to order him to get him an ice yacht,[13] while he still goes to preposterous lengths acting the subordinate, for example by requesting Menshikov, nominally his commander, for a travel warrant.

By the beginning of 1707 it was clear that invasion was only a matter of time. Peter's letters to Menshikov alone reveal how worried he was about anticipating its line of advance. He had decided against standing and fighting the invader. Instead the Russian army would withdraw, opposing river crossings and weakening the enemy by general harassment. The withdrawal was to be supported by a rigorous "scorched earth policy" – originally, it would seem, a Tartar technique. In January 1707 he wrote to Apraksin, ordering him to create a belt 200 versts wide from Smolensk to the south where no corn was to be in evidence – all should be hidden in woods and pits, livestock was to be similarly concealed away from roads. He went on to add that the peasants were to be forewarned of the plan to allay their inevitable doubts and fears! It was typical of Peter that he assumed that a rational explanation could have done anything of the sort. He never really grasped the depths of mistrust he and his policies inspired in his subjects, dismissing such feelings because they were born of ignorance and superstition. He always believed that one day his people would become susceptible to reason – which makes him, in this respect at least, one of the first rulers of the Enlightenment.

Peter's predicament was not improved by further threats from within. In 1707 some Bashkir tribes rebelled, defeated Russian regular troops and posed a serious threat to Kazan. Although they were checked it was to take two whole years to put down the last traces of their resistance. More serious still was a rebellion of the Don cossacks led by a certain Kondraty Bulavin. Peter had sent a small force headed by Prince Yu. V. Dolgoruky to bring in the deserters and runaway serfs, who were moving south in ever-increasing numbers to escape the consequences of Peter's enthusiasm. Bulavin attacked the Russians and killed them to a man. The rebellion grew dangerous enough for Peter to have to detach troops from his main battlefront, since the rebels had gained

[13] *Corr.*, vol. vi, p. 367.

enough ground actually to threaten Azov and Taganrog. However, Bulavin was finally defeated, twice, in the summer of 1708
and prudently committed suicide. Peter had responded to his
threat with a new intelligence and sensitivity. He set Dolgoruky's
son at the head of the punitive force, and reminded him that,
since he would be fighting mounted light calvary, his own infantry and horse would not be able to cope with them in the field.
The proper way to deal with cossack irregulars was to sack their
towns and villages, kill the inhabitants and impale the ringleaders, since "cruelty alone can tame them".[14] However, over
the years Peter had learned the virtues of a selective cruelty. He
ordered his general to be discriminating in his punishments. He
had responded with similar discretion at the time of the Astrakhan troubles, by ordering his servants not to enforce regulations
about dress and shaving too rigorously in the Volga towns.

Charles moved east late in 1707, against the advice of his
generals – but taking advice was never his strong suit. His method
of waging war was not particularly appropriate to Russia. His
engagements with the Saxons, successful though they had been,
had never annihilated his enemy, partly because Charles was
always outnumbered, largely because he drove his cavalry too
hard for pursuit to be possible, so that he would end up holding
a battlefield and observing the backs of his enemies as they disappeared over the horizon. Moreover Charles was accustomed
to living off the land, and Poland was relatively a great deal more
prosperous than Russia.

Charles crossed the Vistula on New Year's Day 1708, and by
January 26 had reached Grodno – two hours after Peter left it.
He now had two choices open to him: to turn north and win
back his lost provinces, or to move into the heart of Russia and
try to bring Peter to his knees.

The next few months were to determine whether or not Russia
could claim to be a European power, meeting the challenge of
Charles, and his redoubtable army. The English resident, Whitworth, assessed the Swedes and their commander as follows:

> The King of Sweden has the advantage of old soldiers, experi-
> enced generals and brave officers, an extraordinary patience
> or even love of fatigue, an invincible courage and resolution un-
> alterable. But then he seems to undervalue all subordinate

[14]*Corr.*, vol. vii, p. 131.

means of proceeding with success and to rely wholly on the justice of his cause.[15]

Whitworth went on to add that his strategies – doing without magazines or large artillery trains – had worked well enough in Poland, "a plentiful country and licentious government where no one had the right to stop the general flame by blowing up his neighbour's house".[16] In Russia of course no one had any rights at all and whole villages might be blown up to "stop the general flame".

The Russian army of 1708 did not impress contemporaries. One officer reported: "The bodies of men are strong, their exercise good, their regiments complete and desirous to engage; but the foot have ill fire arms, the dragoons ill horses, and the army not three able generals; so that a vigorous onset and a bad issue of battle may be expected should it come to that."[17] The shortage of able generals was a frequent complaint. There was increasing tension between Menshikov and Sheremetev, who declared Peter's favourite to be utterly unfit to command cavalry. Of Menshikov Whitworth observed, "his whole character is disadvantageous to say no more, and as for the war, he has neither the experience to know, capacity to learn nor courage to execute".[18] Another slightly later observer was bewildered by the style of the Russian army and guards officers. Senior officers were over-familiar with their juniors, drinking and gambling with them, while at the same time general officers were literally kow-towed to – the proper form of address being to fall on to the right knee, then with hands advanced bow down to the ground in such a way that the head should give an audible thump.[19] He concluded that, although the Russians now looked like somewhat crude versions of the Europeans they aped, "nevertheless within them sits a moujik".[20]

Peter waited to see which line Charles would take. In anticipation of a thrust due east to Moscow he had additional fortifications dug before the capital, and supplies of food laid up in the Kremlin. Instead Charles turned south towards the Ukraine. A second Swedish army under Lewenhaupt, with a large and vitally important supply train, was to travel down from the Baltic provinces and link up with Charles. It is hard to say precisely

[15] Coll., 1886, vol. l, p. 59.   [16] Ibid., p. 61.   [17] Ibid., p. 37.
[18] Ibid., p. 64.   [19] Cht., 1892, vol. ii, p. 79.   [20] Ibid., loc. cit.

why Charles elected to move south. He was apparently alarmed at the ruthlessness with which the Russians had scorched their earth, treating it as if it were foreign territory, and this might have encouraged him to make for the fertile Ukraine. Moreover the south had allies to offer him: Crimean Tartars and, more important, cossacks. The cossack hetman Mazeppa had been in secret contact with Charles's puppet King Stanislas of Poland, and indeed with Charles himself, offering to come across to the Swedes and bring his cossacks with him.

The first serious challenge to Charles's advance was made at Golovchin, where the Russians held an excellent position on a river. They should have stopped the Swedes, but "the foot under general Repnin scarce made a show of resistance, having only kept in order till they gained a great wood on their right, into which they ran to save themselves by the example and command of their general who was some hours after found crying in the middle of it".[21] Several of the ensigns brought their colours with them in their pockets, having thrown the staves away. Once again, as so often in the history of the Russian army, the officers had let down their men. Peter had the general in question downgraded to the rank of cadet and fined him severely.

Despite a victory which had cost the Russians over 3000 men Charles's army was not in good shape. The summer of 1708 was a particularly wet one. The harvest was poor enough as it was and Peter's devastation of his country had proved uncomfortably effective. Moreover the vital link-up with Lewenhaupt was slow in coming. The latter had set off late, and now, owing to bad roads, could not travel more than eight miles per day. In the meantime the main body of the army was beginning to suffer serious shortages. By early autumn there was scarcely any bread, and the army had begun to eat its horses and bullocks, which in turn required them to burn their gun carriages for lack of beasts to draw them. There was a lot of dysentery. Charles's generals advised him to wait for Lewenhaupt to catch up with him, since they were in critical need of supplies, and then to winter in Livonia. Charles paid no heed and pressed on, altering his line of advance.

Lewenhaupt was less than a week away when Charles took a further turn to the south. The Russians succeeded in positioning themselves between the two Swedish armies and now disaster

[21] Coll., 1886, vol. l, p. 38.

struck. They made contact with Lewenhaupt at Liesna and after two days of heavy fighting obliged him to withdraw, leaving 8000 dead, sixteen guns, forty-two standards and between two and three thousand waggons behind him. Peter was overjoyed by his victory, and rightly so. The loss of his supply train was a disaster for Charles; moreover Peter considered the battle to be a turning point in the history of his army. It was the first time that Russian forces had beaten the Swedes without greatly outnumbering them. The Swedes themselves had already noticed a change in the quality of the opposition. In a letter intercepted at the time there were complaints that conditions were growing worse and the Russians proving much more vigorous enemies than had been expected. There were also letters from home intercepted in the same packet, addressed directly to Moscow and reminding various Swedish officers to send off the captured furs they had promised.[22]

Charles's luck had turned now and turned for good. He continued to press south, joined by the remains of Lewenhaupt's army, hoping to link up with Mazeppa and his cossacks. Mazeppa, a character of considerable duplicity, was caught between Charles and Peter, who was now ordering him to proceed against the advancing Swedes. He replied by telling Peter he was a dying man, while making contact with the Swedes and committing himself finally to Charles. Peter sent Menshikov to see Mazeppa – who promptly went over to Charles in person, but without the cossack thousands Charles had been given to expect. Mazeppa brought with him no more than some 1200 men.

On learning of his betrayal Peter ordered Menshikov to move as quickly as possible on the town of Baturin, Mazeppa's stronghold, to raze it and put its population to the sword. Charles too was making for the same objective, and its abundant supplies, but Menshikov beat him by a week and acted decisively. By the time the exhausted Swedes finally arrived they found nothing but embers, rubble and piles of half-burnt corpses. The savagery of the Russian response was enough to discourage the Ukrainian cossacks from following the example of their newly deposed hetman.

Charles continued to travel south, and now, yet again, his situation took a turn for the worse. Many hundreds of miles from

[22] Tumansky, vol. viii, p. 31.

any base or source of supply he found himself in the harshest winter in living memory. His army suffered dreadfully:

> The cold was beyond description, some hundred men of the regiment being injured by the freezing away of their private parts, or by the loss of feet, hands and noses. This besides ninety men who simply froze to death. With my own eyes I beheld dragoons and cavalrymen sitting upon their horses stone dead with the reins in their hands in so tight a grasp that they could not be loosened until the fingers were cut off ... I saw also a foot soldier who being fatigued by the long night march sat himself down, whereupon the ligament of his back broke with a crack like a pistol shot and he fell stone dead.[23]
>
> Nevertheless, though earth, sky and air were against us the king's orders had to be obeyed and the daily march made.[24]

By the time spring came Charles's army was down to a mere 20,000 men totally cut off from their own territories, and in desperate need of provisions and military supplies. On Mazeppa's advice Charles laid siege to the small town of Poltava. Not only was it full of supplies, it was also in a key position, providing possible links with Poland, the Ukraine and the Tartars. Located on a river and defended by three regiments it was not an easy place to take at the best of times, and this was not such a time. Charles simply did not have the resources to sustain the siege which began on May 1. He had already had to abandon or melt down all his heavy artillery, and more serious still his powder had deteriorated so greatly in the course of his wanderings that it was almost useless. The report of the Swedish muskets was said to be no louder than the sound made by two gloved hands clapping together.[25] It was forbidden to mention the shortage of powder for fear of damaging morale.

Reluctantly, Peter recognised that the time had come for his battle. Despite the state of the Swedish army and his own overwhelming numerical superiority he was still less than keen to commit himself. He joined the army at Poltava on June 4, and remained content to watch the Swedes for two weeks, until the Poltava garrison determined him to advance, sending messages declaring that they could hold out no longer. The Swedes could not hold out much longer either—it subsequently emerged that

[23] Bengtsson, p. 319.   [24] Bain, pp. 269–70.   [25] *Ibid., loc. cit.*

they only had enough military supplies to continue their siege for three more days.

Peter crossed the river separating him from the Swedish army on June 17. That day bad luck hit Charles yet again. On a reconnaissance of the Russian positions he was shot in the foot by a cossack bullet. The wound was a clean one and the bullet came out, later to be found in his stocking beside his big toe. However, it was not a good summer for wounds and his turned septic. The leg grew inflamed to the knee and fever ran so high that for two or three days it was not expected that Charles would live.

The wound disabled him as a commander. His presence on the battlefield had no more than a moral value; he was in no condition even to offer advice. Command was assumed by Rehnskjold, who was not nearly as able. Besides, the Swedish generals were so accustomed to obeying Charles blindly that they could not adjust easily to their loss. Nevertheless they decided to attack, considering themselves to be in such a plight that they had no other alternative. It was at this point that the inadequacy of Rehnskjold's generalship declared itself. He issued orders that were less than clear and his commanders were inadequately briefed on the battle plan. Consequently the movements of his troops were poorly coordinated, and as one officer observed, "There was no right command in this battle and every man did as he thought best."[26] Yet it would be simplistic to attribute the Swedish defeat at Poltava to a poorly coordinated battle plan alone. Defeats bring our the inadequacies of a strategy as victories bring out its virtues; one cannot help suspecting that many a battle has been won with worse battle plans than Rehnskjold's, others lost with incomparably better ones.

Rehnskjold planned to surprise the Russians by a sudden move to their north-west, to force them back on to the river Vorskla and cramp their position. However, Peter had anticipated such a tactic and had hurriedly built a series of redoubts to hinder an advance of that kind. Rehnskjold still felt that he would be able to bypass these by means of a night attack. Unfortunately his troops went forward late and the Russians were ready for them. Before the battle Peter had addressed his men with a stirring appeal. Calling on their sense of patriotism in a way that would have been inconceivable at that time elsewhere in Europe he reminded them that they were fighting not for him, but for

[26] Bengtsson, p. 353.

Russia; not only was justice on their side, they had clearly proved that the Swedes were not invincible.

> The hour has struck when the fate of the whole fatherland lies in their hands; either Russia will perish or she will be reborn in nobler shape. And they must not think of themselves as armed and drawn up to fight for Peter, but for the czardom entrusted to Peter by his birth and by the people of Russia ... of Peter it should be known that he did not value his own life his sole concern was that Russia should live in Christian piety, glory and prosperity.[27]

Although Peter had commanded the army up to this point, as the Swedes advanced he handed over to Sheremetev and took on the role of a regimental commander. However, the battle plan and the intial response to the Swedish attack were his own work.[28]

The Swedish infantry was divided into four columns; two were to attack the redoubts, two to pass them by on either side – a bad plan, since coordination between the columns would be impossible, weakening the attack of an army already outnumbered two to one.

The Swedes moved at dawn and two unfinished redoubts fell quickly. But the third could not be taken for all the efforts of Major General Roos and his six battalions of infantry, while Lewenhaupt took his men to the right of the redoubts to mount an independent attack on the Russian camp, thereby losing all contact with the rest of the army for a good two hours.

Rehnskjold succeeded in driving back Menshikov's cavalry, which was placed behind the redoubts, and the Swedes began to draw up in front of the Russian camp. But not all of them. Even after Lewenhaupt had rejoined the main body, the luckless Roos, who had not understood or had not been told that the redoubts were tactical objectives to be bypassed, not taken, was still engaged in an utterly pointless assault, with one-third of the total Swedish infantry. He eventually broke off the attack with forty per cent casualties and set out in quite the wrong direction, *away* from the battle, in order to try to re-form, having no idea of the position of the rest of the army. He was cut off and surrounded by a large Russian force, and when he eventually surrendered he had just 400 men left of his original 2600.

[27] *Corr.*, vol. vii, p. 266.   [28] *Russ. Star.*, vol. xciii, 1909, p. 139.

The main battle was now about to begin. Charles joined the army on a wooden litter which had already been badly shot up as he passed the redoubts. The Swedish infantry line was about 4000 strong facing 16,000 Russians, with four cannon to the Russians' 37. The Swedes went forward, coming under heavy artillery fire. This checked the left, but the right wing pressed its attack home and at one point broke the Russian first line. Peter was quick to see what was happening and at once threw in reinforcements which he brought up and led in person. Before the battle his commanders had begged him not to expose himself, but Peter had replied that he had his obligations. He appreciated that they needed neither his direction nor his example, but he was obliged, in so far as the salvation of his subjects and kingdom might depend on him, to do his duty both as a czar and as a colonel of the guards, for he did not care to bear titles or ranks without acting their part.[29]

Peter showed great personal courage throughout the battle; all trace of his capacity for panic was absent. He was in the thick of the fighting, and was extraordinarily lucky not to be hit. One bullet pierced his hat, another hit his saddle and a third the iron cross he wore round his neck, but this was a battle in which all the luck was on the side of Peter and his men.

The Russians now broke the Swedish line, and essentially the battle was over. The infantry was wiped out almost to a man. Charles's litter was smashed a second time – in all twenty-one of its twenty-four bearers were killed; he was put on to a horse and led away.

The Swedish casualities were considerable. They lost 6917 officers and men on the battlefield, and a further 2678 were taken prisoner.[30] The greater part of the cavalry had survived, however, and together with the troops that had remained outside Poltava there were some 15,000 men left.

It was decided to attempt a link-up with the Tartars. Charles rode on ahead to avoid capture, and together with Mazeppa and some 1500 men took refuge, at Turkish invitation, in the town of Bender. The Russian victory was completed some two days later when the whole of the Swedish cavalry meekly surrendered to a Russian force half its size at Perewoloczna. It is said that certain Swedish veterans felt so disgraced by their commander's decision that they committed suicide out of shame.[31]

[29] Tumansky, vol. viii, p. 93.   [30] Bengtsson, p. 372.   [31] Tumansky, vol. viii, p. 114.

The annihilation of Charles's army was almost complete. "It had suffered the fate of Phaeton," Peter wrote in a triumphant letter to his son. Another contemporary observed that there could be few if any other instances in history of the loss of an entire army, where not a single survivor returned home.[32] The only other example to spring readily to mind is von Paulus' 6th Army at Stalingrad. As always Peter recognised that he and his people had had to learn the hard way; the lessons that began at Narva were now bearing fruit. Peter acknowledged his own part in the victory by promoting himself to contre-admiral and senior lieutenant general.

The European reaction to the news of Charles's annihilation was one of incredulity. Russian successes in the Baltic had not convinced anyone that the Russians could face and defeat the Swedes in a major battle:

> In a word it was a victory that the world thought impossible, the scholars beating their masters. The Russians beating the Swedes was like the Gauls beating the Romans, which was the wonder of the world.[33]

Peter attended a field service to celebrate his victory, and went on to a celebratory feast. He entertained the captured Swedish generals, presenting Rehnskjold with his own sword, and then went on to propose a toast to "his teachers in the art of war", and upon Rehnskjold's inquiry informed him that his teachers were none other than the Swedes themselves.

Of course in one sense Poltava was not unlike some of Peter's earlier victories in the Baltic provinces. Charles was dreadfully outnumbered – the Russian front line proved quite enough to annihilate him – and besides, his army was not in the best of shape. Without wishing to diminish Russian military achievements on the battlefield, which were by no means derisory, the greater achievement was the long-term strategy which had helped to manœuvre Charles into a position in which he could not win. But whatever the merits of the Russian victory Poltava was the kind of event that pleases historians because it can quite properly be considered a turning point in European history. Sweden never recovered from the total loss of Charles's army, even though the war still had more than half its course to run. The battle in-

[32] Tumansky, vol. viii, pp. 121–3.   [33] Defoe, p. 237.

augurated Sweden's decline from a major northern power to a
small nation, and the beginnings of Russia's steady and continuing rise.

A Danish diplomat, Just Juel, who arrived in Russia shortly
after Poltava did not much lik what he found. The only way
to get anything done was to be as rude as possible – good manners
achieved nothing. He found the Russians mean and petty, while
every head in the country had been turned by their recent victory,
making them insufferably arrogant – every head except for
Peter's, that is; he, says Juel, was the only person in Russia to
remain "*sans façons*", unaffected.[34] Peter invited him to attend
the victory procession in Moscow. Inevitably this was an elaborate affair. The city was decorated with triumphal arches and
houses were hung with wreaths of pine branches and allegorical
pictures. The Swedish prisoners were paraded on foot, headed
by their eight generals – there were so many men taken that a
second procession proved necessary in order to display them all.
The procession also included Charles's broken litter. Peter
revealed his cutting sense of humour by riding an English charger
that Augustus had given to him, wearing a sword that Augustus
had given to Charles. He even brought a humorous element to
the procession itself, which included a group of Samoyeds, a
northern tribe, with their "king", a French émigré whom Peter
had introduced as a joke. The Swedes, who have never been
renowned for their sense of humour, were mortified by Peter's
touch of comedy. Juel met Peter on the parade and offered him
a glass of wine:

which he took and embraced me with great friendliness and
demonstrations of esteem towards me, and also kissed me. He
was roaring drunk like all those about him.

He saw him later in the day looking very different:

Riding by at full tilt with a bleak and terrible expression, making many terrible gestures with his arms, mouth, shoulder,
hands and feet [none of which could have been easy at the
gallop], he rode across and beat a soldier, then sat still on his
horse, making horrid faces, twisted his head, foamed at the
mouth, rolled his eyes, jerked his arms and shoulders and

[34] Juel, p. 139.

kicked back and forth with his legs. All his retinue were terrified and kept away until his cook pacified him.[35]

Whatever may have sparked off Peter's rage – he set on one soldier for carrying a Swedish flag and a drawn sword – the cause was almost certainly drink. He had been liberally entertained at every house he stopped at, and he was the kind of heavy drinker whose mood would suddenly change to one of savage violence and rage, making him capable of actions which he was not always able to recall the next day. He sometimes suffered from a heavy drinker's remorse for anything he might have done the night before. In one of his most human and humble letters he once wrote to Apraksin:

> I don't remember leaving last night, being much favoured by the generous gifts of Bacchus. I would like to apologise to anyone I might have angered, particularly those present when I left. May I be forgiven by all.[36]

Peter had a very particular reason to celebrate this victory with enthusiasm. It was not just that he had taught his nation to beat the Swedes, nor just that as a European military power Russia had come of age. Poltava had a special and personal significance for Peter, for in another letter to Apraksin he described the victory as the true foundation stone of St Petersburg, Peter's "earthly paradise".[37]

---

[35] Juel, p. 134.   [36] *Ibid., loc. cit.*   [37] Staehlin, p. 144.

CHAPTER TEN

St Petersburg

Within days of the capture of Nyenskans in 1703 Peter had begun to build. He had fought his way to the Baltic and was and would remain determined never to abandon that bridgehead. In later years he would be prepared to give up all his conquests except for this one, a wild piece of land by a wide river that was frozen for six months every year, and that flowed rapidly and often dangerously for the other six, through flat marshy country which it often flooded. Nothing grew there but scrub, low bushes and the occasional tree. No crops could be sown and the Neva estuary's only inhabitants were a few fishermen living modestly in wooden shacks which they left when the floods ran too high. The nature of the place is well expressed by the name Neva, which is the Finnish for "swamp".

This was the spot that Peter chose to build a fortress, seaport and capital city, and one may well ask why? There had, some centuries ago, been a settlement there which had proved useful as a means of controlling local pirates long before the territory had passed into Swedish hands. However, as a site for a modern seaport it was not especially suitable. The Neva was shallow, its channel no more than eight feet deep in places – when the river was not frozen or rendered unnavigable by the huge chunks of ice that floated down from Lake Ladoga in the spring. Moreover it was only possible to sail out of the estuary on an east wind.[1] With the perpetual danger of floods, the marshy ground, the lack of local building materials and the problems of food supply, the unhealthy climate with its three or four hours of winter daylight,

[1] Cht., 1874, vol. ii, p. 84.

there was much to dislike about the site. Moreover there was the additional disadvantage presented by the Swedes. Sweden held all Karelia to the immediate north of the estuary, and besides it had a Baltic fleet, which was more than Peter did, and was thus in a position to attack the Russian settlers from both land and sea.

Peter displayed an absolute disregard for objections of all kinds. He was so sure of what he wanted that, astoundingly, there is no single document of any kind, not even a private letter, in which he debates the wisdom of building a seaport, or explains his motives for making it his future capital. It was never an issue open to question or discussion. Peter had won access to the sea, and was determined to have his city regardless. In some respects one can see why. A Baltic port was essential to his conception of Russia as a Westward-looking maritime nation. It would be much more convenient in the long run than Archangel, as a base for Western trade. He could not know that within ten years three coastal cities, Narva, Reval and Riga, would pass into his hands. He had won a site that was halfway suitable, and which might be considered the northernmost point in Russia's network of waterways. He would now mobilise his will and his nation's resources to do the rest; it was no more daunting an enterprise than going to war with Sweden.

We do not know when or why Peter decided to remove the capital from Moscow, in the sense that no documents relating to the decision have survived. Yet the rejection of Moscow had begun years before, on the morning that the *streltsy* took the Kremlin; the foundation of a new Westward-looking capital can be seen as the culmination of Peter's long-standing hostility to Moscow, which for him represented centuries of inertia, xenophobia and a perpetual threat to his person. Finally, and by no means least important, was his own genuine and deeply rooted love of the sea. This comes out with clarity and an unusual and touching charm in a brief note he wrote some years later to Zotov's son, who, although there had been a navy of sorts in existence for over ten years, was apparently the first Russian actually to come forward and volunteer to study seamanship! To date recruiting had relied upon that strange blend of reluctance and compliance which was the essential Russian response to Peter's projects. Peter observed that, on the whole, his people do not wish to "abandon their joyous companions in order to listen to the sound of the sea".[2] Peter loved joyous company more than most, but he loved the "sound of the sea" better still. One of the reasons that prompted him to build himself a city on the mouth of the Neva was quite simply because he wanted to live there.

Petersburg began with a fortress, the fortress of St Peter and St Paul; initially built of wood and earthworks, with six bastions, it was rebuilt in stone some three years later. An English naval officer found its design pretty hopeless since its "orbicular" lay-out meant that its batteries could not concentrate their fire.[3] However, Peter's fort never came under serious attack. In 1703 he had to beat off a half-hearted overland thrust from Viborg. A second threat was posed by a Swedish squadron cruising off the mouth of the Neva, which launched an invasion from the sea. This too was beaten off with great ease. The same English-man was amazed at the incompetence of the Swedes. Russian defence were, he felt, so weak that victory was theirs for the taking.

> Had they once pushed in, the batteries could have done little damage, but the Swedes acted as if they had never been upon the coast before. . . . [They landed their troops in the only deep water in the area] taking the soldiers up to the chin and wetting their powder and arms.[4]

Had the Swedes not been incompetent and easily discouraged they would certainly have dislodged the Russians.

In the course of the century St Petersburg grew into a massive city, with extraordinarily broad streets and beautiful ironwork, a city in the grandest neo-classical manner. Yet this was strangely remote from Peter's original conception, which was much more modest and based upon his memories of Amsterdam. His sense of architectural space did not lend itself to grandeur. He loved intimacy, a series of low-ceilinged rooms opening into one another. Later, when his winter palace was being built and it proved necessary to have high ceilings and tall storeys to match adjacent buildings, he had lower false ceilings built in his own apartments.[5] From the start he looked to Dutch models. Within a year of the taking of Nyenskans St Petersburg consisted of

[2] *Corr.*, vol. iv, pp. 85–6.
[3] Bridges, p. 22.
[4] *Ibid., loc. cit.*
[5] Cht., 1874, vol. ii, p. 89.

four rows of wretched wooden buildings, including Peter's own four-roomed house with a small wooden church built in the Dutch style, its bells hand-chimed on every hour, again after the Dutch fashion.[6] Peter intended the centre of his capital to be on an island, Vassilevsky island, opposite the mainland on the north side of the Neva. Within ten years that part of the city had over a thousand inhabitants and ten streets, some of them paved, although the rest of the island was still scrub and woodland with the occasional deer. The city as a whole grew fast, having 8000 inhabitants by 1710. It was not so much that people wanted to go there; they went because they were told to. Merchants and members of the service classes were ordered to go and live in the new city with their families, permanently. Residence was enforced to the point that it was necessary to obtain permission to leave the city at all, and this was only given for a maximum of five months in any one year.[7] Anyone returning late was punished with a fine.

The settlement of St Petersburg in these early years cannot be thought of in terms of the normal way in which a city grows, as a result, say, of its becoming a trading centre. It becomes easier to understand the pattern of its development when it is thought of in terms of the establishment of a colony by means of deportation. The disproportion of population to land mass in Russia, and the ease with which it was possible to escape authority by running away and settling far from its reach, had long made for authority's exercise of extreme coercive pressures upon its subjects' freedom of movement, compelling them to remain where they were or to reside in places where they did not wish to live. The vast majority of Russians have, after all, only enjoyed comparative freedom of movement for the relatively brief period between emancipation of the serfs and Stalin's collectivisation. Yet it is something of a testimony to Peter's authority that he could bring about the population of his city by decree, uprooting merchants of long standing, forcing the greatest families in the land to move. The new city had little to recommend it. Houses were relatively expensive, while problems of food supply meant that prices were very high. The city long retained a half-built appearance, small wooden houses, occasional stone ones, with crooked streets, few embankments by the riverside and lots of blank spaces where houses were yet to be built. Many of the roads

---

[6] Luppov, p. 62.   [7] Predtechensky, p. 135.

were impassable in spring and autumn, at which times they were littered with the carcases of dead horses caught in the heavy ground. The city itself ended abruptly, and beyond it was – nothing, nothing but flat and empty marshland stretching to the horizon. In winter at least inhabitants on the outskirts, and sometimes at the centre of the town, ran a real risk of being pulled down by wolves.

The greatest threat to the city was water. In ground which sometimes flooded after two feet of digging it proved impossible in some parts of town to have cellars or underground storehouses, and where these could actually be dug they were always liable to be filled by the floods which happened almost every year. The Neva flowed very fast and when met by a strong south wind it could back up and reach heights of some thirteen feet above sea level. A five-foot rise made for a little flooding; anything more covered the islands and the town centre. Not that Peter seemed to mind the watery character of his paradise. A letter of 1706 gleefully announces that his own floor was under two feet of water, and that it was funny to see people sitting on roofs and in trees, "not just men but women also".[8]

Petersburg was created and developed as an act of Peter's will, created by decree, and designed along abstract principles of regularity. It was intended that the various professions should each inhabit various quarters. Those living in the military quarter were allocated areas of building land corresponding to their rank. Peter made much use of decrees to establish the character of his city. In order to encourage the construction of stone houses it was forbidden to build in stone anywhere else in Russia; an order that remained in force for over twenty years. To encourage building on the watery Vassilevsky Island, sale of houses there was prohibited. House design was no less controlled, being determined by an architectural office which supplied would-be builders with the plans appropriate to the area and their station. Peter aimed at the start at a regular city constructed according to a predetermined plan. It was not permitted just to grow; its growth had to be trained. Houses were built according to the designs of Peter's Italian architect, Trezzini, which were made available to prospective builders *gratis*. It was forbidden to build in the old Muscovite manner, with houses facing in on closed courtyards; instead they had to look out upon the street. In his

[8] *Corr.*, vol. iv, p. 369.

quest for regularity and the exercise of his will Peter unsurprisingly displayed no respect whatsoever for private property. When it was considered desirable to replan a certain quarter of the city, hundreds of newly constructed private houses were ruthlessly knocked down.[9]

Considering this inhospitable and regimented atmosphere, its wretched climate, and the lack of incentive to Russians to go north and live by the sea on the Swedish border, Peter was quite extraordinarily successful in his attempt to will St Petersburg into existence. He had minor setbacks. He failed to make Vassilevsky Island the heart of the capital, because it flooded too easily, and was much too difficult to get to, residence there requiring constant, tedious and frequently hazardous crossings of the Neva. (In order to instil a love of sailing in the population Peter forbade the use of rowing boats to cross the river, while the ferrymen who were learning to sail as they plied their trade were not the most skilled of sailors. Not only were there frequent accidents, it is said that it sometimes took them almost a whole day to get across.)[10]

The city was built by means of forced labour. Up to 40,000 men worked there every year. They were taken from every province in Russia, including the most remote, such as Siberia and Astrakhan, working usually in two-month shifts – while the journey from Astrakhan must have taken a good six weeks at the best of times. Soldiers were also employed in construction work, as were criminals and deserters who were exiled to labour in St Petersburg "for life". In 1703 Peter wrote to Romodanovsky, saying that for the moment he had enough "good people" working there but that he was short of *criminals*, would Romodanovsky please collect 200 thieves for next year's force.[11] Peter collected the skilled labour he required by press-gang. "If any such man is known to live at a place he is fetched away without consideration of his being settled there, and carried to Petersburg."[12] No great provision was made for the welfare of the workforce, and although no precise figures are available it was generally believed that the death rate was high. This seems likely, though it has recently been pointed out that lists of labourers sent to work on the capital regularly feature the same names year after year. Certainly the conditions of work were adverse. There were few saw-

[9] Luppov, p. 54.
[11] Ustryalov, vol. iv, pt i, p. 242.
[10] Wittram, vol. i, p. 70.
[12] Weber, vol. i, p. 30.

mills, few beasts of burden and the chief resource was human muscle power. Work was rendered harder still in the early years by the fact that the only known wheelbarrow in Russia was in Archangel. Earth was carried about in bags, or more often in the hems of the worker's garments.

While foreigners rightly saw the new capital as the end of Muscovy and the beginning of a modern European Russia, the Russian people saw it as a blighted misery and death trap. Their view is reflected in countless songs and sayings: "On one side the sea, on the other misery, on the third moss, on the fourth ouch!" would be an approximate translation of one such saying.[13] The attitude of the nobility was scarcely different; the most powerful expression of the general loathing being the secret curse uttered by Martha Alekseevna, Peter's sister, "Petersburg will not survive us, let it be barren."[14] Indeed, a sense of barrenness would always remain part of its mood and style. It would go down in Russian literature as the barren, abstract city, the city of the dead, constructed according to principles of manic symmetry and regularity, set down in the middle of nowhere.

Peter loved and gloried in his creation, not just in the massive naval yards and admiralty, begun in 1705 and soon producing ships of the line and galleys in considerable quantities, not just in the "*osteria*", the inn named the Four Frigates, characteristically Peter's first public building, where he would sit and drink with workmen and ships' captains. He conceived of the city as a centre of Western civilisation and his very own creation. He devoted a particular care to it, one which manifested itself in his remarkable and sometimes quirkish sense of detail. For example, he suffered from a peculiar aversion to cockroaches, which were numerous in the Russia of his day and at other times, and it was said that the merest glimpse of one could drive him from a house.[15] One of the many instructions he issued on building techniques for his city prescribed boiling water to treat the moss used for caulking walls in order to prevent cockroaches from settling there.[16]

Peter's conception of his capital was reflected in the institutions he established there, the first of which was a military academy which included geometry and music on its syllabus. He also founded a medical school – something hitherto unheard of in

[13] *Russ. Star.*, 1870, vol. xl, p. 687.   [14] Ustryalov, vol. iv, pt i, p. 274.
[15] Staehlin, p. 62.   [16] Luppov, p. 48.

Russian. Its students were at first recruited by press-gang methods and by no means all of them stayed the course. He also founded two military hospitals and a dispensary, all innovations. The dispensary was free and available to all, and this in turn encouraged the systematic study of botany even before Peter founded the Russian Academy of Sciences. Peter also wanted his city to be beautiful, from the start. He had many trees planted and woe betide anyone who mutilated their branches, while in another of the rare letters of his that could be described as touching he writes to one of his boyars:

Min Her,

As soon as you receive this letter, without delay, send to Petersburg from Izmailov large quantities of flowers, scented mostly, together with gardeners. Also let us know how many recruits you have, how many men are on leave and what the state of the army is in general.[17]

Peter loved his city dearly; as the English resident observed, "The czar is charmed with his new production and would lose the best of his provinces sooner than this barren corner."[18]

*   *   *

Augustus and Frederick IV of Denmark were sufficiently encouraged by Poltava to re-enter the war, and they formed a new alliance with Peter against Sweden. The Danes mounted an unsuccessful invasion of the Swedish mainland, and were obliged to withdraw almost immediately. However, their action enabled Peter to extend his own conquests. He invaded Karelia and captured the fortress of Viborg, making St Petersburg safe from attack from the north. He also extended his conquests in the Baltic provinces. He laid siege to Riga – avenging the insults received on his last visit, and firing the opening shot in person. Riga was eventually reduced, by starvation and a terrible outbreak of plague, in July 1710, and the towns of Pernau and Reval followed soon after, making Russian domination of Sweden's Baltic territories almost complete. The plague that summer was not confined to Riga, the disease was widespread throughout the Baltic provinces, and Peter displayed all his energy and attention to

[17] *Corr.*, vol. iii, p. 42.   [18] Whitworth, p. 127.

detail in his efforts to prevent it reaching Russia. His correspondence of the time is full of instructions controlling the movements of troops and even the transmission of dispatches to prevent the infection from moving east, which indeed it did not. Of course Peter's measures alone cannot account for the halting of the epidemic, yet they do show us an energy, practical concern and meticulousness which command great admiration, and are as much part of his character as his curiously profligate deployment of resources, human and natural, and his readiness to order sacrifice on the most generous of scales in order to fulfil his own and his nation's demands.

However, the following year nearly brought a permanent end to Peter's run of successes. Charles had been encouraging the Porte to break with Russia, and Peter had grown sufficiently confident of his strength to adopt an attitude towards Turkey that was anything but conciliatory, peremptorily asking the Porte whether he wanted peace or war. His ambassador Tolstoy was thrown into prison and the Turks mobilised 200,000 men.

Peter had been in touch with orthodox Serbs and Bulgarians, and whether or not he was prompted by heady visions of pan-Slavism he certainly believed that the orthodox would rise in his support, or at least provide him with supplies. In this belief, and in strange emulation of Charles on his last campaign, he led his army deep into enemy Moldavia, with an inadequate baggage train. In previous campaigns against the Turk the Russians had always taken supplies with them and never expected to live off the land. In the event Peter soon discovered that the enemy had laid the country waste and that the Moldavians and Wallachians preferred collaborating with the Turks to throwing in their lot with Peter.

Pursued by a swarm of locusts the Russians pressed even deeper into Moldavia, largely in search of food. The parallel with Charles is striking enough; more striking still is Peter's new-found confidence, won at Poltava, which encouraged him to echo the manœuvres that had brought about his enemy's defeat. An additional sign of the confidence Peter felt about his Turkish campaign was the presence of Catherine and indeed numerous other officers' wives in the army.

As it turned out, Peter did a great deal worse than Charles. He pressed on, sublimely ignorant of the immediate proximity of the Grand Vizir and an army of 200,000 men. Contact was made on July 17 and Peter's army, by now reduced by "natural wastage" to some 38,000, fought a bitter rearguard action as it withdrew to the river Pruth. The Russians were so pressed and under-horsed, that the cavalry frequently had to fight on foot. Confusion was compounded by the Russian tendency to loot their own baggage train.[19] They eventually took up an indifferent defensive position with their backs to the river, and proceeded to beat off one Turkish attack after another. Poor generalship had to be redeemed by determined junior officers, soldiers and cold steel. On one flank the Turks were able to dig in and take cover behind some rising ground fifty paces from the Russian lines. Repeated assaults failed to dislodge them and almost all the officers in that part of the line were killed or wounded. As the main body of the Turkish army came up to join its mounted advance guard it concentrated on this same flank, with five times as many guns as the Russians, whose supplies were running low after three days and nights of constant fighting. Water and ammunition were dreadfully short and the horses were in a deplorable condition for lack of feed; it was said that some men's eyes ran with blood for the heat and the thirst, and that some killed themselves because they could endure the conditions no longer.

Peter, the architect of this disaster, cut a sorry figure. At a council of war on the first day, before the enemy's main army had arrived, it was decided to dislodge the Turks from their commanding position on the flank and take their guns – until Peter got cold feet and changed his mind.[20] As conditions deteriorated a general panic set in. Peter was observed galloping half-crazed to and fro across the camp, beating his breast and speechless, or sobbing bitterly. The large number of officers' wives present were howling too, and with reason. The situation seemed hopeless. The Russians were surrounded, outnumbered five to one and practically without supplies. They were faced with the prospect of annihilation as an army and quite possibly a lifetime's slavery as individuals – or else they could die fighting. As a last measure it was decided they would try for a break-out west into Transylvania, unless a miracle should occur, and indeed a miracle did.

Peter tried to open negotiations with the Grand Vizir; after his first two envoys were killed a third got through and a forty-eight hour armistice was agreed on. Once it started the Turkish

[19] Cht., 1899, vol. iii, p. 364.   [20] Ibid., p. 366.

troops grew so friendly that sentries had to be posted to keep the lines apart. Peter was prepared to make every kind of concession to save his army and himself, "anything but slavery" he wrote to Shafirov, who was doing the negotiating. Yet despite the ravings of a furious Charles who had arrived too late from Bender to prevent the armistice, and was now observing his old enemy escape the bag, standing powerless on high ground above the Russian camp, the Grand Vizir's terms were preposterously moderate. The Russians were to dismantle Taganrog, return Azov, avoid interference in Polish affairs and permit Charles to return to Sweden; the price was by no means high when the alternative might well have been unconditional surrender. It is not easy to say why the Grand Vizir settled for so little. He was, it would seem, not a warlike man, and probably greatly overestimated the amount of fight left in the Russians. There is reason to believe that he was anxious about his own men, whose discipline was not good, and moreover he resented being hectored by Charles. Finally there is a long-standing tradition that he accepted a monumental bribe. Catherine is said to have contributed all her jewellery and that of the other wives to the nest egg, and indeed to have initiated the whole idea of buying a way through the Turkish lines in the first place. The story of the gift and her initiative is almost certainly apocryphal; however, Catherine certainly made some kind of contribution to the "miracle on the Pruth", for Peter would always express gratitude to her for her behaviour there. Whether or not the Grand Vizir was actually bribed we cannot say, but he was certainly dismissed for his conduct of the campaign and died in exile a year later.

Of course Peter had not emerged entirely unscathed. He had effectively lost all hope of a Black Sea fleet, and the fruits of two Azov campaigns; the Voronezh yards, the Don Volga canal, the harbour of Taganrog, indeed all his early undertakings, had now come to nothing. Moreover the victor of Poltava had suffered considerable loss of face, and it was not considered wise to discuss the Pruth affair openly in Moscow or St Petersburg.

CHAPTER ELEVEN

War and Diplomacy

Peter and Catherine now travelled north together to Warsaw, since Peter, whose health had deteriorated on the campaign, wished to visit the waters at Carlsbad. He left Catherine at the Polish town of Thorn, in the company of a guards battalion, which she greatly appreciated, enjoying the company of hard-drinking officers quite as much, and in much the same way as Peter did, as a *fille du régiment*. We have a rare glimpse of her "in action" during the stay. She entered a Catholic church and listened to the service for a little, grew bored, and wandered around with her retinue, with whom she conversed in a loud voice. She attended to the address for a while, then sent someone to order the preacher to cut it short, but he declined. She then asked to see some relics of the Virgin, said to be there: she wished to take them back to Russia. Here too she was disappointed. The observer, the Dane Juel, says that she and her staff officers behaved as if they were in an inn. But although Catherine startled Juel by her manners and her altogether unregal behaviour, he found that she had considerable charm, and that the coarseness of her character did not prevent her from being a person of great warmth and kindness.

Peter travelled on to Dresden where he dined with Augustus, who, it would appear, was so displeased to see a tarnished silver plate on his table that he bent it in two. Peter thought that he was playing a game and promptly bent his own plate in two. Augustus followed suit and so it went on until the table was littered with bent and crumpled silver.[1] Peter put up at the inn

[1] Maikov, p. 26.

zum göldenen Ring which he left in bad odour, removing the bed coverings and some green curtains that had been specially provided for him, despite the protestations of the staff.[2]

Peter did not care very much for Carlsbad if we may judge from the letter he wrote to Catherine on his arrival:

> Katerinushka my friend, greetings.
>
> We arrived safely, thank God, and start the cure tomorrow. Seriously this place is about as merry as a prison, particularly since it sits among mountains so that you can hardly see the sun. Worst of all there is no decent beer. But let's hope that God will restore my health with the water.
>
> I'm sending you a present, a new kind of clock enclosed in a glass case because of dust, also a seal. I could not get anything more since I was in a hurry and could only spend a day in Dresden.[3]

Peter and Catherine kept up a warm and bantering correspondence. Apparently in reply to a letter in which Catherine had accused him of amusing himself with the opposite sex he replied that he missed her badly and "as for your jokes about amusements, we do without those too here, since we are old and not that way inclined".[4] Catherine replied telling him how much she missed his attentions, begging him to come back soon and bring with him some Hungarian wine since they were so short of it "that we do not even see it in our dreams".[5]

The waters of Carlsbad restored Peter's health rapidly enough, although he made a bad start. His German doctor ordered him to drink three mugs of water per day, and Peter understood him to say "jugs". He managed to down the first two, but observed that he did not think he could do justice to the third, only to learn of his mistake.[6]

Since Poltava, Peter had begun to play at European politics and dynastic alliances, a game at which he was not particularly successful. In 1710 a marriage was arranged between his niece Anna and Frederick William, Duke of Courland. The duke requested a considerable dowry, which Peter arranged to be paid in two parts, the smaller being an outright sum, the latter a loan

[2] *Russ. Star.*, 1874, vol. xliv, p. xi.   [3] *Corr.*, vol. xi, p. 129.
[4] *Ibid.*, p. 1388.   [5] *Ibid.*, p. 1252.
[6] Nagreevsky, pp. 18–9.

at five per cent with which to buy back ducal estates which were to be vested in Anna.

A year later, he embarked upon a second marriage plan, and this time planned to marry his son. Aleksey Petrovich had lived with his mother until Peter put her in a convent, at which point Aleksey was eight. Peter had neglected him completely ever since; his eagerness to resist the conservatism of Muscovy did not extend to removing his only son from its influence or giving any attention whatsoever to his early education. It is true that he had planned to send him to Dresden, but the plan was interrupted by the Northern War. In the early 1700's the czarevich had a foreign tutor, Neugebauer, who was soon dismissed and replaced by a certain Baron Huyssen; however, Huyssen was quickly called upon to act for Peter abroad, suggesting either that there was a severe shortage of persons of any ability or a fair disregard for the education of his son. Perhaps the most surprising aspect of Peter's educational plans is that the person made ultimately responsible for that education, to whom both Neugebauer and Huyssen reported, was none other than the semi-literate Menshikov.

Menshikov's role in the story of Peter's luckless son was sinister from the start. The dismissed Neugebauer painted a dreadful picture of Menshikov flogging the boy personally while the child was "so meek that it made you cry. They young master kisses his hands, and when they are invited anywhere he stands behind Menshikov's chair and waits upon him, which he accepts as his due."[7] On another occasion Menshikov was said to have pulled Aleksey Petrovich to the ground by his hair, in front of his father – who did nothing, thereby encouraging the rumour that Menshikov had bewitched him.

Later Aleksey was to complain that Menshikov had always encouraged him in his weaknesses, notably his weakness for drink. Menshikov and Catherine regarded Peter's first-born as a long-term political threat, and although we cannot say to what lengths they went to assist him in his downfall, one can be sure that Menshikov did not make any effort to turn Aleksey into the kind of son of which Peter would be proud. He was by taste and temperament different from him in almost every way. Weak in character, unwarlike, gentle and terrified of his father, Aleksey in fact acquired a reasonable education, largely thanks to his own

[7] Wittram, vol. ii, p. 303.

love of books. He could speak French and German and had considerable academic interests, reading widely and being particularly interested in religion. Fear of his father and the influence of his mother had made him both pious and sympathetic to the conservative cause. As early as 1698 he was believed to be hostile to his father's innovations. The *streltsy* hoped to put him on the throne and indeed, during their rebellion, he was living with a maternal aunt who was known to be sympathetic to them.[8] In later years he was further encouraged in his hostility to his father by his confessor, Yakob Ignatiev Protopopov, who had great influence over him and introduced him to many conservative priests whose company he enjoyed. Once again one is surprised at Peter's readiness to let his son move in circles that were so clearly hostile to his interests, while demanding of him behaviour and attitude worthy of his heir. In fact as early as 1707 we can see from his letters that Aleksey was conscious of being the centre of a movement of opposition to Peter. The increasing dominance of Menshikov had alienated many members of the traditionally great families, Dolgorukys and Golitsyns, while Aleksey's mother's family, the Lopukhins, had their own well-founded grounds for hostility. By 1709 Aleksey was already proceeding with caution, taking care not to be seen to be in contact with the Lopukhin clan, and his letters suggest that he sometimes thought of himself as a conspirator. Certainly he corresponded with a number of sympathisers, using six different cyphers, and the letters suggest that he enjoyed quite widespread though necessarily muted support.

In 1710 he was sent to live abroad, where he was to remain for three years. Peter had sent him to Dresden, ordering him to "live honourably and study hard at German and French (which you study already), geometry, fortification and some politics. When you have mastered geometry and fortification write to us. May God be your guide."[9] As we shall see, Aleksey did not have much success with his geometry or his fortification. The blend of piety, timidity and guile that shaped so much of his personality emerges in a request he sent from Dresden for the services of an orthodox priest. The priest should be sent to him secretly, beard shaven and disguised as a courier. He would remain in his service, disguised, his sole function being to administer him the last rites should they be needed.[10] The lengths to which he was prepared

[8] Bogoslovsky, vol. iii, p. 48.   [9] *Corr.*, vol. ix, p. 443.   [10] Cht., 1861, vol. ii, p. 40.

to go to conceal the modest desire to have a priest at his side show how great was the gap between himself and the father whom he feared so greatly and with such reason.

Although Aleksey Petrovich hated European life and considered Russian ways incomparably superior, father and son were curiously alike in some respects at least. Not only did he have his father's love of drink, he also had something of his sense of humour. He too had an all-drunken synod of sorts, whose members had nicknames, some blasphemous, some humorous, and he too loved making dignified persons disgustingly drunk.[11] Moreover in due course we shall find him echoing Peter's taste in women by falling in love with a peasant girl and rejecting an arranged marriage.

Peter decided to marry his son to a foreign heretic, Charlotte of Wolfenbüttel, a protégée of Augustus and sister to the empress of Austria; another break with tradition, no czarevich had ever married a foreigner before. For all his aversion to such an arrangement Aleksey agreed, even though Charlotte would be permitted to remain a Protestant. He even accepted the humiliating assignment of trying to beat her relatives down on the matter of her pension and settlement. After months of haggling an agreement was reached and the marriage ceremony held. Peter wrote to his senate to announce that "I beg to notify you that the marriage of my son took place here to-day at Torgau, in the house of the Polish queen, a fair number of distinguished persons being present. Our kinsfolk of the house of the princes of Wolfenbüttel are reasonably respectable."[12]

After three days of celebration Peter ordered Aleksey to Thorn to help with provisioning the army. Peter followed on after a meeting with Danes and Saxons, to find that his son had not yet arrived. He had tried to bring his bride with him, but she had declined to proceed until she had taken delivery of a travelling bed. Aleksey was eventually obliged to leave alone and Charlotte only arrived six weeks later. In four months' time Peter ordered his son away again, while early in the next year he made public his own marriage to Catherine. After the public celebration Peter went first to Menshikov's house and then to his palace. "His Majesty left his sled with some impatience a little before they came to the door, so that he might have time to hang up a sconce

---

[11] Cht., 1861, vol. ii, p. xvi.
[12] Graham, p. 210.

with six branches of ivory and ebony which he had turned him-self."[13]

Peter had delayed dismantling his Black Sea ports as long as possible, but it took all Peter Tolstoy's ingenuity and largesse to prevent the Porte from renewing the war – Tolstoy was both ambassador and hostage and had grown to recognise that un-expected stays of unpredictable duration in Turkish dungeons were a seemingly inevitable part of his lot as Russian ambassador in Constantinople. A peace treaty was finally signed in April 1712. Peter was to remove all his troops from Poland, respect the inde-pendence of the Ukrainian cossacks and refrain from building fortresses on the Don. The Turks were free to hold, banish or escort Charles through Russian territory as it should please them. The treaty was a second humiliation for Peter, confirming, indeed amplifying, his already considerable loss of face.

There was little enough to cheer him about the Northern War, which now entered a peculiarly messy and inconclusive phase. Whatever the consequence of Poltava, it had not left Sweden defenceless. Moreover the maritime powers, notably England, were disturbed by the rise of Russia, and would do all they could to prevent an overwhelming Russian victory. The pattern of the war during its second half is a series of halting and largely half-hearted campaigns. The Russians were desperately anxious to hang on to their gains and somewhat uncertain as to their future policies. As Charles Whitworth wrote in 1712.

On one side their vanity and insatiable desire of new conquests, on the other the fear of losing what is already gained, hang on them like the ague and the hot and cold fits have been very violent on the last alternation.[14]

The campaign of 1712 had proved unsatisfactory. The fighting had moved west; the Saxons wished to take the island of Rügen, the Danes wanted Wismar, while Menshikov was attempting to take Stettin, unsuccessful at least in part thanks to his allies' re-fusal to supply him with any siege artillery.

Peter, who, in these later years, suffered increasingly from despondency and bad health, returned to Carlsbad that autumn. En route he passed through Berlin, where he attended a state ban-quet and surprised his observers by his failure to belch, break

[13] Cht., 1861, vol. ii, p. 145.   [14] Coll., 1888, vol. lxi, pp. 177–8.

wind or pick his teeth in public.[15] On his return to Carlsbad he seemed in better spirits. He offered a prize for the best marksman at a local shooting contest and carried it off himself, nearly gunning down a spectator who was so impressed by the czar's shooting that he jumped for joy, a movement Peter misinterpreted as mockery.[16] Another characteristically Petrine episode was his encounter with a gang of workers plastering the façade of a house from scaffolding. Peter observed them briefly, then climbed up and joined them. Once again he seems to have been somewhat over-sensitive. When one of the workers reacted to the sight of the czar of Muscovy plastering the façade of a Carlsbad house by letting his jaw drop in amazement, Peter once again suspected that he was being laughed at and hit the poor plasterer so hard that he nearly knocked him into the street, subsequently accepting that he was not being teased at all and giving him some money.[17]

In the meantime Peter was behaving strangely towards his son and new daughter-in-law. No arrangements of any kind had been made for their residence. They lingered in Thorn, living off Aleksey's army pay, while not a penny was seen of Charlotte's supposed annuity. Even Menshikov declared himself shocked by the condition in which he found them and lent them some of his own money. Peter now once again ordered Aleksey away to join the army, while Charlotte went to the city of Elbing, near Danzig. Her move did not please Peter, who wished her to proceed to Russia. Charlotte refused unless the money owing her should be forthcoming, which it was not. Peter then proposed that Catherine and Aleksey should take her back to Russia with them, but by the time they had arrived at Elbing Charlotte had run home to her mother.

In the meantime Charles, in Bender, had new dreams of conquest. A Swedish army under Stenbock would attack Poland from the north while Charles and the Turks would advance from the south. Indeed in September 1712 Stenbock managed to land an army on the island of Rügen. However, it was the last Swedish army and not to be ventured in campaigns of extravagant Caroline fantasy. Moving west Stenbock defeated the Danes at Gadebusch and turned north into Holstein. Pursued by the allied armies under Peter's command he took refuge in the fortress of Tönning, where some three months later he surrendered.

[15] Graham, p. 218.   [16] Nagreevsky, p. 34.   [17] Ibid., pp. 43–4.

In search of new allies Peter turned now to Frederick William I, who had just succeeded to the Prussian throne. He promised him arms, and Russian giants for his military guard, and, in due course, Prussia too came in against Sweden. Peter did not leave Berlin empty-handed. When in Mon Bijou he saw the king's famous amber room and other treasures. Frederick William recalled: "He immediately demanded this statue and then several others from the king, who was in no position to refuse. He did as much with a room which was panelled entirely in amber. Its sad fate was to be taken to Petersburg much to everyone's regret." It took twelve waggons to transport it.[18]

Ever since the foundation of the admiralty in 1705 Peter had been steadily building up a Baltic fleet. The first oak timber, unobtainable in the north, arrived all the way from Astrakhan three years later. By 1712 Russia had a navy, of sorts. It was by no means perfect. Inferior powder made its gunnery less effective than that of the Swedes, whose guns outranged the Russians by a full third. Russian seamanship was poor too, while many of the ships rode badly and could not keep up with the rest of the fleet. None the less by 1714 there were twenty ships of the line with sixty or fourteen guns, including the *Poltava*, the *Randolph* and the *Oxford*. More to the point there was a large galley fleet. Galley service carried less prestige and privilege than naval service proper, yet the galleys proved, in the Northern War at least, a great deal more useful than the sailing ships. They were essentially troop transports, extensions of the army as opposed to part of the navy, and by the end of the war virtually any army ensign was capable of commanding one. The Russians were in advance of the Swedes in galley design and the vessels would prove invaluable in subsequent campaigns. The Russian navy proper was well aware of its limitations. It never attempted a blockade or any major engagement on the open sea. The galley fleet, however, was able to move unchallenged round the shallow coastline of Finland and Sweden, under the eyes of Swedish ships of the line which could do nothing to prevent the shallow draughted galleys from manœuvring as they pleased off the coast.

Now in 1713 Peter turned his attentions to Finland, and by the end of that year he held Abo, Helsingfors and all the southern part of the country. Then, after the bloody battle of Storkyrko on November 9, 1714, which saw the annihilation of the Swedish

[18] Coll., 1878, vol. xxiii, p. 86.

defenders, the rest of Finland fell into Peter's hands. It was in the course of this campaign that he enjoyed his first naval triumph proper. The battle of Hangö was a modest enough affair, essentially fought by galleys, yet for Peter it took on the proportions of a second Poltava. The Russians actually captured a Swedish admiral, who was featured in the elaborate victory celebrations, obliged to wear a splendid uniform with silver thread lent him by Peter to betoken his rank. Peter made official report of his victory to his "king" Romodanovsky in the senate house and was promoted to vice-admiral for his services, his first promotion for five years. The parade passed under a magnificent triumphal arch covered with significant emblems such as a Russian eagle seizing an elephant – the name of a captured Swedish frigate.[19]

The allies also met with some success in the west. After Tönning fell Menshikov occupied both Hamburg and Lübeck, and in each case collected large sums of money from merchants anxious to continue their Swedish trade. He went on to take the fortress of Stettin, though on peculiarly disadvantageous terms. Allthough stormed by a Russian army it was to pass to Frederick William in return for a vague commitment to the anti-Swedish alliance.

In the meantime Charles, in Bender in 1713, gave the last and most startling display of his warlike energy. The Turks had decided to repatriate him and came with 800 men and eleven guns to advise him of their decision. The Swedes were taken by surprise and many surrendered. Not so Charles, who fought his way into his house, narrowly escaping having his brains blown out. With some fifty others he cleared the house of enemy and then came under heavy fire. Six hours later, when the house was burning, Charles came out fighting, but had the good fortune to slip as he approached the enemy, who promptly seized and bound him. Turkish casualties numbered over 300 men, ten accounted for by the king in person. The Swedes lost thirty.[20]

Yet for all the Russian successes, the war in the West had lost momentum as the various allies or would-be allies, Saxony, Denmark, now Prussia and Hanover too, found themselves at variance in their interests. In the meantime Queen Anne of England died, to be succeeded by George I, who as Elector of Hanover was eager to involve his new country in the Swedish dismemberment. A new coalition was formed against the Swedes in 1715,

[19] Weber, vol. i, p. 36.   [20] Jeffreyes, pp. 40–1.

which included an English fleet committed to providing limited assistance to the Russo-Danish effort. Elaborate plans had been drawn up for the eventual partition of Sweden's remaining possessions on the mainland, and by the end of that year Charles, who had returned to Europe and was now in Stralsund, was at war with England, Hanover, Russia, Prussia, Saxony and Denmark. After twelve months of fierce fighting Stralsund fell and Charles escaped to Sweden.

His prospects were not spectacular; an allied invasion of Sweden, in force, appeared more than likely. However, Peter, continuing his diplomatic and dynastic experiments, now committed a major blunder. His allies were suspicious enough of one another and supremely suspicious of him, such suspicions coming to a head when Peter failed to respect the freedom of Danzig, seizing all Swedish ships in port and compelling the city to build him privateers. He then proceeded to guarantee Wismar and Warnemünde to the gross and unlovely Duke Leopold of Mecklenburg, to whom he also gave his niece Katerina Ivanovna in marriage. This overt meddling in German affairs was a terrible mistake. By giving the duke his support he antagonised Hanover and hence England and Denmark too. His own diplomats had advised him most strongly against the step, but he had paid not the slightest attention. It is not easy to see what his motives were, unless he felt it important to have a sphere of influence in that part of Germany. Whatever his reasons, the result was an immediate weakening of the alliance.

Russian troops sent to help Danes and Hanoverians take Wismar were neither wanted on the siege nor admitted to the city when it fell. None the less Peter, together with Frederick IV of Denmark, still planned to invade Scania, where Charles had made camp with an army of 20,000 men. Peter was to provide a squadron of galleys and the crossing would be made under the protection of English, Danish and Russian fleets. Peter proceeded to Copenhagen to arrange the conduct of the campaign. He had expressly asked to reside in Charlottenburg, the castle of Charles, the king's brother. The king was deeply distressed by the suggestion and immediately ordered all objects of value to be put away. The brother was no less alarmed at the prospect of his unwanted guest, but fortunately for him Peter eventually chose to lodge elsewhere.

We have a glimpse of him during this time of preparation for the invasion from a Danish apothecary who saw him, late in July, going for a walk with Menshikov and others. They suddenly commandeered some peasants' horses, rode to a village inn and kicked the innkeeper out of bed, thus enabling Peter to take his place, boots and all. Peter looked like an NCO or headsman, in a dirty blue coat with brass buttons, and a broad leather belt, high boots, velvet cap and a cudgel. He was, however, undeniably handsome. When buttering his bread he would lick the knife clean.[21]

Despite their assembly of a massive invasion force the allies could not bring themselves to invade. There was too much mutual mistrust, and too much respect for Charles, well dug in on his home ground. In early September Peter decided to abandon invasion plans for that year. When his allies heard of his decision they accused him of treachery, even of trying to take Copenhagen, and ordered the English fleet under an Admiral Norris to fall upon Peter's ships – which he declined to do. Peter went into winter quarters in Mecklenburg and contracted a defensive alliance with Frederick William of Prussia. Early the next year, in April 1717, in search of further support Peter journeyed west once more, this time to France.

Peter's visit to Paris is of considerable interest. As a diplomatic mission, seeking to weld France to the alliance, it failed. Yet the visit to Paris marks another stage in Peter's own development. He visited the most sophisticated city in the world, one whose inhabitants had the keenest and most critical of eyes, and were always ready to perceive ridicule in others. In general he was considered by them to be a savage but great ruler; no longer the eccentric young czar of Muscovy hob-nobbing with workmen, Peter was now considered over-direct perhaps and going beyond the bounds of *politesse*, yet a force none the less, the leader of a major power. The consideration afforded him in Paris was the final proof that Muscovy was no longer a large, faraway country about which one knew very little and which was anyway something of a joke.

En route for France Peter made a brief stop in Brussels where the Austrian resident found him unaffected but very changeable.[22] While there he indulged a favourite habit, the inspection of relics deemed to be sacred. In this case he inspected a piece of the true cross said to be $15'' \times 7''$ – Peter removed a rule from

[21] *Russ. Star.*, 1915, vol. clxii, p. 161.   [22] Gachard, p. 497.

his pocket, measured it and observed that it was 18″ × 12″.[23] We next see him at Dunkirk, observed by a French diplomat assigned to him, who describes him as follows:

> The czar is very tall, with a slight stoop, the head a trifle bowed. He is swarthy with a wild look about him. He seems to be intelligent and quick to grasp things, and has a certain occasional grandeur in his manner. He is melancholic and distracted, though easy to approach and frequently familiar.[24]

The diplomat in question did not find the Russian party easy to deal with. "This little court is very changeable, undecided and capable of great anger at every level from throne to stable."[25] They objected especially strongly to being referred to as Muscovites. They were much less organised than most royal embassies, living from day to day without predetermined plans. They complained regularly, the principal complaint being the transport provided them; rejecting the massive four-wheeled berlins as too slow, they insisted on two-wheeled two-place chaises, in which they travelled to Paris as quickly as possible, incidentally giving considerable offence to local dignitaries who had made elaborate plans for their reception, by passing through their cities unannounced and often at night. Peter's aversion to crowds was as strong as ever.

In Paris he was to find the most civilised and cultured city of the West, and to be subjected to the most critical of scrutinies – which left him entirely unabashed. On the day after his arrival he received a visit from the regent, the duc d'Orléans. Four days later the seven-year-old Louis XV called and paid him a formal compliment, which delighted Peter so greatly that he kissed his hands, hugged him and ruffled the young monarch's hair. When paying his return visit Louis came out to meet Peter, who, displaying his disarming disregard for protocol, bounded up the stairs of the Louvre to meet him, swept him into his arms and bore him inside.

While his ambassadors pursued their quest for an alliance Peter explored Paris and its environs. He was most impressed by the Gobelins tapestry factories, so much so that he subsequently set up a comparable installation in Russia, regardless of the fact that the kind of wool appropriate, or rather essential, to such weaving

[23] *Ibid.*, p. 495.   [24] Coll., 1881, vol. xxxiv, p. 147.   [25] *Ibid.*, p. 150.

was not obtainable. The waterworks of Marly caught his eye too. As usual he was more interested in technical matters than in the arts, and his comments on the manuscript treasures of the Royal Library have not been recorded, although we know that he was delighted when the royal mint produced a medal bearing his likeness. He had been preceded by his reputation for drunkenness and after one dinner and four bottles of champagne he had to be carried to a carriage in which the duc d'Antin prudently declined to join him. Peter was indeed thoroughly sick on the way home and had to be cleaned up before being put to bed.[26]

The French reaction to Peter is most interesting. They found him poorly dressed, and were surprised to learn that he slept in the dressing room of his apartment. They were equally nonplussed by his willingness to abandon his retinue and hail a cab – or even to turn total strangers out of their carriages.[27] Used as they were to the style of kingship set by Louis XIV, they found Peter's casual *sans façons* altogether bewildering. Yet if it is characteristic of the French national character to expect the external trappings of *gloire*, the Frenchmen of Peter's day were no less true to character in another respect; they were universally appalled by the meanness of Peter's tipping! By the second week of his six-week stay he had the reputation of being "less than generous". There were also complaints that he walked so fast it was not possible to keep up with him. By the end of his stay his parsimony had made him so unpopular that he was held to have the soul of a "petit bourgeois".[28] On the whole the court found him too unusual to be impressive – with one notable exception; one of the keenest observers of the age, the duc de Saint Simon, has left us both a vivid description and one of the most penetrating appreciations of Peter ever made. Saint Simon, for one, understood his true quality:

He is very tall, well made, thin enough, with a roundish face, large forehead and fine brows; the nose is quite short . . . and thick at the end; the lips are quite fleshy; his complexion is a reddish brown, fine black eyes, large, lively, piercing . . . a gracious and majestic gaze when he cares, but otherwise severe and wild, with an occasional twitch that distorts the eyes and his entire countenance and which inspires fear. It would last for a moment, giving him a wild and terrible expression, from

[26] Buvat, p. 268.   [27] Saint-Simon, p. 367.   [28] Lortholany, p. 19.

which he would at once recover. His whole manner announces wit, intelligence and grandeur and is not without a certain grace.[29]

Saint Simon alone understood that beneath his simplicity there lay a genuine greatness:

> In a most surprising way he displayed the loftiest, most proud, most delicate and sustained majesty, which was at the same time the least embarrassing . . . always the master but with degrees of familiarity according to the company. He possessed a kind of familiarity deriving from liberty; but he was not free from a strong touch of his country's erstwhile barbarity, which made his manners abrupt not to say brusque, his will uncertain, refusing to be constrained or contradicted by anyone.[30]

Paris did in fact have a certain "civilising" influence on Peter, which extended beyond tapestry. He bought numerous pictures, seascapes mostly, and porcelain and came away from the city with a somewhat deeper appreciation of the gentler aspect of European civilisation than he had possessed before. The French army did not impress:

> I saw dressed up dolls, not soldiers. They perform acrobatics with their muskets and do not march, they dance.[31]

On France in general he observed:

> It is a good idea to borrow their arts and sciences from the French, however sooner or later Paris will pay dearly for its luxury and licence and moreover it stinks.[32]

---

[29] Saint-Simon, p. 368.
[31] Maikov, p. 85.
[30] Ibid., p. 368.
[32] Nartov, p. 34.

CHAPTER TWELVE

Peter and Aleksey

There is darkness enough in the life of Peter, and failure too, but no darkness, no failure can equal the dreadful story of his miserable and hopeless son, *un jeune prince pas des plus rusés* as the French ambassador Campredon described him.[1]

Peter never appears to have treated him with much warmth. Not one of the surviving letters show any hint of affection. When they do not hold terrible warnings they consist of bald matter-of-fact instructions. Peter reserved warmth for Catherine and for Menshikov.

One can only assume that from the outset Peter assumed his son to be "one of them", one of the old guard, a Lopukhin, a Muscovite at the least. Indeed he was all these things, but the onus was on his father to make him into a worthy heir, and this he entirely failed to do. The treatment handed out to the newly married Aleksey and Charlotte is puzzling enough. He appeared to have no consideration whatsoever for the young couple, being determined that his son should spend more time with the army than with his bride. He eventually persuaded Charlotte, who it will be remembered had returned to her mother, to go to St Petersburg, by dint of much reassurance and a large sum of money. Aleksey also returned home, after his three-year stay abroad. He returned in dread of his father, knowing how little he had learnt, and how different he was from what the czar would have him be. He was so terrified that Peter might ask him on his return to demonstrate the skill he was supposed to have acquired at drawing fortifications that he fired a pistol at his

[1] Coll., 1881, vol, xxxiv, p. 305.

hand; even then the bullet missed, so that all he got was a powder burn. It is a terrible little story, eloquent of the fear and the weakness of wretched Aleksey, and his view of his father. As he put it later: "From which [i.e. the wounding attempt] it can be seen that although I was afraid of you it was no filial fear."[2]

Aleksey cared little for his wife. and soon started drinking heavily and muttering in his cups that things would be very different when his father was gone:

> The czarevich was entirely given up to low sensual pleasures and mean vicious company, and had no desire at all to marry ... and the princess, whose amiable person and engaging accomplishments deserved a better fate, entirely missed her road to happiness.[3]

Charlotte was indeed no happier in St Petersburg – and not much wealthier. Her allowance was paid to her piecemeal and she often found it difficult to settle her bills. Aleksey was later to complain that his father and Catherine treated his wife little better than they might a serving girl.[4] In July of 1714 she gave birth to a daughter, the czarevna Natalya, and fourteen months later bore a son, the future Peter II. Four days later the luckless mother was dead.

Aleksey, for all his weakness, drunkenness, terror of his father, was still perfectly aware that he would probably follow him, although it was ultimately up to the czar to nominate the Romanov who was to succeed. Many of the old families looked to him to restore the old ways, and he had his own set of close friends and advisers who encouraged him in his tacit opposition to Peter. One of the most important of these was a certain Alexander Kikin, once a protégé of Peter but who had lost his favour through dishonesty.

Peter's dissatisfaction with his son had clearly been building up for years, and now, on the death of Charlotte, it emerged in a dire letter of admonition. This accused him of being a hopeless soldier, displaying not the faintest interest in military affairs. It was not a lack of natural ability that he was reproaching him for, but a lack of goodwill. He clearly saw his son as the epitome of that deadly inertia which he had fought to overcome in others all his life, and which must needs set in again were Aleksey to

[2] Ustryalov, vol. vi, p. 34.   [3] Bruce, p. 82.   [4] Ustryalov, vol. vi, p. 68.

succeed him unless he could be persuaded to mend his ways. He offered this last warning; should it not be obeyed he would deprive Aleksey of the succession, "cut off like a gangrenous growth". The letter ended characteristically. The demands Peter made of others were no different from those he made of himself: "I have never spared nor do I spare my own life for my people or my country, so how can I have mercy on one as useless as you?"[5] Aleksey reacted hopelessly. Instead of promising to change his ways he weakly agreed with his father's assessment of his inadequacies and unfitness to rule, begging to be deprived of the succession in favour of the son recently born to Catherine – who was, however, to die some months later.

Soon after this Peter fell so seriously ill that he received the sacraments. Captain Perry was in no doubt as to what would happen were he to go:

And this is certain that if the present czar should happen to die without the greater part of his old boyars go off before him, the generality of things wherein he has taken so much pains to reform his country will for the most part revolve into their old form. For it is believed that his son the present prince of Russia, who is of a temperament very much differing from that of his father's and adhering to bigotry and superstition, will easily be prevailed on to come into the old methods of Russia, and quit and lay aside many of those laudable things that have been begun by the present czar.[6]

Peter knew this too, and the knowledge must have made him despair. Aleksey was bound to undo most of his work, and it was virtually impossible to ensure that he did not succeed him. Whatever provision he might make could scarcely avoid the possibility of a disputed succession and possible civil war. Ironically enough, a few months earlier Peter had told the French ambassador that his considerable admiration for Louis XIV was tempered by the latter's failure to secure the succession on his death. "I call it the greatest of cruelties to sacrifice the well-being of the state to a mere right of succession."[7] Peter was resolved to avoid that particular "cruelty", at all costs.

On his recovery he wrote a second letter to his son accusing him of hating all his works and ordering him either to mend his

[5] Ustryalov, vol. vi, p. 49.   [6] Perry, p. 261.   [7] Busching, 1769, vol. xix, p. 186.

ways or to become a monk. Aleksey answered briefly that he was ready to enter a monastery. There seems to have been duplicity here. Aleksey knew that there was nothing irrevocable about such a step. "The cowl is not nailed to your head," Kikin had reminded him. Peter again refused to admit that his son was prepared to go to any lengths rather than be the kind of son he wanted. He wrote to him once more from abroad, ordering him to join the army in Germany at once.

Kikin had previously advised Aleksey to remove himself from Peter's authority by living abroad till his father's death. The twenty-six-year-old czarevich now believed his father to be seriously ill, thinking it unlikely that he would live more than a year or so longer. He decided therefore to take Kikin's advice and await his father's death in safety. He subsequently said that he had taken his renunciation of the throne seriously, but hoped to be the regent to Peter's young son for many years, since he was sure that there were many persons of influence who would rather be governed by him than by Menshikov, whom he rightly saw as his chief rival. Shortly before setting off, ostensibly to join his father, he had gone to the senate to take his leave and whispered to Prince Yakob Dolgoruky, "Do not forsake me." "I will always oblige, but please say no more, people are watching us," the prince replied.[8] He also knew that many other senators and also Boris Sheremetev, commander-in-chief of the army, would, if it came to it, support him against the upstart Menshikov.

He now told the latter, in his capacity as governor of St Petersburg, that he was going to join his father. Accompanied by his mistress, a Finnish peasant girl Efrosinya, to whom he was devoted, as it will appear, unwisely, he set off in the direction of Copenhagen. However, Kikin had advised him to make for Austria, since the emperor would protect the husband of his late sister-in-law, and would be most unlikely to hand him back to Peter; on no account should he return, for if he were to do so, Peter would most certainly kill him.

At the time of his flight there were rumours of a plot against his life, headed by Menshikov, with the possible connivance of Catherine. Certainly now she had borne Peter a son she had an additional reason for wanting Aleksey out of the way. Moreover, there could be little doubt that were he to succeed Peter and restore the Muscovite tradition neither she nor Menshikov would

[8] Ustryalov, vol. vi, p. 54.

retain their positions for an instant, and would probably lose their heads, for it is difficult to conceive of either of them in a monastery. Certainly Peter would subsequently blame Catherine for the flight of his son, complaining that the world would think that it was he who had driven him away.[9] Menshikov's comment on the flight was to observe that Aleksey was incapable of ruling and to hint that he might anyway be of suspect and illegitimate birth.[10]

On November 10 1716, Aleksey arrived at the Viennese residence of Count Schönborn, the Austrian vice-chancellor, travel-stained and in a state of tearful panic. He demanded to be taken to the emperor – it was late at night – and repeatedly stated that Peter wanted to kill him, that he surrounded himself with evil and bloodthirsty people, believing that like God he had the power of life and death, that he had spilt much innocent blood, that he was immeasurably irascible and vindictive and altogether without mercy. Were the emperor to compel him to return, his life would be forfeit; and should his father spare him his step-mother and Menshikov would not rest until he was dead.[11] He was dissuaded from seeing the emperor, who summoned a meeting to decide what to do with this extraordinary embarrassment. It was decided to keep his presence a secret, maintain his incognito and hide him in a castle in the Tyrol. Aleksey agreed to the plan, begging the emperor to keep him hidden. He knew Peter's powers well enough to believe, and rightly, that it would suffice for him to know where Aleksey was hiding for his fate to be sealed.

When Peter learned of the disappearance he guessed that his son would make for Vienna and ordered Veselovsky, his minister there, to look out for him. Aleksey's arrival was indeed confirmed but then the trail went cold. After casting about for some time Alexander Rumyantsev, a guards captain, picked up the scent again and tracked Aleksey down to the fortress of Ehren-berg in the Tyrol. Now Peter could put the pressure on. His minister informed the emperor that the czarevich had been discovered, and demanded his immediate return. The emperor stalled for as long as he could, but Veselovsky was demanding "repatriation" with an increasing insistence, even threatening that Peter might resort to force of arms to ensure his son's return.

---

[9] Wittram, vol. ii, p. 376. [10] Cht., 1861, vol. ii, p. 223.
[11] Ustryalov, vol. vi, p. 68.

The emperor responded by trying to make Aleksey disappear a second time. In order to convince him of that need, he was shown the original of Peter's letter to the emperor demanding his return. This frightened Aleksey so much that he was unable to speak, he simply ran around the room crying, waving his arms, and then fell to his knees, imploring the emperor to protect him for otherwise he was doomed.[12] He was taken secretly away, with Efrosinya disguised as a page, to Naples, which was at that time in Austrian hands, and the castle of St Elmo. The scheme might have worked had not Rumyantsev had the party followed. They arrived in Naples on May 6, 1717.

Peter responded to the news of the second flight by sending his ablest diplomat, Peter Tolstoy, to Vienna. Tolstoy brought extreme pressure to bear upon the emperor. Torn between Christian duty and *raison d'état* the latter called a meeting of his ministers. It was eventually decided to allow Tolstoy and Rumyantsev to visit Aleksey in his asylum and let them try to persuade him to return – the presence of a Russian army in Germany was one very good reason why they were prepared to expose the weak and pathetic Aleksey to Tolstoy's brutal pressure. It was too dangerous to assume that Peter would not use it. However, conscience was salved by the determination not to countenance an enforced repatriation.

Tolstoy and Rumyantsev arrived in Naples in late September. They brought Aleksey a letter from Peter promising him before God that if he obeyed and returned he would be forgiven and shown his father's "best love". Otherwise he would curse him and denounce him as a traitor. Aleksey should recall that Peter had never forced him to do anything, although "I could have done whatever I wished".[13] Tolstoy impressed upon Aleksey that wherever he might run to he could not hide from his father's eye for long; sooner or later he would go back. This was precisely the kind of argument likely to weaken the wretched Aleksey, who was quite frightened enough of his father's power and his all-seeing eye as it was. Tolstoy had a series of interviews with Aleksey. He knew he had to convince him that he could never be safe anywhere, that his only hope was Peter's mercy. In other words he made Aleksey play rabbit to his stoat.

At first, to Tolstoy's rage and disgust, Aleksey stood firm, but

[12] *Ibid.*, p. 87. For "senate" see *infra*, p. 228.
[13] *Ibid.*, p. 112.

then the ambassador played his trump card. He had suborned the secretary to the viceroy of Naples, whom Aleksey trusted, offering him a considerable sum of money to exert the appropriate influence. The secretary now told Aleksey in confidence that the emperor would not protect him very much longer. Tolstoy had also won over the viceroy himself, and now he threatened to have Efrosinya, who was four months pregnant, taken away. The combination of pressures broke Aleksey, who loved his peasant girl very much, Tolstoy reported. He agreed to return provided that he be allowed to marry her. Tolstoy recommended that Peter agree, cleverly pointing out that this would alienate the emperor, who would besides lose confidence in Aleksey for having changed his mind.

Tolstoy was duly authorised to agree to the marriage and to bring Aleksey home. The emperor believed him to be returning willingly, but when Tolstoy took him back in great haste and secrecy, rushing him through Vienna without giving him the chance to have an audience with the emperor, the latter grew suspicious. He instructed the governor general of Moravia, Count Coloredo, to hold the party up in Brünn and satisfy himself that Aleksey was returning of his own free will. When Coloredo called Tolstoy at first brusquely denied that Aleksey was there at all. He then announced that there was no time for a meeting, and, when Coloredo insisted, grew truculent. The count found him "hard and rude".[14] After a lot of acrimonious discussion he was eventually permitted to see Aleksey, but not alone; Tolstoy insisted on being present throughout the interview. Aleksey was dreadfully subdued and under the influence of his escort. When Coloredo asked him why he had not called on the emperor, inviting him to admit that he was under duress, Aleksey was too frightened to speak up. He muttered some excuse about the condition of his clothes and carriage being such that he was too embarrassed to call. Almost immediately afterwards Tolstoy brought the interview to a close and the party left at once; Aleksey's last chance to save himself was gone.

Aleksey was now separated from his pregnant Efrosinya. She followed on slowly and Aleksey wrote to her tenderly, urging her to buy a really well-sprung carriage, and to make sure she got the right kind of medical advice. He also wrote to her attendants urging them to amuse her, or else he would have

[14]Ustryalov, vol. vi, p. 130.

the skin off their backs. The letters have a naively optimistic tone.

Thank God all is well, and I think they will let me off everything, that God will allow us to live together in the country and they will leave us alone. Do not believe what you read in the newspapers about me when I arrive, for you know that the German newspapers do not always write the truth.[15]

Efrosinya stayed for some time in Berlin and it was there that she received a still more ironic communication – from Peter Tolstoy, who congratulated her on the safe arrival of Aleksey, "God willing he would soon be seeing Peter."

The supporters of Aleksey Petrovich were dismayed at the news of his return, as were the common people – reported the Austrian resident Pleyer.[16] It was generally believed that he would be dispatched to a monastery forthwith. He returned to Moscow on January 31, 1718, and on February 3 Peter received him in the Kremlin – with three battalions of guards standing to with loaded weapons. He appeared under arrest without a sword, fell to his knees before Peter and begged him for "mercy and his life". The czar agreed, provided he renounce the succession and name everybody implicated in his flight. Once more Peter scented conspiracy. Aleksey agreed to everything and that same day signed an act of renunciation in the Cathedral of the Assumption. Leading dignitaries were also required to sign. Many of them were in tears as they did so, and the entire congregation sobbed as if bereaved.[17]

Next day Peter's interrogation of his son began. He set him a list of questions accompanied by terrible threats should he fail to disclose all. Peter wished to know whether Aleksey really intended to become a monk. He wanted full details of his plans for flight, the names of anyone who had helped him run away. He wanted to know the names of his correspondents. Peter rounded off the package by requiring him to confess anything he might be guilty of which was not included in Peter's questions.

Aleksey, whose courage was unequal to the business of protecting his friends, immediately named Kikin and an ex-tutor, Nikifor Vyazemsky, as his chief accomplices; he also named Prince Dolgoruky. Vyazemsky succeeded in exonerating himself.

[15] Ustryalov, vol. vi, p. 437.   [16] Ibid., p. 142.   [17] Wittram, vol. ii, p. 382.

Dolgoruky, brought to Moscow in chains for all his princely title, escaped with exile; not so Kikin who was tortured dreadfully. The interrogation of Aleksey and his circle, who naturally named all the names they could think of in order to escape further and still more enthusiastic questioning, gave Peter the impression of a steadily branching plot that was vaguely reminiscent of the affair of the *streltsy*. Yet all this "Plot" consisted of was little more than a series of names of persons who had, at one time or another, expressed sympathy for Aleksey and wished for his succession. This was quite enough to meet Russian conceptions of high treason, or "*Word* and Deed" (i.e. against the czar) as it was known. It was sufficient that Peter should discover that certain persons close to his son were guilty of what might, in later years, be termed a "negative attitude" towards him and all his works.

The czar now got wind of an additional ramification of the conspiracy which reached out to include his ex-wife Evdokiya Lopukhina, now the nun Elena. Peter sent an officer to interview her. He found her living in a state of considerable "disorder", by monastic standards that is to say. She wore secular clothes, did not live by the monastic rule and was treated as the czaritsa. Moreover she had a lover, in the shape of a certain Major Stepan Glebov. He was immediately arrested, together with other sympathisers including the bishop of Rostov, one Dosifey. In order for him to be tortured the bishop had first to be stripped of his office and reduced to a simple monk. Under subsequent torture he named further "conspirators", such as Aleksey Petrovich's uncle Avraam Lopukhin, whose principal crime was to be heard to wonder whether his sister would recover her rank on Peter's death. When his turn came he admitted under torture to wanting Peter to die; no further admission of guilt could be extracted.

Evdokiya had effectively remained without a voice ever since Peter had sent her to her convent under military escort, but now she makes herself heard with a piercing clarity. When Glebov's house was searched a series of letters from her were found in which her hitherto shadowy character leaps into vivid and tragic focus. The letters, which she dictated, are the spontaneous words of a desperate, overwrought woman, a prisoner, uncertain of the allegiance of her lover, writing in a manner that is urgent, hysterical and repetitive, undershot by moments of occasional optimism when she thinks Glebov might be able to bring about her release:

> Please, please my light, do what you can for me, in the proper quarters, as you know, only do not put yourself in danger for my sake. Please, please try anyone who might help. Even if it be only the slightest use to me in my misfortune. Help me. You are my only hope. Help me and write and tell me everything. Please solicit for me as you know best. Only do not endanger yourself . . . I am full of hope. You act for me, you think as I do, your word is my word, your word is my head, I am in your hands entirely and for ever . . . I do not lie . . . I beseech you with tears in my eyes. Avoid having to go on active service. I will send you some 700 roubles . . . and you make sure you do not serve. [However, Glebov was unable to bribe his way out, for a subsequent letter reads] . . . So now the accursed hour draws near when we must part. It would be better if my soul were to part from my body. Oh my light, how can I go on, how can I live without you? Wear my ring and love me, I have had another made just like it for me to wear . . . For a long time you have changed in your love for me . . . Why do you not come to see me? What has happened to you? Who has set you against me? Will you forget me? I shall never forget you, my friend. [The letter continues in a hysterical vein asking Glebov to come to see her the following day.]
> I have sent you a kerchief, wear it, my soul. You wear nothing of mine, I'll give you anything. Or do I no longer please you? Oh my light, my soul . . . I don't know how I shall live without you. I feel sick . . . Send me, my heart Stepanushka, my friend, send me your favourite shirt. Why have you left me? Please God do not leave me. I'll kill myself. Don't forget me . . . don't love anybody else. How did I make you angry? Why have you left me so cold, so miserable, so alone?[18]

Emotion and character come through more strongly in these disjointed lines than in any other document of the age. The letters are unique, and their despairing entreaty is the last we hear from Evdokiya, whose husband is shortly to kill both her lover and her son, while she returns to live out her own life in the silence of the convent.

[18] Ustryalov, vol. vi, pp. 327–34.

Glebov was tortured dreadfully and then impaled. Dosifey was broken on the wheel, as was Kikin. Others implicated lost their tongues, had their noses slit and were exiled to Siberia. (It was alleged afterwards that Dosifey had been broken by mistake, they had got the sentence wrong and he should have been beheaded.[19]) When Lopukhin was executed a little later, Peter is said to have picked his head up by the hair and examined it carefully; this would be his final confrontation with the last of old Muscovy.[20] An eyewitness to the execution recalls that the victims "had been obliged to lay their heads on the same block and in the blood of those that had suffered before them".[21] Two months after her husband's death Lopukhin's widow burnt herself alive in her own bath-house.[22]

The affair of the czarevich had aroused all Peter's insatiable suspicions once again, and once again he responded with a cruel rage that almost defies belief. Yet even now he was not convinced that he had extracted all the truth from his son, whom he moved from Moscow to St Petersburg for still further interrogation. Efrosinya had arrived in St Petersburg in April 1718 and her interrogators had waited for her to have her child before they commenced. We know absolutely nothing about the baby, we only know that she had it. Ironically enough in view of his feelings for her, it was her answers to Peter's questioning that finally sealed Aleksey's fate. One can only assume that fear, stupidity and the peculiar psychological condition that can follow the most normal of childbirths combined to have her produce such damning testimony. She repeated a whole series of highly treasonable observations that Aleksey had made. He was said to have rejoiced in a rumour that the army was in a state of mutiny; he had promised to restore all the old ways, to transfer the capital back to Moscow, to reduce the army. He would abandon all the conquered territories and disband the navy. He foresaw civil war on his father's death.

Aleksey, who had hitherto merely been kept under surveillance, was now placed under close arrest. As far as Peter was concerned he had forfeited all guarantees of mercy by failing to make a full confession. Peter charged his son with these omissions and Aleksey, terrified, confessed to anything and everything. He would have joined a mutiny if asked to. He

---

[19] Ustryalov, vol. vi, p. 226.
[20] Wittram, vol. ii, p. 461.
[21] Weber, vol. ii, p. 243.
[22] Coll., 1888, vol. lxi, p. 487.

longed, like Ivan Karamazov, for his father's death; he would have restored the old ways and abandoned the navy. Perhaps at no other time does the character of Aleksey come through quite so clearly as in this pouring out of admission. So great was his terror of his father that he was perfectly prepared to do anything, even sign his death warrant, if only he could make the process of paternal interrogation cease.

After these confessions Peter felt he could no longer permit his son to live. The remotest possibility of his succeeding him was a threat to a lifetime's work. Yet at the same time Peter could not bring himself to assume responsibility for his son's death. He first consulted his clergy as to what should be done with him, particularly with respect to whether or not Peter was bound by his promise to show his son mercy if he returned. The clergy were remarkably non-committal – it was not for them to judge such an affair – however, they were inclined to recommend mercy. Nothing was said of the oath. Peter then turned for his mandate to a secular court consisting of 127 dignitaries, addressing them in similar terms. They unanimously condemned his son to death. Menshikov was the first to sign the sentence.

In the meantime Aleksey was being tortured. Peter was still not satisfied that he had learnt everything. He received twenty-five lashes at a first interrogation, relating to his secret correspondence. Three days later Peter sent Tolstoy to him with questions of a final and different kind. Peter wanted to ascertain the fundamentals. Why had Aleksey gone against him in all respects, why had he disobeyed him, how had he found the courage to do so? Aleksey, despite his physical condition wrote a long reply to these questions in his own hand. It is a miserable document in which as always he makes haste to blame himself, as if admission of unqualified guilt might somehow bring the whole affair to a close. He seeks to explain his behaviour by his own weakness, his innate evil, and his education. He blamed the bad company of priests. Perhaps the most pathetic feature of this "confession", which seems designed entirely to tell his father what he thinks he wants to hear, is his praise of his mentor Menshikov. Two days later Aleksey was tortured again but found little more to say. He received fifteen lashes. The court passed sentence on that same day, June 24. On June 26 the czarevich died. All kinds of reports and rumours circulated about his death, which was officially put down to apoplexy. There is, for example, a letter purporting to be from Rumyantsev, written two days later, in which he says that he, Tolstoy and two others suffocated Aleksey by Peter's order.[23] Popular rumour suggested that Peter beat him to death in person.[24] The historian Ustryalov has recorded nine different versions of the death. He concluded that it was probably the result of the forty lashes he had received in the course of his last weeks. However, the one certain and sinister fact seems to be that, on the morning of his death, the czarevich had received a visit from Menshikov.

Although Peter tackled the conspiracy he believed to be centred upon Aleksey Petrovich in a familiar manner, the killing of his own son should not be thought of as a final piece of old Muscovite barbarity, of the same nature as the rule that wives who murdered their husbands should be buried alive. It was a ruthlessly cruel act of a new and different kind. Peter had his son killed in order to ensure that the new Russia he had created would survive him. One can conceive of earlier czars going to great lengths to guarantee a succession, and Ivan the Terrible of course killed his own son too; yet to murder in this way to ensure the survival of a certain conception of the state would have hitherto been inconceivable Although the cruelty and the ruthlessness were a part of the Muscovite inheritance, the motives themselves were new; political as opposed to dynastic. His son was sacrificed to something closely akin to a European idea of absolutism and to Peter's urgent desire to build a certain kind of Russia. His treatment of Aleksey is a ghastly proof of the price he was prepared to pay to make the future of that kind of Russia secure.

[23] *Russ. Star.*, 1890, vol. lxvii, pp. 412–16.
[24] *Ibid.*, 1885, vol. xlviii, p. 460.

CHAPTER THIRTEEN

Victory: The Pleasures of Petersburg

In its latter years the Northern War took on a new complexion. Russia had defeated Sweden in the field. There were no more great battles, or even sieges. The real issue now was whether Russia would be allowed to keep her gains or whether diplomacy and the possible threat of an anti-Russian alliance would bring some restoration to Sweden. Peter had brought his country into modern Europe with a vengeance. Henceforward she was a force to be reckoned with, having already supplanted Sweden as the major northern power, while it was only a matter of time before she would make herself felt in the south. Accordingly there was a certain reluctance among the maritime powers, and other states, such as Hanover, to see Russia keep all she held. Peter's dynastic marriages and the presence of his army in Mecklenburg suggested to many that he might have enduring designs upon German territories too. Consequently, although he encountered little effective military opposition, Peter now found himself having to deal with the intricacies of a European diplomacy frequently directed against Russian interests.

The Russians seem to have found war easier than diplomacy, one of the resons perhaps why the war dragged on and on for years in a peculiarly uneventful way. Peter himself was considered an able negotiator. He tended first to reject any proposal out of hand, but would eventually turn to careful reasoning. To negotiate with him, wrote a Prussian diplomat, one must be able to state a case in full, argue it logically, speak German and be resilient enough not "to be put off by the vestiges of old Muscovite manners that are still to be found in this court".[1]

[1] Wittram, vol. i, pp. 306–7.

After the failure of his attempt to invade Sweden Peter had hoped to enlist the support of the Royal Navy to "bring the king of Sweden to reason", but although there was a squadron cruising in the Baltic it was made plain to Peter that they would not assist him in any way.

Peter had gone to France in search of an ally. He did, in August 1717, gain her promise that she would mediate, and enter into no treaty that would be contrary to the interests of Russia and Prussia. This, however, was so much less than the Franco-Prussian-Russian alliance that he had hoped for that it was tantamount to diplomatic failure. Peter, in his search for the right sort of peace, was now obliged to turn elsewhere.

He turned to Sweden herself; laying down the basis for direct negotiations via a Holsteiner, the Baron von Görtz, one of Charles's principal advisers. The Swedes initially agreed to relinquish some of their German territories in return for compensation in Norway, which Charles had invaded in 1716 and was now attacking once more in 1718. In May of that year Swedes and Russians met at the peace conference of Åland, a Baltic island. Peter was represented by one of the few really able men in his entourage, Ostermann, a Westphalian who had served Peter for ten years and would serve Russia for many more with great intelligence and a virtually unique honesty. His only "treachery" was to contrive to be sick at times when it might have been imprudent to commit himself or give advice.

Peter wanted peace badly – but he wanted to have his cake too. He was ready to restore Finland, but Ingria, Livonia, Estonia were to remain his. Görtz knew that Charles would never accept such severe terms, and kept them from him. Ostermann argued that Sweden could scarcely continue to fight on, and urged an invasion or raid to bring her to her knees. In the meantime the conference dragged inconclusively on.

On December 12, 1718, Charles was killed – shot in a trench while besieging a Norwegian fortress. The next day Görtz was arrested, and in February 1719 executed for high treason. In March Charles's sister Ulrica Eleonora ascended the throne and negotiations continued. However, Swedish policy now changed. Since it was clear that Russia intended to keep what she had won by force of arms, Sweden sought to isolate her by concluding treaties with her allies instead. In 1719 she made peace with Hanover, Prussia and Poland. Now there was every prospect of an anti-Russian alliance being formed. Even this did not frighten Peter into making concessions.

The key to any effective coalition was England – Hanover, and George I was trying to bring Saxony, Poland and the Empire together with his own countries in an alliance against Russia and Prussia. Peter managed to lower the tension slightly by withdrawing his forces from Mecklenburg. However, Augustus had his eye on Courland; technically ruled by Peter's niece since the duke, her husband, had failed to survive the wedding celebrations held for the young couple in Petersburg, in effect the territory was under Peter's own control. George I backed Augustus and sought a peace that would put some restraint upon Russian power in the Baltic. An alliance was therefore concluded with Sweden. The Royal Navy was to be used to curb Peter, the Baltic squadron being given secret orders to combine with the Swedes to destroy the Russian fleet.

However, the British navy was singularly unsuccessful. Although Britain and Russia had been in a state of armed hostility that stopped just short of war, Peter was quite unmoved by letters from the English admiral Norris calling on him to stop fighting the Swedes. He fought them to considerable effect for three whole summers, 1718, 1719 and 1720.

Peter had discovered the way to bring Sweden to her knees. She did not have anything like sufficient forces to protect her coastline, so for three summers Peter mounted limited invasions with his galley fleet. Able to lie close inshore well out of reach of Swedish and British men-of-war, troops could be transported and landed quickly at any point along the coast, and long before the Swedes could move up sufficient forces to check their ravages they would be gone. The raids were designed to hurt as much as possible, and the raiders were ordered to avoid major engagements and stick to the coast. In 1720 they destroyed towns, villages, farms and manufacturies, demonstrating that the country was indefensible. These were not particularly glorious military actions and the commander, Apraksin, apparently carried out the order to sack the countryside with considerable reluctance.[2] The strategy worked, however. Sweden was obliged to negotiate and talks opened at Nystad in May 1721. Once again Peter was asked to make concessions – Viborg and Livonia – and once again he

[2] Bridges, p. 69.

declined. Instead he made another landing on the Swedish coast and in September 1721 the Swedes finally signed.

The treaty of Nystad saw the end of the twenty-one years of war on which Peter had embarked so lightly. Not only had he fought his way to the Baltic, he had expanded his first narrow bridgehead so as to win the whole coast down to Riga. Moreover, he had never allowed himself to be intimidated into yielding any of the territories he had won by the sword. There can scarcely be a greater contrast between the tearful panic-stricken Peter, surrounded by Turks and prepared to give up virtually everything when cornered on the Pruth, and the adamant tenacious negotiator from strength of a few years later, who declined to be intimidated by diplomacy into making concessions of any kind.

For twenty-one years war had taken up some 95 per cent of the nation's budget. Some 280,000 conscripts had been raised for a war that remains the longest fought in Europe since 1648. In the course of those twenty-one years the Russians had changed from the army that had taken two years to capture one fortress, Azov, and showed at Narva that there was still scope enough for jokes about the Muscovite military. By the end of the war matters were very different; a French officer serving Peter observed that the Russian army of 1720 would be invincible, if only the officers possessed the courage and determination of the men.[3]

Peter also had a navy – of sorts. The galley fleet was most effective, but many observers considered that Peter had many more ships of the line than was necessary. After all, Russia had no merchant fleet to protect. However, it would be wrong to expect Peter to moderate himself in any matter concerning the navy. His Baltic fleet was somewhat better than the strange and disproportionate creations of Voronezh. Oak timber had started to arrive in quantity from Kazan, though much of it was rotten on arrival. One of the disadvantages of the Neva estuary was that its brackish waters proved deadly to ships' timbers, while the actual ships themselves were not all perfect. They were often badly designed and built in haste. They tended to ride badly and were not particularly fast. One, the *Hangö Head*, for example, launched in 1719, could "bear no sail if it blowed anything hard".[4] More serious still was the lack of seamen. If Peter was short of crew he would simply make the ship's complement up with soldiers,

[3] Coll., 1884, vol. xl, p. 56.   [4] Bridges, p. 67.

so that in one fifty-four gun ship of the line, of a crew of 400 "not thirty are to be found that deserve the character of able seamen at their going out to sea".[5] Russian seamanship was not good; they could not handle ships in a strong wind and indeed the navy never engaged in any sea fight during the war. Russia would have to wait until the reign of Catherine the Great for her first naval victory proper. Of the seventy ships built for the Baltic fleet between 1703 and 1724, forty-seven were either lost, broken up or unseaworthy by the latter date.

Yet characteristically Peter's celebration of his victory over Sweden had a thoroughly nautical air to it:

the Russians in general had a strong aversion to shipping or maritime matters. In order to apprise them of the great advantages arriving from a massive force, in his triumphant entry into Moscow, he represented to his people that the peace, the rejoicings for which were now being celebrated, was obtained by means of his naval strength . . .

The first of the cavalcade was a galley, finely carved and gilt, in which the rowers plied their blades as on the water. The galley was commanded by the high admiral of Russia. Then came a frigate, of sixteen small brass guns, with three masts, completely rigged, manned with twelve or fourteen youths, habited like Dutch skippers, in black velvet, who trimmed the sails and performed all the manœuvres as of a ship at sea. Then came the most nicely decorated barges, whereon sat the empress and the ladies of the court. There were also picket boats heaving the lead and above thirty other vessels ... It was in the month of February, at which time all the ground was covered with snow, and all the rivers frozen. All the machines were placed on sledges, and were drawn by horses, through all the principal streets of Moscow. The ship required alone forty horses to draw it.[6]

The major celebration of victory took place not in Moscow but in St Petersburg. The senate, with the grandees and chief clergy of the empire, went in a body and thanked His Majesty for his fatherly care and the unremitting devotion which he had applied to advance the happiness and prosperity of the empire. They prayed that he would be pleased to receive the grateful

acknowledgement of his faith people and accept the titles
of father of his country, emperor of all the Russias and Peter
the Great.[7]

*   *   *

In 1721 Freiherr von Bergholz accompanied the Duke of Holstein
to St Petersburg, where he was to remain for some years. As he
travelled closer to the capital he found it increasingly difficult
to obtain any food for himself or his horses, since St Petersburg
absorbed all the produce for miles around. He had been to the
city once before, some five years previously, and now found it
so altered that he could scarcely recognise it. The Nevsky Prospekt impressed him the most; stretching across the city with its
double rows of trees on either side he found it the most imposing
sight he had seen in his life – and it is interesting to note that Bergholz had just come from Paris. He was most impressed by its
cleanliness – it was regularly swept by Swedish prisoners of war –
and by the stone paving.

Stone paving was indeed almost essential both on the Nevsky
Prospekt and elsewhere. The process had begun in 1710 because
the streets would otherwise be impassable after any rain. Initially
an order went out to all inhabitants to collect stones, but there
was unfortunately little stone to be had locally so that a second
order was issued: all carters, bargees, boatmen entering the city
were ordered to bring so and so many stones with them on every
journey. The decree was only revoked in 1766.[8]

The Nevsky Prospekt was impressive enough, but not all the
city lived up to it. Petersburg had been somewhat unevenly developed. Another visitor who first went there in the 1720's considered that, far from being a city, it had the appearance of a
"heap of villages bunched together like some plantation in the
West Indies".[9] There were, it is true, some stone houses to be
seen now, notably along the banks of the Neva, "but in the
majority of instances the interior of the houses has not been completed . . . streets have been laid out but are scarcely built on,
just the occasional houses here and there".[10] Many observers
commented on the unfinished quality of the houses; stone façades
there might be, but there was often little else. Buildings stood

[7] Bruce, p. 261.   [8] Luppov, pp. 114–15.
[9] Weber, vol i, p. 4.   [10] Luppov, p. 44.

without floors or ceilings, while in other cases the house itself might remain half-finished, rotting in the cold. This was especially the case on the Vassilevsky Island. Elsewhere it developed more quickly and notably along the banks of the Neva. Rather than the island capital which Peter had envisaged it was becoming a city facing across the river from the "mainland" with an impressive façade of stone buildings and a steadily increasing number of wooden ones behind. Developed with insufficient preparation the houses themselves were not always very sound, however impressive they might appear:

> Those that are built with stone are but indifferent, some others are built with brick covered with mortar on both sides; they seem at first very fine, being built according to a new architecture half French and half Italian, but when that mortar falls to pieces which happens shortly after by reason of the great frosts and other injuries of the air, they have but a disagreeable aspect.[11]

Built in haste to meet the requirements of Peter's plan, it was said that their foundations were so poor that a passing carriage could make them shake.[12]

Peter had continued his policy of peopling the city by decree; for example a decree of October 1715 ordered 12,000 families to settle there. Living conditions were hard, problems of supply made food prices in those years from five to eight times as high as those of Moscow, and the cost of food made it desperately difficult for the poor to feed themselves. They lived on roots and cabbage and scarcely ever saw bread. The city was largely supplied by water and one could regularly see hundreds of barges coming down the Neva from Lake Ladoga laden with food – whenever, that is to say, their passage was not checked by the regularly unfavourable winds. The obligation to reside in the capital, observed the English Captain Perry, "Makes the generality of the nobility uneasy ... There are tears and water enough at Petersburg but they pray God to send them to live again in Moscow."[13] It is incidentally fascinating to see that the famous contrast between Moscow and Petersburg, the one being warm, natural, friendly, cosy, the heart of old Russia, the other cold,

[11] Gordon, A., p. 295.   [12] *Russ. Star.*, 1879, vol. xxv, p. 267.
[13] Perry, p. 263.

artificial, affected, contrived, which runs through so much 19th-century Russian literature, notably the novels of Tolstoy, is already to be found within a few years of the city's foundation. Bergholz, in Moscow for the first time, left a party at the Kremlin to spend three hours with his landlady and her women friends drinking tea and eating jam. He was astounded to find how pleasantly and sociably the inhabitants of Moscow lived, in contrast with those in the capital, having an abundance of food, good cheer and no shortages of any kind.[14] Yet for all the well-founded hostility to St Petersburg, for all the murmuring, Peter's decrees were obeyed without serious question, and much to the amazement of foreign observers who could only conclude that "as far as fear and blind obedience rather than the wisdom of government can carry things the Russians surpass all other nations".[15]

For all its ramshackle development, its gaping patches of waste land and its miseries, the city continued to expand along rational and regular lines. Peter made a serious attempt to oblige all persons of particular trades or professions to reside in particular quarters. It was thus decided that only those working in the docks could live on Admiralty Island, and anyone not so employed was ordered to move to an appropriate quarter.[16] Certain parts of town were designated for the "base people", others for the military. Peter extended his conceptions of order and regularity to the moral sphere, for St Petersburg was the first Russian city to be policed. Peter created the post of Polizeimäster, the first incumbent being a Portuguese Jew from Holland, Anton Devier, whose responsibilities extended well beyond the modern conception of police work. Devier was appointed "to transform the imperial capital into a European city",[17] a task which extended from overseeing the proper conduct of public assemblies to hunting down the wolves which, in 1714, were still to be found on the outskirts and indeed in the centre of town, for in the winter of that year a sentry on duty outside the foundry, near the present Liteiny Most, was pulled down by wolves, together with a comrade who tried to save him.[18]

Peter was determined to civilise his nation, if necessary by decree, and was anxious that his upper classes should adopt European manners. In the latter years of the Northern War they

[14] Busching, 1785, vol. xix, pp. 334–5.   [15] Webber, vol. i, p. 20.
[16] Luppov, p. 590.   [17] Wittram, vol. ii, p. 158.
[18] Weber, vol. i, p. 341.

appeared a strange blend of European and Muscovite. In 1714 the ladies of St Petersburg "wore the French dress, but it seemed to fit uneasy on them, particularly the hoop petticoats, and their black teeth were sufficient proof that they had not yet weaned themselves from that notion so fast riveted in the minds of old Russians that white teeth only became blackamoors and monkeys".[19] In an attempt to impose European manners Peter issued a decree ordering that "every great man at court was to give an assembly a year".[20] Notice to do so would be served on him by the chief of police. The decree went into considerable detail as to the form the assembly should take. It was to begin at 4 p.m. and end at 10. The host was not obliged to meet his guests nor to see them out, simply to provide facilities, tables, chairs, pipes, tobacco, music, food and drink. Assemblies could be attended by nobles, officers, merchants, civil servants, leading figures in the manufactories, not by servants or lackeys. They were by design neither noble nor bourgeois, offering a mixture of conditions, craft, trade and nobility that was unique in the Europe of that time.

They were not initially an unqualified success. Bergholz complained bitterly that smoking and gambling were permitted in rooms reserved for dancing, which made for a terrible "stink and clatter", and that it was impossible to converse with Russian ladies. Between dances one could do no more than eye them in silence as they sat apart from the men on the far side of the room.[21] Peter considered the assemblies to be an interim measure which could be suspended once his subjects began to entertain one another in the appropriate manner of their own free will. Yet for all their aspirations to a European *politesse*, Peter's assemblies were peculiar. One of the most popular attenders was a lieutenant in the guards who was renowned for his ability to laugh very loud and long. Then there was the old courtier who was passionately fond of jelly. He would consume enormous quantities at great speed. On one occasion Peter held open his mouth and then filled it with helping after helping of the stuff. When he was in a good mood Peter would laugh, joke and, according to a contemporary, "act like a child", for example imitating a dancer who was performing in a singularly maladroit albeit vigorous manner. Yet if anyone should happen to annoy him the consequences could be unpleasant. On one occasion Peter

[19] *Ibid.*, p. 27.   [20] *Ibid.*, p. 188.   [21] Busching, 1787, vol. xx, pp. 400–1.

listened for some time to a foreign colonel talking about the war. Clearly his words displeased the czar, who signified displeasure by spitting in the man's face and walking silently away.[22]

Social life in the capital was indeed a strange and somewhat grotesque mixture, combining elements of carnival, court life conducted along recognisably European lines and elaborate ceremonies, almost always accompanied by ringing salvoes of celebratory gunfire and truly daunting quantities of drink. Peter loved to play, by his rules, in the city he had created, and insisted that the rest of the population play with him. For example when flags were flown from certain points in the city all boats of a particular kind, according to the flag in question, had to assemble by the fortress of St Peter and St Paul and process up and down the river. Defaulters were severely fined.[23] Peter's love of gunfire was intense; although in all other respects he was parsimonious to the point of being mean, when it came to the burning of powder in celebration he was prodigal, and ever ready to stage the most elaborate cannonades – to celebrate the anniversary of Poltava, for example – regardless of expense. More private occasions also made ample use of artillery. A guest of Peter's recalls dining to the sound of gunfire as pieces were discharged to accompany each of the numerous toasts.[24] One observer, quite amazed at the amount of powder squandered on public holidays, remarked that the Russians "value powder as if it were sand".[25]

When Bergholz first arrived at court he was surprised to find that in appearance and manners it did not seem to differ vastly from anything he had seen in Germany. There were differences, however. It was strange to feel that all the buildings and gardens were brand new, and had appeared out of nowhere. Besides, not all of them worked. At one banquet he found himself thoroughly drenched because the wooden palace had a leaking roof.[26] Yet leaking roofs were a minor hazard; at his first court gathering in a garden Bergholz suddenly noticed that the guests were showing signs of alarm at the sight of six guardsmen bearing down on them carrying trays with glasses of a vodka which, Bergholz says, could be smelt at a hundred paces. All were obliged to drink, and drink themselves silly, anyone seeking to avoid that fate being denounced by numerous "spies". A suspicious Russian

[22] Knyaz'kov, pp. 625–7.
[23] Busching, 1785, vol. xix, p. 82.
[24] Le Bruyn. pp. 61–2.
[25] Cht., 1892, vol. ii, p. 191.
[26] Busching, 1785, vol. xix, pp. 51–2.

even smelt Bergholz's breath to be sure that he really had had his dose. On this occasion, and indeed regularly, guards were posted on the gates to ensure that no one left before Peter allowed them to do so. Peter's entertainments were all informed by this bullying pattern of enforced hospitality which lay halfway between an entertainment and the deliberate infliction of pain. On Weber's first visit to court:

> After having gulped down at dinner a dozen bumpers of Hungarian wine, I received from the hands of the vice czar Romodanovsky . . . a full quart of brandy and being forced to empty it in two draughts I soon lost my senses, though I had the comfort to observe that the rest of the guests lying already asleep on the floor, were in no condition to make reflection on my little skill in drinking.[27]

The obligation to attend the innumerable banquets, the impossibility of leaving before permission was given, made the foreign population bewail their lack of a pack of cards to pass the time, while the Russians, observed Bergholz, simply drank themselves quietly into a stupor. Anyone who could or would not drink was automatically a target for Peter's bullying and teasing. The Danish resident Just Juel was a favourite butt of the czar, having a weak head and an uneasy sense of dignity which was perpetually at threat. Peter would regularly torment the luckless diplomat for his inability to drink. On one occasion Juel tried humour, begging Peter to allow him to get away with no more than a litre of strong Hungarian wine. Peter insisted that it would have to be two. Jokingly, Juel fell to his knees and asked for one and a half. Peter, observing that he could kneel as well as the next fellow, joined him on the ground, where they both remained, each reluctant to be the first to rise, and drinking themselves silly, until Juel lurched to his feet and heard his request refused.[28] He promised a priest close to Peter that if only he could persuade the czar to stop forcing him to drink he would finance the building of a monastery.

Peter's mocking and elaborate sense of humour comes through in the accounts of his enforced entertainments. There is the well-known occasion when he ordered his entire court together with foreign representatives to assemble to see a demonstration by a

[27] Weber, vol. i, p. 5.　　　　[28] Cht., 1899, vol. ii, p. 266.

strong man on April 1, 1719. The audience was obliged to wait for two whole hours before a cloud was let down on to the stage bearing the word "April" on it in German and in Russian.[29] The same author tells an even stranger tale of Peter's behaviour as a host. After a drunken evening, "Whereupon we quite lost our senses and were in that pickle carried off to sleep, some in the garden, others in the wood, and the rest here and there on the ground", they were woken at 4 a.m., each given a hatchet, and the czar and his guests proceeded to cut a walk through some trees to the shore. After three hours' hard chopping they got through and had recovered from their hangovers. Peter thanked them. At supper they were once more obliged to drink themselves senseless, only to be roused at midnight and made to proceed to the bedside of the Prince of Circassia and his wife where they drank till four in the morning. At eight they were invited to court for breakfast, where brandy was drunk again, then they were obliged to ride past under the czar's windows mounted on eight comically miserable jades. There was more drinking before they went on board Peter's yacht just as a gale was getting up. Crew and visitors alike prepared themselves for death, but they reached their destination safely after seven hours' rough sailing, whereupon Peter said "Good night, gentlemen, this was carrying the jest too far".[30]

At public gatherings Peter was both playful and unpredictable. He was in the habit of announcing his departure from such occasions by beating out the appropriate tattoo on his drum. Yet play was accompanied by a certain alertness, awareness of what he was doing. There are times when his behaviour seemed calculated to put his subjects, and foreign diplomats, where he wanted them: at a disadvantage. On one occasion Juel contrived to leave a gathering early and by 10 p.m. was asleep. Peter noticed his absence shortly after midnight and sent two officers to fetch him back. Juel sadly observed that ambassadors had to drink and comply if they were ever to hope to catch the czar's ear. Peter's merciless teasing and bullying of the luckless Dane derived partly from his sense of fun, but was also an exercise of his authority. Rejecting out of hand traditional protocol and court ritual he imposed what amounted to a ritual of his own, which he created, controlled and enjoyed, as was the case with the all-drunken synod. He was its master and it gave him a considerable measure

[29] Weber, vol. i, p. 264.   [30] *Ibid.*, p. 93.

of control – in this case over an ambassador. Whatever persons such as Juel might think of their ambassadorial dignity, they were obliged to cast such dignity aside when dealing with the "all-joking czar".

Even more alarming than this enforced drinking was Peter's enthusiasm for various skills and crafts, especially medical ones. He prided himself on his prowess as a dentist, and woe betide anyone who entered his presence with toothache, for Peter would have the offending tooth, and possibly others, out in a trice. Bergholz's diary contains numerous entries of the following sort:

> The duchess of Mecklenburg is very worried in case the emperor should come to see her soon about her bad foot, because he believes himself to be a great surgeon, he gladly undertakes operations of all kind.[31]

The operations were dangerous. Peter persuaded the luckless wife of a Dutch merchant to let him operate on her dropsy, and boasted that he had extracted at least twenty pounds of liquid. Unfortunately the patient died soon afterwards. Peter's enthusiasm and wilfulness were thus a perpetual threat to his entourage. Small wonder that some acrobats who entertained Peter should have given his courtiers cause for alarm:

> The czar took particular note of everything, especially of one that danced to perfection on the rope; this has given some jealousy and fear to some of the boyars lest they should be forced to learn that art.[32]

The coarse atmosphere of the court, and notably the acute and universal drunkenness which was a necessary element in all assemblies that Peter attended, was the cause of frequent and violent public quarrels. There were numerous fallings out that sometimes came to blows, wild punches or hopeless grapplings between Russians and foreigners alike. Yet curiously there was remarkably little duelling. Peter's decrees forbidding it had been almost totally successful – in contrast with similar prohititions in France. This would suggest that his courtiers were both more obedient and less concerned with their *point d'honneur* than their Gallic counterparts. Thus actions were allowed to pass which would have led either to a duel or utter dishonour anywhere else

[31] Busching, 1786, vol. xx, p. 417.   [32] Coll., 1881, vol. lxi, pp. 509–10.

in Europe. At one shipboard celebration where a great deal had been drunk Admiral Cruys gave one of his flag officers such a smack in the face that he knocked him under the table and took his wig off into the bargain.[33] On another occasion, when a ship was being launched, Peter had closeted himself in an upper cabin with a lady, and had sentries posted. Below the rest of the company continued to drink:

> The admiral was so drunk that he wept like a child … Prince Menshikov was so drunk that he fell to the floor deadly sick … In a word nobody was sober and if one were to recount all the foolishness that occurred in those hours it would fill a few sheets of paper.[34]

Inevitably it was left to the luckless and solemn Juel to fall foul of Peter on such an occasion. He was very drunk and made three attempts to escape from the ship, but Peter always had him brought back. He went on deck to be sick, but Peter sent for him once more. On this occasion Juel protested that he was too ill; Peter's officers tried to force him below but he clung obstinately to the rail. They were joined by others who prised him away and cursed him in the coarsest language. Peter then joined in, very drunk and no less coarse, threatening to complain to his king that he had laid a hand to his sword in his presence – which he had, in order to discourage the abusive officers. Juel replied that he had still greater grounds for complaint, at which an intoxicated emperor asked him for his sword and had him put ashore in a rage. The sword was returned that evening, and the next morning Peter sent his apologies, saying, with the regular reply of the drinking amnesiac, that he could remember nothing of the previous day's proceedings but would like to apologise for any offence he might have caused.[35]

Besides such private occasions Peter prescribed elaborate entertainments of a more public kind, which sometimes lasted for several days. There were frequent fancy-dress parades arranged at his command: witness entries in Bergholz's diary such as the following:

> The fourth was a rest day [i.e. from the masquerade], but we all had to go about in our masks all day.[36]

[33] Busching, 1788, vol. xxi, p. 301.
[34] Ibid., 1785, vol. xix, p. 94.
[35] Cht., 1899, vol. ii, p. 198.
[36] Busching, 1788, vol. xxi, p. 318.

The masquerade in question was an eight-day affair, carefully planned with the movement of the thousand masked participants regulated by cannon shots. Peter was disguised as a Dutch skipper or a ship's drummer; Catherine was a Friesian peasant woman; Menshikov and several others went as the mayor of Hamburg (apparently a particularly ornate costume). Others dressed as babies, or even birds. Solemnly the masks processed around the city – Peter had ordered that every house should be illuminated for the masquerade's duration. The chief of police had been ordered to ensure that no one, including women, returned home sober. Some ladies who attempted to escape were arrested and obliged to drink themselves silly on the very worst wine.[37] The occasion coincided with an entertainment of a more grotesque sort; the marriage of the new Prince-Pope Buturlin, who succeeded Zotov, to the latter's eighty-year-old widow. The ceremony was followed by a meeting of the Pope and his chapter of cardinals, who were reduced to the statutory state of abject drunkenness. After a banquet the newly married couple were conducted to a wooden pyramid built in front of the Senate House to celebrate the victory of Hangö. It was illuminated within and contained a marriage bed made of hops, surrounded with barrels of wine, beer and spirits. The couple were obliged to drink still more in the presence of the czar, from vessels made in the shape of the male and female sexual organs – both, observed Bergholz, of fairly considerable size. They were then left alone in the pyramid with the company observing them through holes in the sides made to that end.[38]

Crueller still was the wedding Peter arranged, against their will, between a couple of dwarfs. They were given an elaborate send-off. It began with a procession led by a richly dressed dwarf, the marshal, then came bride, groom and thirty-six couples of dwarfs, the property of Peter, Menshikov and Catherine. Onlookers found the procession particularly funny since the dwarfs had to wear foreign dress and being mostly peasants were unable to walk or behave properly. Peter held one of the crowns over the married couple in church; all six foot seven of him. There was much giggling during the service and the priest could hardly speak for laughter. After the marriage the guests processed to Menshikov's palace. Six little oval tables had been prepared in the centre of the hall, with miniature chairs and cutlery, while

[37] *Ibid.*, 1785, vol. xix, pp. 126–7.   [38] *Ibid.*, *loc. cit.*

the "grown-ups" sat around the sides to watch the dwarfs disport themselves. They entertained the company by dancing in the Russian style, much to the general amusement. One eye-witness found them reminiscent of dachshunds.[39] They were so drunk that they could scarcely crawl, let alone dance; however, there were many amusing sights, Juel considered, as they slapped one another's faces and tore at their beards. The only pity of it was that they could not fire off the miniature cannon that had been specially cast for the occasion, since Menshikov's son, his only son, was not very well. In fact he died that night. Bride and groom spent their wedding night in Peter's apartments. She would later die in childbirth and marriages between dwarfs were forbidden from that moment on.

Peter's masquerades, pageants, ceremonies and entertainments had more than a streak of cruelty in them. They went well beyond Russian traditions of aggressive hospitality, and can really amaze us by their callousness. Curiously, it is Menshikov's dying son that really sticks in the craw – he gave a magnificent party to celebrate his own name day a week or so after his bereavement. Yet beyond such particular details there remains Peter's taste for the spectacle of human weakness, his own included, and his grotesque and playful sense of pageantry and carnival. One of carnival's principal characteristics is that it should turn the world upside down, reverse roles, put slaves above their masters for a day, and upset all conventions of order, dignity and piety. Blasphemy and profanity too are integral features. Traditional carnival frequently involved the election of a king or pope, who was accompanied by his bishops and enthroned with suitable solemnity.[40] All these features are to be found in the social life of Peter's capital. One cannot attempt to deny Peter's ceremonies their crude and cruel aspects, but nor can one deny them a certain rude exuberance, energy, a humour of sorts and the great charge of ironic glee and gusto which Peter devoted to the turning of his subjects' world upside down.

[39] *Russ. Star.*, 1882, vol. xxxvi, p. 309.
[40] Bakhtine, *Le Poétique de Dostoevsky*, Paris 1970, pp. 170–1.

CHAPTER FOURTEEN

The Reforms

Peter is sometimes referred to by Russian historians as the czar transformer, and properly so. The transformations he brought about were both wide-ranging and far-reaching, if not invariably successful. They vary in scope tremendously, from extensive changes in the pattern of government to edicts drawn up in Peter's hand concerned with details that ought to have been beneath the czarish notice, but all are measures inspired by his extraordinary if haphazard and restless energy, and by the desire to improve his people whether they liked it or not. If any one aim emerges from the confused assortment of measures and decrees it is the desire to use his absolute authority to make government more efficient, to encourage his people, using force if necessary, to devote themselves to the service of Russia, to develop the economy of the country, to educate the upper classes, compelling them to acquire skills necessary for the country's continuing well-being. Peter's transformations are the products of an absolutist paternalism which brooked no resistance. He was always ready to hope that others shared both his energy, his vision and his unqualified devotion to his country. Regularly he would discover that this was anything but the case, at which point he would resort to force. He was well aware of the extent of his nation's capacity for what he would consider to be sloth, but which others might view as lack of curiosity and innate resistance to change. He was not always complimentary about his subjects. The Brunswick resident, Weber, recalls him referring to them as:

A herd of beasts whom he put into the shape of man, but

despaired of ever breaking their obstinacy or rooting up the perverseness of their hearts.[1]

Elsewhere he compared them to children who had to be forced to learn the alphabet, but would one day be grateful for their lessons.[2] He once wrote in a letter:

> You know well that our people do not accept innovation, however greatly it benefit them, unless they be compelled.[3]

Peter seems to have seen himself, and certainly others saw him, as pitting his colossal energies against the massive sum of his nation's inert resistance. The contemporary economist Pososhkov described him as trying to pull his way up a mountain with the strength of ten men while a million sought to hold him back.[4]

This image of one man pitted against a nation is not too preposterous an exaggeration: Peter's greatest mistake was his failure to surround himself with sufficient numbers of likeminded persons who would carry through both spirit and letter of his reforms without getting their hands caught in the till in the process. Peter's natural violence and impatience with all who failed to share his tastes and sympathies comes out all too clearly in the style of his government; he never hesitated to use cruelty and compulsion in case other methods should fail. Peter knew quite well that he was considered by many to be a cruel tyrant. The charge of cruelty he rejected out of hand, while feeling authority to be essential to the government of Russia:

> They say that I am cruel; that is what foreigners think of me, but who are they to judge. They do not know what the situation was at the beginning of my reign, and how many were opposed to my plans, and brought about the failure of projects which would have been of great benefit to my country, obliging me to arm myself with the greatest severity; but I have never been cruel ... I have always asked for the cooperation of those of my subjects in whom I have perceived intelligence and patriotism, and who, agreeing with my views, were ready to support them.[5]

[1] Weber, vol. i, p. 18. [2] Knyaz'kov, p. 150.
[3] Wittram, vol. ii, p. 128. [4] Pososhkov, p. 41.
[5] Staehlin, p. 224.

As for the charge of tyranny:

> Foreigners say that I rule over slaves. I rule over subjects that obey my decrees. The decrees do good, not harm to the country. English liberty has no place here ... You need to know the nation and how it must be governed ... Whoever does no evil and pursues the good is free ... I do not increase slavery through wanting the good, I correct the obstinate and wish to soften the hard of heart; when I change the way my subjects dress, bring order to the army and to the citizenry and teach them social graces I am not being cruel. I am not being a tyrant when justice condemns an evil man to death.[6]

The passage is revealing, exposing not only his dedication but also his most critical limitations. His people had to pay a heavy price for Peter's generally well-founded and quite unshakeable belief that he was right and that anyone disagreeing with him must needs be wrong. This often had a narrowing effect, making him intolerant of any kind of opposition. Opposition to his reforms, he considered to be a form of sin, witness the talk of good and evil above. Indeed, in a conversation with Pososhkov Peter referred to resistance to innovation as literally evil, considering his policy of reform to be a battle against sin itself. He justified the violence of his methods also: "Without such terror I do not believe that it would be possible to seek out and destroy the root of evil."[7]

For all his cruelty the results of Peter's activities impressed foreign observers tremendously. Charles Whitworth, writing in 1710, found that in ten years he had improved his empire more than any other had done in a hundred "merely by the strength of his own genius, observation and example".[8] Of course there was more to it than that. The fact that many of his reforms took root and survived him suggests that his nation was perhaps more ready for them than appeared the case; an eventual Westernization was inevitable. However, there can be no doubt that Peter personally accelerated the process to an astonishing degree.

By no means all the reforms can be considered the work of a cruel but benevolent despot forcing his people into enlightenment. Many of the early ones in particular were simple ways

[6] Maikov, p. 82.   [7] Soloviev, vol. viii, p. 532.   [8] Whitworth, p. 58.

of raising revenue to pay for Peter's navy and his war. A whole host of new taxes were devised in the early years of the century, ranging from government-stamped paper for legal transactions to taxes on funerals, marriages and baths. Besides these, there were lucrative state monopolies in salt, tobacco, rhubarb; taxes on beards, Muscovite harness, dress, and even coffins. Old Believers were allowed to keep their faith, but paid double rates of taxation, and like the Cathars before them and others later had to wear a yellow star designating them as heretics.

Fiscal considerations also brought about another kind of reform which affected the raw material of all Peter's undertakings, the peasantry. In pre-Petrine Russia there had been various categories of peasant: personal slaves, serfs bound to the land, serfs bound by temporary contract, and freemen. One of the advantages of personal slavery was exemption from tax. By the end of Peter's reign these distinctions were abolished. Slaves and serfs became one single category, bound to their master in perpetuity and obliged, of course, to pay taxes. Various categories of peasant that had previously enjoyed a certain degree of liberty were now incorporated into a new class, the state serf, which formed half the peasant population and belonged to the state as other serfs belonged to their masters. A third and final category was the factory serf, assigned to work in the new industries that Peter was trying to build up. In short Peter had simplified and transformed the nature of human bondage in his country. There had hitherto been various types of bondage, with varying degrees of limitation of freedom; the peasants were now all turned into slaves proper, whose sole right seemed to be the right to pay. The power of their owners over them was unlimited; they could be bought and sold as cattle. For peasants there were now only three possibilities: slavery, the galleys or the army. Peter's reforms might have simplified their position, but could scarcely be said to have improved it. Henceforth they would enjoy a degree of servitude more complete than any they had known before.

By no means all Peter's reforms were fiscal; from the earliest years he had concerned himself with education, establishing schools of mathematics and navigation in Moscow, and yet another teaching geography, ethics, politics and dancing. He also encouraged the development of printing, and took a great interest in the design of a new Russian alphabet with a reduced number of letters of simplified nature, entering into the detailed discussion of the form of individual characters at the height of the Northern War. It was also in the early 1700's that the first Russian newspaper or gazette appeared – *News of Military and Other Events Deserving of Knowledge and Recollection*. Plans for education and dissemination of knowledge grew increasingly ambitious, culminating in a decree of February 24, 1714, establishing compulsory primary education for the children of noblemen and civil servants. They were required to learn arithmetic and elementary geometry and were forbidden to marry until they had done so,[9] a marriage licence only being granted on production of a certificate of competence. However, all pupils had to leave school at fifteen: the time when their obligatory and lifelong service to the state began. The decree, as was sometimes the case with Peter's edicts, did not have much effect. A school inspector of Pskov, Novgorod, Yaroslav, Moscow and Vologda reported in 1719 the existence of twenty-six pupils, all the sons of priests, at the Yaroslav school, while all other schools were empty. We do not know whether there was any falling off in the rate of marriages.

Peter was always ready to try to mobilise the youth of his nation on a generous scale. "In 1704 Peter personally interviewed over 8000 youths who had been summoned to Moscow from the provinces. The interviews were followed by the distribution of the youths among regiments and schools. In 1712 those living at home or studying in schools were ordered to present themselves at the chancellery of the senate in Moscow, from here they were sent by carriage to St Petersburg to be examined, and there were divided into three categories according to their ages. The youngest were sent to Reval to study navigation; the next group were sent to Holland for the same purpose; the eldest were turned into soldiers."[10] It is a splendidly arbitrary Petrine gesture – reminiscent of the occasion on which he turned the cab drivers of Moscow into a regiment of marines.

The sending of young men abroad had already begun in the latter years of the preceding century. The process had mixed results, usually being initiated by decree:

We have received news from Italy that in Venice they wish to accept our young people into naval service training, today the French have also replied saying that they too are willing to

[9] Klyuchevsky, p. 96.   [10] *Ibid.*, p. 93.

accept our trainees. Consequently select immediately in the Petersburg schools children of well-to-do nobles, bring them to Reval and place them aboard ships.[11]

The unfortunates so selected did not have the easiest of times. The British ambassador was appalled to learn that Peter, who was sending thirty young noblemen to England at his own expense, expected them to earn their keep as common seamen, excused no labour or duty.[12] However, or possibly as a result, residence abroad frequently failed to have the desired effect, or at least not immediately. Weber found the Russians sent abroad "largely brutish and full of vice, while those who achieved politeness soon cast it off on their return".[13] Peter seems to have resigned himself to occasional failures. He sent a favourite, I. M. Golovkin, to Venice to study Italian and galley construction. On his return Peter interrogated him and found that he had learnt nothing of galleys.

"Did you learn Italian?"
Golovkin conceded that he had not picked up a lot.
"What did you do?"
"Sire, I smoked tobacco, drank wine, had fun and learnt to play the bass, and went out seldom."

For once Peter was amused, not enraged. He christened Golovkin Prince of the Bass and had him painted smoking a pipe, surrounded by musical instruments, while his tools lay neglected in a corner.[14]

Neplyuev was another young man sent abroad for naval training. He saw a little service on Venetian galleys in the company of some twenty other Russians, before being sent to Cadiz naval academy. There the Russians were kept terribly short of funds. They pleaded for active service, only to be told that Spain had just seven galleys in all and that they were in Sicily. One of the Russians died, another went mad. Earlier, in Corfu, one had killed another after an evening at cards. Yet another deserted to become a monk on Mount Athos, whence he wrote to his ex-colleagues asking them to send on the money he was expecting from his father. On his return Neplyuev and his companions

[11] Dmytryshkin, p. 12.
[12] Coll., 1884, vol. xxxix, p. 294.
[13] Weber, vol. ii, pp. 18–19.
[14] Maikov, p. 135.

found themselves unpopular among their contemporaries for having been away, mocked by friends and relations for the alteration in the manners.[15]

The most significant of Peter's reforms concerned the pattern of government; from the administration of towns to the administration of the country as a whole, everything was reworked more than once over the years, in a manner that was frequently confused and insufficiently thought out. We have already seen one wave of urban reform in 1699 designed to increase taxation yield. In the course of the Northern War it became clear that the traditional administrative machine could not meet the demands that Peter placed upon it. The old system had been headed by the council of boyars, or *duma*, which administered a series of offices or *prikazy*. These had spheres of competence that frequently overlapped with one another, making for considerable confusion. For example many offices were responsible for justice in various areas, and it could happen that one office administered a particular town in one capacity, another in a different one. Certain offices were responsible for some aspect of government throughout the nation, others had localised responsibilities. Into the bargain each office was assigned a certain number of towns from which it collected taxes to pay for its own running. There were some forty such offices in the late 17th century, making for a considerable degree of confusion and malpractice, particularly since there was nothing approaching the separation of powers — executive and judicial functions not being distinguished in any way.

Some remodelling took place in Peter's early years. The Admiralty Office was formed to deal with the fleet, the Military Naval Office with foreign seamen, while the most interesting addition, the Preobrazhensky Office, was the father of the Russian secret police. In addition Peter had established a Privy Chancellery to control all state finance. This was eventually incorporated into the *duma*. Originally a council of boyars with some authority, it had gradually been reduced in size to become a purely administrative body, working directly under Peter and not confined to persons of rank — something in other words not unlike the French *conseil d'état*.

Among the many disadvantages of this administrative system was the fact that taxes raised locally had to go to Moscow before

[15] Neplyuev, p. 90.

they could be returned to meet local needs, and the taxes tended to evaporate en route. Peter's solution was to decentralise. Many of the offices were already responsible for the administration of vast areas, e.g. Siberia. Peter now extended the principle, dividing his country up into nine provinces and appointing local governors to administer them. His chief aim was to create a system of taxation whereby "everybody should know from where the required receipts were coming".[16] In 1708 a total of 341 towns were variously assigned to the eight enormous provinces which made up Russia. Three years later an extra province, Voronezh, was formed, based on a group of towns whose contributions were to go entirely towards naval construction. The army, on the other hand, was divided among the eight provinces for its maintenance, total military expenditure being similarly divided. The actual provinces were broken down into smaller units. The governors were at first supposed to work with small boards of persons known as *landraty*, in theory elected by the nobility but in fact chosen from lists drawn up by the selfsame governors. However, this attempt to combine governors and local administrators was singularly unsuccessful, since the *landraty* were supposed to be the equals of the governor as members of the executive council, while remaining his subordinates as provincial administrators.

The historian Klyuchevsky was not impressed by Peter's provincial reforms which, he said, "show neither forethought nor wisdom. The aim of the reforms was purely fiscal. The provincial institutions had a repulsive characteristic, they were presses to squeeze money out of the taxpayer and were concerned less and less with the well-being of the people."[17] We find a similar degree of confusion in urban administration. Peter encouraged the towns to manage their own affairs. However, by encouraging or insisting upon participation in local government, it should be realised that Peter was conferring obligations, forms of service, and not privileges or exemptions of any kind, as was the case in the France of the *ancien régime*. Here too his system was confused. While making urgent efforts to have the towns administer themselves, he restored to local governors all the powers that they had enjoyed before the reforms of 1699, giving them authority over the officers of local government. On the one hand he intended local merchants' guilds and the urban administration to be subordinate solely to the central authority of the capital; on

[16] Klyuchevsky, p. 192.   [17] *Ibid.*, p. 198.

238

the other, he also subordinated them to the local authority of regional governors. Inevitably the attempt to establish local government along such lines proved a failure.

When he created eight, later nine, provinces Peter had left his country without a central administrative body. There was a council of ministers, but this met casually and was not a permanent affair. It would appear that it was in order to fill this gap that Peter created the senate. This body was to be responsible for the administration of domestic affairs, though it had nothing to do with foreign policy or the military. Peter intended it to run the country in his absence, and accordingly gave it authority over the provincial governors. However, it had no privileges, no legislative powers, and would always remain accountable to Peter for the authority it exercised. It soon became clear that the senate needed subordinate departments if it was not to get bogged down in detail. After much investigation, and partly on the recommendation of the philosopher Leibniz, Peter chose the system of administrative colleges based upon the Swedish pattern. These were collective bodies which would be responsible for foreign affairs, state revenue, justice, the army, the admiralty, commerce, mines and manufactures, state expenditure. Unlike the earlier offices, their fields of competence were carefully delineated and their authority covered the whole country. Business was conducted on the principle of collective consultation, a principle Peter had come to believe in even for the army. No general was ever authorised to take a decision without a preliminary council of war "even if this had to take place on horseback".

The czar had high hopes for his new institutions. He announced that the year the colleges were founded would be as important as the year of Poltava. He expected the system, which was tantamount to government by executive committee, to be a marvellous training ground for young administrators; it would be imbued with the spirit of "justice and liberty".[18] Each college was to consist of a board of eleven, president and a vice-president. Understandably enough in view of the total lack of native understanding of the new system, Peter had recruiting difficulties. Attempts were made to recruit Slavs from the Austrian empire to staff the bodies, but these failed. In 1717 Peter invited volunteers from the large population of Swedish prisoners of war

[18] Knyaz'kov, p. 196.

throughout the country, but here too he was not especially successful since the war seemed to be drawing to a close and they could hope for early repatriation.

The system finally went into operation in 1720. However, Peter was to be disappointed with his reform. It did not produce the instant improvement he had hoped for. There was interference between the colleges and the senate, notably because the collegiate presidents had been promoted senators which meant that they did not have the time to fill either office properly. They were in due course ordered to keep their places in the senate and to appoint successors in the colleges. Other kinds of confusion arose from the lack of a properly coordinated plan. The change in administrative structures had taken place in a somewhat haphazard fashion. For all the work Peter and his collaborators had put into the system they had not thought matters through adequately. "When commencing their reforms they did not first impose limits to them. Borrowing the college system from the West, they did not understand that they would have to restructure the senate, and did not realise at once that all the colleges concerned the provinces, which made it necessary to coordinate those two administrative levels."[19] In short there was a certain lack of foresight and overview. Indeed at no stage did Peter appear to have any grasp of the overall patterns of administration. His practical and impulsive mode of thought did not lend itself easily to abstract thinking and planning. He remained content to string together a series of piecemeal solutions. The first results were short of perfection and disappointed him bitterly, yet the system came right in the end, as senate and colleges learned to cooperate and formed the basis for the pattern of Russian administration for many years.

Along with such major reforms Peter regularly issued various decrees detailed almost to the point of triviality, and which bear witness to his peculiar sense of perspective – or lack of it. Thus he announced the discovery of some waters near Olonetz which contained iron and had curative properties. He laid down the most elaborate set of orders as to their use. These involved resting for several days before taking the water and resisting the temptation to sit or lie down after consuming the dose. Patients should have a good meal afterwards, with a glass of vodka before, and a glass or two of hock or burgundy with it. The decree also goes

[19]Knyaz'kov, p. 202.

into some detail as to the proper diet to be pursued.[20] Patients should obey the instructions strictly, since the waters were God's gift and must not be used irrationally. A year later he declared his anger at the discovery that certain persons had failed to observe the rules. They were thus abusing the priceless gift of God. Henceforth no one would be permitted to take the waters without medical supervision.[21]

Peter brought his sense of detail to agricultural improvement. An edict of 1721 ordered peasants from the western provinces to be sent into Russia at harvest time in order to teach the use of the scythe to local, sickle-bearing peasants. By next year all peasants were to use scythes. He also concerned himself with details such as the proper way to tan leather. A decree of December 1715 ordered the discontinuing of the traditional method of tanning by birch bark. This was inefficient, since the leather was insufficiently waterproof. Henceforth leather was to be tanned with fish oil and anyone caught using the old method would be expropriated and sent to the galleys for life.[22] Other decrees concern matters such as how to build a stove, stipulating the proper circumference of the stove pipe and insisting the stove be built upon the foundations of the house and not upon the floor.[23]

He also went to considerable lengths to develop domestic industries – with mixed success. Thus as we have seen he failed to establish a tapestry factory; owing to the lack of the right kind of wool the master craftsmen imported from France had nothing to do. He was no more successful in his attempts to establish the manufacture of silk. In his attempts to build up domestic industries Peter often resorted to compulsion. His regular method was to create a monopoly and oblige someone to take it up. Thus a decree of 1711 establishes a linen factory in Moscow complete with plant and skilled foreign labour. It was to be given to the merchants Andrei Turka and Stepan Sinbalshikov. Should they make a profit they would be rewarded, and fined were they to make a loss. The principle of coercion was taken to the point that actual force was exerted. One cloth factory required the presence of soldiers to make a reluctant company agree to take it on.[24] The notion of a government encouraging private enterprise

---

[20] Tumansky, vol. ix, pp. 203–8.　　　[21] Wittram, vol. ii, p. 127.

[22] Ibid., p. 135.　　　[23] Knyaz'kov, pp. 148–9.

[24] Wittram, vol. ii, pp. 35–6.

by armed force is an unfamiliar one. In the short run and by dint of various kinds of stimulus and coercion Peter succeeded in setting up a whole series of new industries. By the time of his death some 230 different factories had been established,[25] although not many of them survived him. There were successes though, notably in the field of mining and metallurgy which expanded greatly during his reign and continued to flourish as Russia's major industry. Metal works were developed in Tula, Olonetz, the Urals and St Petersburg, while the ordnance factory at Tula provided weapons for the entire army. Peter's reign also saw the extensive development of copper mining and working. In 1718 Russian foundries produced 104,464 tons of iron and 3214 tons of copper.

In some respects certainly the edicts, reforms and decrees of Peter seem haphazard, the work of impulse. Something – peasants in a field with scythes – would catch his eye, and a decree would go off; next year it was to be scythes for all Russian peasants or the galleys for life. Certainly a great many of such "impulse decrees" never got beyond the statute book, and yet there is a sense in which Peter did have an overall design, or at least a vision, a sense of thrust. Very much, in this respect, a ruler of the enlightenment, he believed in the power of authority to compel his subjects to improve their lot, combining compulsion with education. In some ways he anticipated the attitudes of the 18th-century French *économistes* who believed in the use of the unrestrained power of the state to change its subjects for the better through benevolent authoritarianism. "*L'état fait des hommes ce qu'il veut*" is one of their principal tenets.

Peter wanted a regulated, indeed a regular kingdom, a regularity reflected in a different way in his conception of St Petersburg, with its architecture governed by decree and official design. Moreover, he conceived of a Russia in which every citizen would devote his entire adult life to service, in emulation of Peter's own example. Service went together with regularisation. We have already seen how he regularised the position of the peasantry – by creating three simple categories of servitude. He applied similar principles of regularity and service to the status of the nobility to create one of the most important of all his reforms. He decreed that all members of the landowning classes were to "appear" at court, from all over Russia, half at Moscow, half at St Petersburg. This was partly intended as a form of census,

[25] Klyuchevsky, p. 148.

partly in order to make suitable appointments. All landowners were obliged to serve, from the age of fifteen to death: two-thirds in the armed services, one-third in the more lucrative and less onerous civil administration. Thus, where in past reigns service had been largely intermittent and military service confined to times of war, Peter now formalised his conception of service as a lifetime obligation. He did so through the so-called Table of Ranks, by which all officers and officials, civil and military, were classified according to fourteen parallel grades. Just as Peter himself had "risen from the ranks" and just as all his officers began their military service as privates in the guards or even in line regiments, so every state servant had to begin on the bottom rung. Promotion was gained by a combination of seniority and merit. Moreover, standing in the service was to take precedence over privilege of birth in every respect. Peter conceived of his hierarchy as the basis of a genuine service aristocracy *ouvert aux talents*. Anyone of any origin, Russian or foreign, who reached the eighth grade in the hierarchy, "whatever their birth become the equals of the best and the most ancient noble families and enjoy the same dignity and advantages together with their children". Thus in place of an aristocracy based on birth, Peter substituted a service bureaucracy open to talents and foreigners, paving the way for that steady influx of Germans who would play an increasingly prominent part in the government of Russia over the years to come.

Peter also altered the status of the nobility in another respect: by changing the laws of succession. He did not, as has sometimes been said, establish the principle of primogeniture. Rather he established the principle of sole succession whereby estates could no longer be divided up among a series of sons. A particular son had to be designated as the sole heir in order to avoid excessive subdivision of inheritance. "Disinherited" sons of landowners were exempt from their service obligations since these were directly attached to the holding of land. Peter decreed that it should not be held a dishonour to himself or his family should any such person become a merchant. However, it would seem that the edict was not entirely effective. Landowners continued to subdivide their estates as if it had never been executed.[26] In the words of Klyuchevsky, the decree "merely succeeded in complicating property rights and in bringing economic chaos to agriculture".[27]

[26] *Ibid.*, p. 111.   [27] *Ibid., loc. cit.*

Peter reduced the authority and prestige of the old families, putting in their place a bureaucracy largely dependent upon the recognition of its achivements by the state. The shift assisted the evolution of a kind of absolutism that was largely independent of European models in which the nobility possessed rights and privileges, indeed a prestige and moral authority, which enabled it to constitute some kind of check upon the power of the central authority: Montesquieu's conception of an aristocracy forming an "intermediary body" which might act as a brake upon the power of the throne. The Russian nobility was simply incorporated into an administrative system designed to execute the sovereign's will. It should be recalled, however, that in Petrine Russia, the gap between intention and effective execution was always greater than it might seem on paper. One suspects that the burden of a lifetime's service with only occasional bouts of leave to supervise the administration of one's estates was less crushing than it might seem, and the obligation to "appear" at Moscow or St Petersburg to be registered for service was not impossible to avoid. "Russia is great, you cannot master her", as the serfs of Moscow once observed to the mutinous *streltsy*.

As important as Peter's reform of the nobility was his reform of the church, also conducted according to principles of regularisation, which in this case meant the incorporation of the church into the administrative framework of the state. The principal architect of Peter's ecclesiastical reform was a Ukrainian, Theophan Prokopovich, head of the Kiev Academy. Learned, intelligent and utterly sympathetic to Peter's intentions and principles, he was the author of a textbook of moral and religious instruction which would remain the last word on the subject for a century. It is a fascinating document which stresses throughout that the first moral duty of a citizen is obedience – to the czar. Thus in its commentaries on the commandments it qualifies "Thou shalt not kill" with the observation that this does not apply to soldiers when they are obeying orders, for "It is the duty of kings to see that war is undertaken for just causes".[28] The commandment to "honour thy father and thy mother" is expanded to include "others who exercise parental authority over us ... Subjects like good sons must honour the czar."[29] All lesser authorities were to be accorded appropriate veneration. The chief

[28] Garrard, p. 97.   [29] *Ibid.*, p. 91.

purpose of the text was to establish a hierarchy of power which culminates "under God" in the czar, to whom the ecclesiastical, civil and military authorities of the state were subject and to whom all the lesser "Orders of paternal authority and their subjects owed ultimate obedience".[30] Prokopovich shared Peter's view of the proper relationship of church and state, whereby all power, both religious and secular, were ultimately vested in the hands of the monarch. This was the attitude which formed the basis of his *Ecclesiastical Regulation* of 1721, a reform which placed the Russian orthodox church in unequivocal subordination to the state – a position which it has enjoyed ever since.

The regulation formally abolished the office of patriarch, which would not be restored for some two centuries, putting in its stead an "Ecclesiastical College". Prokopovich produced nine good reasons for the decision, almost all of them practical rather than spiritual, based on administrative convenience and the advantages of the college system which was preferred to "one man rule" and suited to "a monarchical state such as our Russia",[31] because "simple people cannot distinguish the spiritual power from the sovereign power, and suppose that a supreme spiritual pastor is a second ruler, the spiritual authority being regarded as higher and better than the temporal".[32] The administrative body which was to head the Russian church was established as the Holy Governing Synod, a title of Peter's own devising. It consisted of a President, Vice-President and eight other members appointed by Peter, although unlike the other colleges it was not subject to the authority of the senate.

It is remarkable that Peter met so little resistance to what amounted to the total elimination of any kind of ecclesiastical independence. The little there was he dealt with characteristically. On one occasion when the synod actually submitted a request to re-appoint a patriarch, Peter is said to have drawn his hunting knife, slammed it on the table and, striking his chest with his other hand, shouted angrily, "Here is your patriarch!"[33] Lack of resistance was accounted for by contemporary observers by the indifferent quality of the orthodox clergy[34] and by the continual sapping of orthodox energies through the schism. For

[30] *Ibid.*, p. 94.
[31] *Ibid.*, p. 102.
[32] Bain, *Pupils*, p. 379.
[33] Staehlin, p. 216.
[34] Cht., 1874, vol. ii, p. 17.

those critics of Peter who, to the present day, hold him responsible for destroying the unified and spiritual society that they claim to perceive in old Muscovy, where in contrast to the godless West secular authority was always controlled and mitigated by a profound Christian awareness, this ecclesiastical reform was the czar's greatest villainy. Thus Solzhenitsyn, in his examination of how his country had come to be barbarised by ruthless authoritarianism, regarded Peter's reforms as a lamentable milestone marking a new phase in the evolution of Russia's patterns of absolutism:

> Should we console ourselves with the thought that for a thousand years Russia lived with an authoritarian order – and at the beginning of the twentieth century both the physical and spiritual health of her people were intact? However in those days an important condition was fulfilled; that authoritarian order possessed a strong moral foundation; embryonic and rudimentary thought it was – not the ideology of universal violence but Christian Orthodoxy ... before it was battered by Patriarch Nikon and bureaucratized by Peter the Great. From the end of the Moscow period and throughout the whole of the Petersburg period, once this moral principle was weakened and perverted, the authoritarian order, despite the apparent external successes of the state, gradually went into a decline and eventually perished.[35]

An earlier critic of Peter, Prince Shcherbatov, writing in the 18th century, complained that Peter's reforms, ecclesiastical and sumptuary, did untold damage to the spiritual fibre of the nation. Peter is taken to task for imposing reforms upon an ignorant people "when the people were not yet enlightened, so that while extirpating superstition from an unenlightened nation he also took away faith in God's law". He goes on to compare the reforms to the work of an unskilled gardener pruning weak trees injudiciously.[36]

Peter was, and remains, the supreme target of the Slavophils who consider that his reforms broke the back of old Christian Russia, making it a "cold" (Moscow is warm, Petersburg cold) and spiritless place governed by German bureaucrats and an aristocracy which had lost its intimate organic contact with the

[35]*Letter to Soviet leaders*, p. 52.   [36]Shcherbatov, p. 29.

"people", whose language it was unable to speak, preferring to converse in indifferent French. By forcing it to the West, and a particularly Germanic and militaristic kind of West at that, the reforms created divisions in Russian culture from which it was never to recover. The reform of the church was simply the most malignant instance of this destruction. It must be said that to this day Russian Slavophils have always been capable of remarkable heights of eccentricity. It is still accepted in some circles that Peter was indeed a reforming Antichrist whose assault on Christian culture has mysteriously been incorporated into the Jewish World Conspiracy, whereby Wall Street, the Politburo and the Elders of Zion plot feverishly with Freemasons in a bid to rule the world – a view held with passionate intensity by many of the present-day Moscow intelligentsia, not to mention increasing numbers of non-Russians who ought to know better. Certainly Peter's reforms did create divisions. They were the origin of the so-called "Accursed Questions" which haunted the writers and thinkers of the early 19th century. "What is Russia, a European or an Asiatic State?" "Why does it have the unique mission of saving the world?" "Who are we?" It may also be said that Peter created an Accursed Question of another kind. At a time when the institution of serfdom was breaking down in most of the rest of Europe, Peter's "reform" of the peasantry was a reinvigoration of the principle, formally recognising that the vast majority of his subjects could be bartered as slaves. However, this, like all Peter's reforms, was essentially an accentuation of already existing trends. Peter did not create serfdom, he simply reinforced it. He did not actually impose any fundamental change upon Russian society. As Klyuchevsky wrote:

> The reform was a revolution not in its aims and results, but solely in its methods, and the impression it created upon the minds and feelings of contemporaries. It was a convulsion rather than an upheaval.[37]

For the aim was an ever-increasing dominance of the unmitigated authority of the central government over all its subjects. It proposed the notion of service to the state as the sole duty of noble and peasant alike, and made sure that, whatever man might render to God, his first duty was to render unto Caesar. In this

[37] *The Russian Tradition*, p. 110.

respect Peter's principal achievement was to reinforce the patterns of absolutism by means of his regularisations and, in the words of Plekhanov, to develop to its final logical conclusion "the condition of complete helplessness of the population vis à vis the state that is the characteristic of oriental despotism".[38]

[38] *The Russian Tradition, loc. cit.*

CHAPTER FIFTEEN

The Last Years

The years after the peace of Nystad saw one last foreign adventure, a final war, which, though modest, prepared the way for Russia's future expansion in yet another direction, towards Persia. Peter had always shown interest in the Far East, although the Northern War and the recasting of Russia had occupied most of his attention. He had made attempts to develop the overland trade with China, sending two large if unsuccessful missions to Pekin. He had also succeeded in expanding Russian holdings in the Far East by acquiring Kamchatka. His reign saw the development of Siberia – mining and now agriculture too increased rapidly. Peter also wished to bring areas of Central Asia under his control. He had heard tales of much alluvial gold to be had, and thought also in terms of trade routes and extending Russian influence to India – a dream of Russian foreign policy that was to die hard over the next two centuries. In 1714 he had sent an expeditionary force into Central Asia to attempt to subdue the rival Khanates of Khiva and Bokhara, and if possible press on to India. Unfortunately the leaders, after beating the troops of an unfriendly khan in the field, were taken in by his overtures of peace. They allowed their men to be divided at his suggestion and thereby ensured that the entire force was put to the sword.

Peter also sought further contact with Persia. In 1715 he sent one of his supposedly ablest men, Volynsky, on a mission to the shah, which included proposals for a commercial treaty. He was also ordered to make as full a report as possible on the state of the nation. Not only was a treaty concluded, which improved the basis on which Russian merchants traded, Volynsky also reported that Persia was on the verge of collapse, and that a small army could easily annex the silk provinces that lay along the Caspian. When in 1721 the shah was deposed by Afghan rebels Peter took his chance to intervene, ostensibly to restore order, in fact to gain control of the western and southern Caspian seaboard, and above all to deny it to the Turks.

Peter led his last campaign in person, once again accompanied by Catherine. In 1722 he joined an army of 30,000 regulars and a large quantity of cossacks. He took his infantry across the north-western corner of the Caspian by sea, leaving the cavalry to go round by land – which was a mistake. There was little water, less fodder and the horses suffered dreadfully in consequence. However, Peter eventually succeeded in capturing Derbent, a trading town on the west coast of the Caspian. He had hoped to press further south, with the help of Georgian and Armenian Christians who professed themselves to be ready to rise and flock to his standard – as the Balkan Christians had once promised – as Peter advanced to the river Pruth. However, this time Peter did not over-extend himself so readily. The climate and its attendant diseases had already accounted for too many of his men and he had lost thirty supply ships in a storm at sea in which Peter himself nearly drowned. Accordingly he elected to withdraw, having in fact achieved remarkably little. Human opposition had proved weak yet his losses had been severe. Estimates vary, but the most modest talks of 15,000 horses, 4000 men and a million roubles.[1] Other reports suggest that he lost a third of his effective forces through sickness and fatigue.[2] At all events the campaign was not a success. The French ambassador, Campredon, suggested that had it not been for the intercession of Catherine, Volynsky, now governor of Astrakhan, might well have been flogged to death for advising it and assuring Peter that it would be easy. Nevertheless there were advantages. Later that year the Russians took Baku and a year later they reached the Persian port of Resht. Indeed, Russian expansion in this quarter alarmed the Turks enough to bring them close to a declaration of war until it was finally agreed that Russia should keep a strip of the Caspian coast and would not seek to expand its influence westward into Georgia and Armenia.

Peter's principal concern in these later years was to regulate and reform his own kingdom as he had tried to regulate and

[1] Coll. vol. xl, 1884, p. 280.   [2] Bruce, p. 356.

"reform" his son. Tireless and utterly committed to the service of his nation he expected no less of others, an expectation which was disappointed with an ever-increasing regularity. If there is tragedy in Peter's life beyond his destruction of his first-born then it lies in his gradual discovery that the corruption and self-interest which were so foreign and repugnant to him, and which he had fought throughout his reign, were as prevalent as ever, and that no one, not even those closest to him, were free of this taint. There are times when Peter must have felt, with more than a little justification, that he was the only honest man in a nation of rogues.

Official corruption had always been a feature of Russia's public life, and for good reason. Just as the tax farmers of France made a profit from the collecting of indirect taxes on the crown's behalf, so in old Russia it was accepted that an official appointment was a source of revenue. Officials received little or no regular salary and looked for "*kormlenie*", or "nourishment", to the opportunities conferred upon them by their office. Corruption and abuse of official privilege were as prevalent in Russian public life in Peter's day as they would appear in, say, the portrait of small-town officialdom painted by Gogol a century or so later in *Dead Souls* and *The Government Inspector*. Peter was obliged to tolerate the principle of *kormlenie* to some extent, yet he would not readily accept either corruption or a degree of inefficiency and sloth amounting to moral turpitude at the head of government. After establishing his senate he set up a body of men to police both it and Russian official life at every level, the body of so-called "fiscals" under the control of an "ober-fiscal". Essentially their job was to protect the revenue of the state by spying, investigating and denouncing. The need for such policing is illustrated by one foreigner's observation that households in St Petersburg were taxed at double the official rate whereas he estimated that perhaps a third of the moneys paid over might reach their proper destination.[3] Peter encouraged his fiscals to be extreme in their diligence. When the first ober-fiscal asked Peter: "Should I just prune the branches or should I sink the axe to the roots?" "Cut it to the very roots," he replied. In the circumstances it is not surprising that the fiscals were less than popular. Indeed they were hated even to the extent of being denounced from the pulpit by one of Russia's leading churchmen.

[3] Weber, vol. ii, p. 72.

The loathing has left its mark upon the language, in which the verb *"fiskalit'"* means to "tell tales".

Ober-fiscal Nesterov, a one-time serf, relentlessly pursued some of the highest figures in the land. His greatest triumph was the unmasking of tremendous abuses in the administration of Siberia, under Prince Gagarin. He had involved many of the country's leading figures in his corrupt practices, as it began to emerge in the "Great Inquisition" which began in 1715. Some of those involved, Apukhtin, Volkonsky, had their tongues branded with red-hot irons, some were flogged and exiled, while other, more august figures escaped with severe fines. Among the latter we find Menshikov, of whom more later, Apraksin, described by the English ambassador as "very vengeful and no enemy to presents", and Shafirov who "has more experience than natural qualifications ... it is said that his private interest will not always let him distinguish the merits of the cause".[4] Peter did not feel that he could rely upon the nation's leaders to conduct a proper and impartial investigation of their own affairs. Instead he looked to his army, placing the investigation in the hands of junior officers:

> And so things have come to pass in Russia that the members of a venerable senate composed of the heads of the greatest families in the czar's dominion were obliged to appear before a lieutenant as their judge and be called to the account of their conduct.[5]

Peter's sense of carnival, of the world turned upside down, sometimes extended well beyond the world of play.

Guards officers were also used for a time to supervise the senate's actual conduct of business, having the right to arrest any senator they considered to be at fault. Their place was later taken by a new official, the *General Prokuror*, whose task was to supervise the conduct of business, dealing with problems such as that set by Shafirov: "Who will never permit his vote to be recorded so that his prejudiced findings may pass unnoticed, moreover he shouts at the secretary heaping insults and abuse upon him."[6] Indeed, the senate seems to have been a hotbed of malpractice and corruption. When the senate house burnt down in 1718 it was widely supposed that this was an act of arson designed to destroy

[4] Whitworth, p. 71.   [5] Weber, vol. i, p. 193.   [6] Knyaz'kov, p. 175.

incriminating evidence.[7] Nevertheless, despite this and other attempts to frustrate the Great Inquisition, Gagarin was eventually convicted of corruption on a monumental scale: trading privately with the Chinese as opposed to on the government's behalf, permitting merchants to do as much themselves and even selling the government his own goods. Despite his pleas for mercy and his noble lineage Gagarin was hanged – opposite the senate house.

In 1723 his crimes caught up with Shafirov, who had served Peter for some twenty years. He was convicted of robbing the late Gagarin, whose son had married his daughter, of money and jewels later found in Shafirov's house, of forging senators' signatures to increase his brother's salary, thereby causing an innocent clerk to be flogged twice, raising postal charges on his own initiative and pocketing the proceeds, and other lesser peculations. He was led out to a place of execution opposite the Kremlin, on a simple sledge, wearing an old fur coat and carrying a candle. His indictment was read to him followed by a sentence of death by the axe. His wig was removed and he turned to face a church, crossing himself and showing great dignity he lay down upon his great belly with his head upon the block as the headsman's assistants held his feet. The axe went up and came cracking down into the wood beside his ear, and Shafirov was informed that, in view of his past services, the death sentence was commuted to destitution and exile.[8] He had in fact been subjected to that well-known Russian punishment the mock execution, an institution that would be familiar both to Dostoevsky and countless later inhabitants of the Gulag Archipelago.

Peter was dealt yet another blow the following year when it was discovered that Nesterov, the ruthless and seemingly incorruptible rooter-out of malpractice, was himself corrupt. He was condemned for accepting bribes, broken on the wheel and executed in 1724. Yet the most corrupt, and indeed most powerful, figure of them all was Menshikov. "He was an exceedingly artful fellow of a vast memory but wicked above what can be imagined."[9] As governor of St Petersburg he was in a position of which he took the most spectacular advantage, in both war and peace. His appetite for wealth was insatiable and his vanity equal only to his appetite. Fiercely jealous of Peter's favour he was

[7] Coll., 1881, vol xxxiv, p. 305.   [8] Busching, 1786, vol. xxi, pp. 195–6.
[9] Gordon, A., p. 280.

extraordinarily adept at securing the disgrace of anyone he felt might be a potential rival, never hesitating to stoop to acts of the most base dishonesty to get what he wanted.

He governed his province by arbitrary exercise of power, quite beyond any concept of legality. No one enjoyed rights or guarantees of any kind, any more than they did elsewhere, but his subjects were especially vulnerable to his acquisitive appetites. Thus we find a nobleman severely beaten, stripped of all he owned and sent to the galleys for life for failing to illuminate the windows of his house on Menshikov's birthday.[10] Besides he seems to have practised something not entirely removed from a "personality cult" if we are to go by incidents such as the arrest and flogging of someone found drawing "celestial Signs" upon Menshikov's printed portrait.[11] The Danish visitor Juel reports that anyone whose wealth caught Menshikov's eye stood in dire danger of losing it *instanter*, by confiscation, and without appeal. All it required was a simple false accusation or even suspicion of "failure to denounce". It was only possible to secure immunity by passing massive bribes over to Menshikov. Juel suspected that some of these went to Peter, but this was on the whole unlikely, since it is hard to conceive of the czar trafficking in guarantees of immunity.

Menshikov, quite unlike Peter in this respect, was addicted to magnificent display. He travelled like a monarch: his retinue could number some 250 attendants, 370 horses, sixteen waggons, with outriders, Moors, dwarfs, pages, scribes and a grand total of nine cooks.[12] Indeed he was so unlike Peter in his tastes that it is hard to understand how he managed to retain such a hold over him. The electress Sophie, who had first met Peter on his grand embassy, found it inexplicable, wondering how Peter could favour someone "*qui lui est tout à fait contraire en toute chose*".[13] Peter himself appreciated that Menshikov's abilities had their limits. He did not allow him to participate in foreign negotiations, for example, since he spoke German and, as the French ambassador put it, "could thus reveal his lack of ability and the stupidity of which he is uniquely capable".[14] For years he continued to enjoy Peter's favour, although the czar gradually began to discover the extent of his dishonesty, an extent great enough

---

[10] Coll., 1884, vol. xxxix, p. 344.　　[11] Bozhernyanov, p. 118.
[12] Wittram, vol. ii, p. 256.　　[13] *Ibid.*, p. 260.
[14] *Ibid.*, p. 448.

to have cost anyone else his head. Yet Menshikov was never entirely disgraced, nor punished beyond a series of severe fines, and this even though it was Peter's usual custom never to give anyone found guilty of great corruption a second chance, let alone a third, fourth or fifth. He remained curiously reluctant to bring down his one-time companion; this partly out of gratitude for past services and, almost certainly, partly thanks to the regular intercessions of Menshikov's protectress and protégée, Catherine.

Peter first began to complain of Menshikov's corruption as early as 1711, when he chided him for being over-enthusiastic in his personal looting of Poland:

> I am most surprised to learn that your waggons are still in Poland a year after your departure. I urgently request you not to risk your reputation and credit for such trivial gains.[15]

He also began to find his judgement suspect, if not corrupt, complaining: "You present scoundrels to me as honest men, honest men as scoundrels",[16] and warning him to mend his ways. The following years are punctuated by Peter's repeated warnings to Menshikov, who seemed to have paid little enough attention to them. Thus in 1714 Peter called on him to deliver yet another severe warning. He and his subordinates of Petersburg province were overdoing their malpractice, growing too rich too fast at the expense of the state and its citizens. A year later Peter had his vice-governor and two other officials publicly flogged, and everybody expected to see Menshikov join them and fall at last. Yet once again he escaped with a severe fine. On this occasion Peter was heard to observe that the offence was a capital one, yet Menshikov's guilt was outweighed by past services. Nevertheless he gave Menshikov a beating in private and warned him, once more, that this was to be the last time.[17]

The wretched business of the czarevich served to restore Menshikov to temporary favour; Peter clearly valued his support, a support Menshikov lent for good reasons of his own. Neither he nor Catherine would have survived a week had Peter's son succeeded him. Yet once again Menshikov proved unable to resist temptation. By 1722 he was once more in the deepest trouble, and in the following year disgrace seemed inevitable. On his

[15] Soloviev, vol. viii, p. 499.   [16] *Ibid.*, p. 500.   [17] Maikov, p. 50.

return from Persia Peter discovered that Menshikov was once more involved in various forms of malpractice. He was prudent enough, knowing how to reach Peter as he did, to make a full confession on this occasion, and as a result his punishment was restricted to various fines and confiscations. However, he had finally forfeited any remaining vestige of Peter's favour, and it was only thanks to the empress that he lost nothing more. Nartov, Peter's lathe-master and a privileged intimate, recalls the following scene:

> On this occasion the empress interceded for Menshikov; she saved him from total disaster by her persistent pleas for mercy, to which the monarch paid heed, saying as he pardoned him, "Menshikov was conceived out of wedlock, born in sin, and will die a scoundrel. And Katinka, if he does not mend his ways he shall lose his head. I forgive him this once for your sake."[18]

Catherine was indeed empress now. Ever since his eldest son had shown himself unworthy to succeed him Peter had been faced with the growing problem of the succession. Matters were further complicated by the death in 1718 of the son that Catherine had borne him, that year thus being marked by the death of both his boys. The obvious successor, his grandson Peter, Aleksey's son, would clearly serve as a conservative rallying point. His daughters Anna and Elizabeth were too young. Thus Peter's thoughts gradually turned to his Katinka, the loyal wife who had shared his campaigns, knew just how to soothe him and scratch his back and who alone, of all those close to him, had never let him down.

He prepared the way for designating her his successor in a decree of 1722 which declared that the czar had absolute freedom to nominate his heir — in the past it had been essential that the successor be a Romanov. Along with the decree all Russians and foreign residents were required to swear that they would recognise the title of whoever Peter might designate to succeed him. "The order", relates an observer, "struck a damp upon the spirits of everybody",[19] since it quite clearly meant the disinheritance of his grandson. Indeed many schismatics refused to take the oath, and one group of twelve locked themselves in a church which they proceeded to blow up rather than make what was

[18]Maikov, p. 98.   [19]Bruce, p. 262.

tantamount to a pledge to a German czarina. For Peter now issued a second decree announcing his intention to crown Catherine empress. He alluded particularly to her services on the Pruth, when "with great self-sacrifice she shared all the trials and discomforts of a soldier's life, encouraging us and our entire army by her valour and heroism ... Whereupon by the authority given us by God we have resolved to reward such great services of our consort by crowning her with the Imperial Crown."

Yet again Peter was offering an outrage to Muscovite tradition. To crown a czarina at all was virtually without precedent, and what kind of ruler could Catherine be over Holy Orthodox Russia – a foreigner, a peasant and the erstwhile lover of Menshikov?

Yet Catherine enjoyed the support of all those committed to Peter's cause, and, most important, was extremely popular with the guards, who would soon take on the role of czar-makers, a role they would continue to fulfil throughout the century and attempt for the last time in December 1825. Catherine, like Menshikov, was far from hostile to magnificence, and her coronation on May 7, 1724, was a truly splendid affair. It took place in the Cathedral of the Assumption in the Kremlin. Her crown, specially made in Paris and based on the Byzantine Imperial Crown, carried 2564 stones, some of the diamonds being taken from Peter's own crown which he had had stripped for the occasion. The finest gem of all was an enormous ruby which Menshikov had acquired from Pekin for 60,000 roubles. Catherine's triumph now appeared complete, for it could only be a matter of time before Peter proclaimed her his successor. Yet time nearly ran out for Catherine as another case of corruption came to light, one in which she herself was most dreadfully compromised.

For many years she had been close friends with the brother and sister of Peter's lover Anna Mons, Wilhelm Mons and Anna Balk. Mons was, it would seem, a strikingly handsome man, and as Catherine's chamberlain was close to her, although it is not possible to say whether or not he was her lover. In the autumn of 1724 Peter discovered that Mons and his entourage had long been profiting from their position. Catherine was supremely well placed to grant favours – or have Peter grant them – since she had his ear as no one else did. It transpired that anyone wishing to secure her support had first to gain the backing of Wilhelm Mons, and that cost money. An investigation showed that Mons and his sister had been trading for years upon their positions, most probably with Catherine's connivance. Mons was tortured twice, and then beheaded on November 16, 1724, for malversation, peculation and usurping the authority of the senate. His sister, sister-in-law and wife were also arrested, flogged and exiled while certain pages involved in the corruption were degraded and made to serve as common soldiers. The extent of Catherine's actual involvement in Mons's practices and indeed the nature of her involvement with Mons was never established. Yet it was clear enough that to Peter, and to many others, she was distinctly suspect. Reporting on Mons's execution the French ambassador observed discreetly:

> There are conjectures on other subjects about which one dare do no more than think.[20]

Although Peter did not mount a direct attack on Catherine, he punished her with characteristic cruelty. He is said to have had her driven past the dangling corpse of Mons, so closely that she brushed against it, while he stared hard at her to observe her reaction – she was controlled enough to show nothing. He also had Mons's head preserved in alcohol and introduced into her apartments.

The Mons scandal and the partial disgrace of Catherine also saw the final discrediting of Menshikov, who proved to be guilty of yet further extensive frauds. He was immediately deprived of his office in charge of the Department of War, and, on this occasion, Catherine's pleas for mercy were of no avail. It was generally felt that Catherine and Menshikov had had only a foretaste of Peter's rage, and the atmosphere at court in late 1724 was electric. Peter was deep in a mood of overwhelming and universal suspicion, so much so that the French ambassador thought it prudent to suspend his regular practice of seeking advantage by means of bribes. He described Peter as being:

> Highly disturbed by the infidelities which he had discovered reaching right into his own household. Menshikov was threatened with imminent disgrace, if nothing worse, while Catherine too was dreadfully nervous, making every effort to hide her grief and apprehension. Everyone anticipated that Peter would move against her decisively at any moment.[21]

[20] Coll., 1886, vol. lii, p. 344.   [21] Ibid., p. 358.

Whatever one's opinion of Peter, his situation in these last months of his life can only command sympathy and pity. He alone, it would seem, of all those he had chosen to surround him, had devoted himself whole-heartedly to serving his people. Everyone else, whatever their capacity to charm, or play, or convince him to the contrary, were hopelessly corrupt and out for themselves. His sons were dead, his wife no better than the rest of them, and to make her his heir would be tantamount to putting Russia in the hands of Menshikov. No wonder in the circumstances that people believed that at any moment the heads of Menshikov and Catherine would roll.

These years were further darkened for Peter by the deterioration of his health. He had had bouts of serious illness before, scarcely surprising when one considers the demands that his work and play made upon his constitution, but this was now showing signs of definitive decline. In the winter of 1723 he had experienced pain in the urinal canal, which he ignored, making no concessions, eating and drinking his fill despite increasing discomfort. By September 1724 he found it very difficult to pee. He accordingly went to take the waters at Olonetz, and afterwards, reports the French ambassador, passed large numbers of stones. However, as always, he refused absolutely to let the condition of his body dictate to him. He continued to drive or walk about Petersburg virtually unattended, always anxious to do and see for himself, particularly in these last months when he was overwhelmed by suspicions. "He was not contented without going to the bottom of things and therefore, instead of making people wait on him, he watched them, so that he was seldom to be found in the palace."[22]

He also retained his capacity to work. On his return from Olonetz, where as well as taking the cure he had "played" in the iron works, digging out a piece of ore weighing 120 pounds with his own hands, he went sailing in the Gulf of Finland. Coming into the port of Lachta he saw a boat with soldiers and sailors on board in serious trouble. It was a dark autumn day with high seas and the boat had run aground. Peter ordered another boat to go and get them off, but to no avail. The men worked so slowly and incompetently, being half dead with fear, that Peter grew increasingly frustrated, until he reckoned that the time had come to take a hand himself. He went in up to his waist, and quickly

[22] Gordon, A., p. 315.

got the boat refloated. The Gulf of Finland, in November, was no place for a fifty-two-year-old in poor health to take a soaking, and the waters of the Baltic rapidly undid the work of the waters of Olonetz. Peter's health grew steadily worse, so that for much of the time he was in agony. Yet even now he was still able to seek amusement:

> One of his pleasures was a train of … little children's sledges. Twenty or thirty were tied together so that they were only a foot apart from one another. Common people were placed on them, having to sit like orientals with their knees almost touching. They held on to the sides of the sledges and awaited their fate. Five or six horses side by side were hitched up to the sledges and they galloped off. All was well along straight streets but if they had to turn in narrow streets it may be easily imagined that many of the sledges and especially the last ones knocked together and hit the sides of the houses, and since the horses never stopped it happened that some of the passengers, broken and bruised, were unable to get back on the sledges, which was held to be a misdemeanour, that was variously punished.[23]

Peter's sense of fun retained its cruel streak. A boyar, M. A. Golovin, had incurred Peter's disfavour. The czar ordered him to play the part of the "Archbishop of Kazan" at a gathering of the all-drunken synod in the last days of 1724. Golovin turned up late for the ceremony and was duly punished by being placed naked on the ice – and dying seven days later.

The all-drunken synod had recently lost its Prince Pope, who died late in 1724. For all his dreadful health Peter had ordered the election of a new one. The conclave was called for January 3, opening with a most elaborate ceremonial procession including a marshal, fife players, sixty choirboys, 100 officers, generals, cardinals, dwarfs, six stammerers – the papal orators – a dozen bald men carrying a large barrel and bearing pigs' bladders, and a huge statue of Bacchus filled with wine. The cardinals were brought to their "Vatican" and Peter stayed to drink with them till midnight. The czar, who had less than a month to live, showed as much attention to the details of his play ceremonial as he had

---

[23] Golitsyn, pp. 109–10.

ever done, and was still able to drink and disport himself with that extraordinary seriousness that informed his carnivalesque extravagance.

Shortly after, on the feast of the Epiphany, Peter attended the blessing of the waters on the Neva, where he caught a severe chill, and his condition deteriorated steadily. He was being treated by two doctors, Blumentrost and Bidleau, and their treatment was proving ineffectual. Peter summoned a third, an Italian, Azzariti, for a consultation. He subsequently told the French ambassador that Peter's urine was obstructed by "the remnants of an old venereal infection" which formed ulcers at the entrance to the bladder. He did not at the time think it dangerous. However, although Peter's urine cleared temporarily, the ambassador, who was keeping a close watch, observed that on January 26 he grew worse, and had two litres of pestilent urine full of pieces of rotting flesh removed by force. That morning he tried to take some gruel but was overcome with fever and fainted. On coming to he said he felt as if he had a house on his chest, and ordered the release of 400 prisoners.[24] Azzariti was now less than happy with his patient's condition. His presence was moreover resented by the two other doctors, who were reluctant to admit him to Peter. He considered them ignorant, and believed that they were contributing to Peter's decline, treating symptoms with palliatives and rejecting his recommendations for treatment of the ulcers that he believed to be doing the damage. It was he who had insisted on pumping out the urine, despite their protestations, and even this took place twenty-four hours after he suggested it. Azzariti eventually recognised that Peter was dying. He advised Peter Tolstoy that the time had come for the czar to make his final dispositions. Although Catherine was with him constantly and he had taken communion three times in a week, this particular piece of news was kept from him. As soon as Catherine appreciated that he really was dying she set Menshikov and Tolstoy to work.

Almost to the last Peter remained aware that he had left one major problem unresolved: the succession. At about 2 p.m. on January 27 he called for pen and paper, and wrote "Leave all to ...", unfortunately the rest was an indecipherable scrawl. He then called for his eldest daughter so that he might dictate to her, but by the time she was brought to his side he was already

[24] Coll., 1886, vol. lii, p. 414.

unconscious. Between 5 and 6 a.m. on the morning of January 28, in a series of dreadful convulsions, Peter died.

As he lay dying Menshikov busied himself, persuading officers of the guards to pledge themselves to the Empress Catherine. She had issued sixteen months of back pay to the local garrison, doubled the palace guards and posted troops in the streets by the time she closed Peter's eyes.[25] Menshikov also addressed himself to the civilian and ecclesiastical dignitaries assembled in the palace, using an equal balance of threats and promises. Next day Catherine was proclaimed empress and Menshikov had triumphed again.

Peter's death could not have been more timely for his wife and ex-favourite, so timely that it might appear suspect. A medical study of his case in this century suggests that he probably died of acute cirrhosis,[26] at all events he seems to have died of natural causes. Yet there is a lingering suspicion that Catherine and Menshikov did not strive to keep Peter alive. The treatment of Peter prompted the French ambassador to observe that "their ignorance is not without suspicion".[27] Nothing we have seen of Menshikov suggests that he would have been acting out of character had he taken steps to advance the end of his erstwhile protector, who died in agony and very much alone.

On the night of Peter's death an open confrontation took place between conservative elements, the grand old families of Russia, Repnins, Golitsyns, who wanted Peter's grandson to succeed, and the supporters of Catherine, such as Peter Tolstoy. At the height of the altercation the drums of the guards were heard to roll, and Catherine's opponents were urged to swear allegiance to the empress, which, very prudently, they did.

So Peter was succeeded by Catherine, and Menshikov, whose first step was to annul all the corruption charges pending against him. He continued to use his position as Catherine's favourite to increase his own wealth, setting examples of venality unprecedented even by Russian standards.

Catherine, who devoted a considerable proportion of her time to riotous banqueting, found her health beginning to decline towards the end of 1726. She caught a severe chill in December of that year when the Neva rose unexpectedly and flooded her palace. She eventually died on May 28, 1727, having reigned a

[25] Coll., 1886, vol. lii, p. 434.   [26] Wittram, vol. ii, p. 499.
[27] Coll., 1886, vol. lii, p. 434.

little longer than two years. She was succeeded by Peter's grand-son Peter II, aged eleven. Effective authority remained with Men-shikov, until he finally fell from favour in September 1727. Although accused of treason and fined 500,000 roubles, on this occasion his daughters secured a final pardon from the young czar, who allowed him to depart to his Ukrainian estates – with sixty waggons of baggage. However, less than a year later the conservative faction brought about his complete ruin; he and his family were finally exiled to the village of Berezov, and Menshi-kov had come to Siberia at last.

*   *   *

"What a tragedy could be made of Peter's life," Napoleon once observed[28] – and it will be recalled that Peter himself regarded his own life as a *roman*. Certainly it had some of the stuff of tragedy about it, especially towards the end, its last act beginning with the killing of his son. One of the necessary in-gredients of tragedy is that it should concern itself with human greatness. Whatever one may think of Peter – his cruelty, his violence, his crudity, his terrors, or even his sense of humour – his greatness is beyond dispute. Campredon describes him as having a capacity to apply himself and to work which was super-human, so that had he had more able ministers his achieve-ments would have been greater still.[29] Whitworth provides a portrait of him that is touchingly human without diminishing his stature:

> Good-natured but very passionate, having learnt restraint when sober, suspicious of other people, not over-scrupulous in his engagements or gratitude, violent in the first heat, irreso-lute on longer deliberation.[30]

His lathe-master Nartov described himself as devastated by Peter's death, and rightly so:

> This monarch put our fatherland on an equal footing with others and taught us to know that we too were human.[31]

[28] Posselt, vol. ii, p. 545.   [29] Coll., 1886, vol. lii, p. 145.
[30] Wittram, vol. ii, p. 59.   [31] Knyaz'kov, p. 156.

Peter was great through generosity of spirit, and scale, above all the scale of his service, his devotion to a certain conception of what his nation should be. He was sometimes the victim of his own single-mindedness, and this made him a poor judge of people; he was better at understanding things. Thus because he devoted himself utterly to service he expected everybody to follow suit, and if necessary he would apply force to make them want to. Peter was a great believer in taking horses to the water and obliging them to drink.

Yet curiously, for this biographer, the real extent of his greatness, his largeness of spirit, comes out in his modesty and lack of vanity. He never had that maniacal conviction that he was infallible that one finds in a Napoleon or a Hitler. Instead there was a much calmer confidence in his vision of Russia. His sense of czarish dignity never checked his capacity to play, with water and with fire. Whether he was sailing on the Neva, in a storm, with a shipload of terrified diplomats, drinking toast after toast to the sound of artillery, or solemnly participating in the ceremonies of his drunken synod, Peter never forgot how to clown. This is one of the fundamental and most admirable of his characteristics. His sense of his own stature was so secure that nothing he might do could threaten it – in church one day in Danzig, feeling the cold, he silently borrowed the wig of the mayor of the city for a time, and then returned it with a nod of thanks.[32] His greatness required no ceremonial, no pomp to amplify it. He was happy to play the part of the most modest of men, bombardier, captain or drummer boy, for no role he might adopt could in any way diminish him, it could only teach and enrich.

Along with this lack of vanity was an amazing and inhuman ruthlessness. He proposed to transform his country, make it modern, whatever the pain or cost. It would be wrong to talk of a master plan for Russia, since this would imply a degree of coherence that Peter never had. Instead he possessed a kind of instinctive sense of direction, the direction which he was determined to oblige his nation to take. Rather than work to a coherent scheme of things he threw himself indiscriminately into a whole range of enterprises, some more trivial than others, all of which, however, fitted that sense of direction. Leo Tolstoy, who planned to write a novel set in Peter's time, was unflattering on this subject:

[32] Staehlin, p. 35.

Do you know I once wrote about Peter I and there was one good thing I wrote. It was the explanation of Peter's character and of all his evil deeds by the fact that he was constantly terribly busy, working at a lathe, travelling, issuing decrees etc. It's a truism that idleness is the mother of vice, but not everyone knows that feverish hasty activity is the habitual handmaid of discontent with oneself and especially with other people.[33]

Certainly Tolstoy is right to emphasise Peter's capacity for restlessness and discontent. He was prodigal, not to say wasteful, of his own energy and resources, and indeed of those of his subjects too. He caused great misery by placing his trust in the scoundrel Menshikov. His neglect of his son had the most tragic consequences and brought about the succession of Catherine, not the most suitable person to rule Russia. Yet his shortcomings are easily outweighed by his achievements. Although Russia would have turned to the West without him, the part he played in its turning requires no further comment. There can be few rulers in history who have brought about more widespread and enduring transformations than Peter's turning of Muscovy into imperial Russia. Future generations have not always thanked him for his work, but that is another matter.

The study of his life is rewarding in another and particular aspect. I have not always resisted the temptation to draw parallels between Russia past and present–for example the fact that "failure to denounce" was and is again a criminal offence. The style of Peter's rulership, his absolutism, his lack of regard for "the human factor", his treatment of his critics and potential enemies all have their analogues in this century. Of greater interest still, when it comes to comparisons, is the fact that Peter got away with it. He did great violence to his most traditionally minded nation, violence both physical and spiritual, and yet his people assented to it, however much it went against the grain. They have assented since, still assent, to much more of the same. It would be preposterous to maintain that Peter invented a style of rulership which set the pattern of Russian government up to the present day. For all his innovations Peter was part of the Russian tradition and not its source. Yet the extraordinary energy and enthusiasm which he brought to bear upon his nation had a most peculiar effect upon it, bringing to the surface some of

[33] L. Tolstoy, *Correspondence*, London 1978, ed. Christian, vol. ii, p. 374.

its most essential characteristics, making Russia declare its essential Russianness. He gave it victories, anniversaries, landmarks and its enduring crisis of identity. So many of the events of his reign, major and minor, seem archetypical of Russia: Romodanovsky's bear, the courage and endurance of Russian soldiers and labourers, the various rituals of the orthodox church and the all-drunken synod, the peasant who tried to fly with mica wings, the casual appropriation of the mayor of Danzig's wig, the vistas of the Nevsky Prospekt and the fortress of St Peter and St Paul.

The ultimate testimony to Peter's greatness, albeit an ambiguous one, is this fact that the pressures he put on Russia, the questions he asked of her, made her more than at almost any other time so fundamentally herself that the study of Russia under Peter is tantamount to a study of quintessential Russianness. Peter's reign illustrates those articles of faith which make Tytuchev observe that Russia cannot be judged, only believed in, while Peter himself actually achieved the ultimate dream of a great leader. Ceasing to be a mere historical figure, the part played in the creation of his country was so fundamental, so colossal, that Peter, his achievements, his actions, his words, the style of his rulership, transcend mere history to become incorporated in the very essence of Russia; just as the heroes of antiquity were sometimes rewarded by mythic metamorphosis into a constellation, Peter, the man of fire and water, goes beyond Russian history to pass into the realm of Russian myth.

BIBLIOGRAPHY

Unless otherwise stated all English titles are published in London.
M = Moscow, L = Leningrad, St P = St Petersburg.

Adelung, Fr. v. *Augustus Freiherr von Meyerburg und seine Reise nach Russland.* St P, 1827.

Anderson, M. S. Peter *the Great.* 1977.

Aristov. *Moskovskie smuty v pravlenii tsarevny Sophii Andreevny.* Warsaw, 1871.

Avril, P. *Voyages en divers états d'Europe et d'Amérique.* Paris, 1693.

Baddeley, J. F. *Russia, Mongolia, China.* 1919.

Bain, R. N. *The Pupils of Peter the Great.* 1897.
 The First Romanovs 1613–1725. 1905.

Banks, J. *History of the Life and Reign of Peter the Great.* 1740.

Barrow, J. A. *Memoir of the Life of Peter the Great.* 1832.

Bell, J. *Travels from St Petersburg in Russia to Diverse Parts of Asia,* 2 vols. Glasgow, 1763.

Bengtsson, F. G. *The Life of Charles XII.* 1960.

Bogoslovsky, M. M. *Pyetr velikiy, materialy dlya issledovaniya,* 5 vols. L, 1940–8.

Bouvet, J. *The Present Condition of the Muscovite Empire.* 1699.

Bozheryanov, I. N. *Sankt Peterburg,* St P, 1903.

Bridges, C. A. G., ed. *The Russian Fleet during the Reign of Peter the Great.* Naval Records Society, 1899.

Bruce, P. H. *Memoirs ... containing an account of his travels in Germany, Russia, Tartary, etc.* 1782.

Burnet, G. *History of his Own Time.* 1888 ed.

Busching's Magazine, vols xix–xxi for Diary of Freiherr W. v. Bergholz.

Buvat, J. *Journal de la Régence 1715–23*. Paris, 1865.

Buxhoeveden, Baroness Sophie. *A Cavalier in Muscovy*. 1932.

Chteniya v imperatorskom obschestve istorii i drevnostei rossiskikh pri Moskovskom universitete, 1849–1917. (Abbreviated Cht.)

Collections of the Russian Historical Society, 1867–1916. (Abbreviated Coll.)

Collins, S. *The Present State of Russia*. 1671.

Crull, J. *The Antient and Present State of Muscovy*, 2 vols. 1698.

Dashkov, P. Y. *Pyetr velikiy v evo izrecheniyakh*. St P, 1910.

Defoe, D. *An Impartial History of the Life and Actions of Peter Alexowitz written by a British Officer in the Service of the Czar*. 1723.

Dmytryshkin, B. *The Modernisation of Russia*. 1974.

Fegina, S. A. *Pyetr velikiy, sbornik statei*. M, 1947.

Gachard, L-P. *Etudes et notices historiques concernant l'histoire des Pays Bas*. Brussels, 1890.

Garrard, J. *The Eighteenth Century in Russia*. 1973.

Gilyarovsky, V. A. *Moskva i moskvichi*. M–L, 1959.

Golikova, N. B. *Politicheskie protsesy pri Petre velikom*, M, 1957.

Golitsyn, E. M. *La Russie au 18-ème siècle*. St. P, 1863.

Gordon, A. *History of Peter the Great Emperor of Russia*, 2 vols. 1775.

Gordon, P. *Passages from the Diary of General Patrick Gordon of Auchlechries*, edited for the Spalding Society by J. Robertson. Aberdeen, 1859.

Tagebuch, 1655–1699, ed. Posselt. M, 1849–53.

Grey, I. *Peter the Great*. 1962.

"Peter the Great in England", in *History To-day*, April 1956.

d'Haussonville, G. "La Visite du tsar Pierre le Grand en 1717", *Revue des deux mondes*, vol. xiv, p. 137. 1896.

Howard, Charles, Earl of Carlisle. *A Relation of Embassies*. 1669.

Jeffreyes, Captain J. *Letters to the British Government*. Stockholm, 1897.

Juel, J. *En Rejse til Rusland under Tsar Peter*. Copenhagen, 1893.

Kafengaus, B. B. *Rossiya pri Petre velikom*. M, 1955.

Klyuchevsky, V. *Peter the Great*. 1958.

Knyaz'kov, S. A. *Ocherki iz istorii Petra Velikovo i evo vremeni.* M, 1909.

Kurakin, V. I. *Istoriya o tsare Petre Alekseevichem.* St P, 1890.

Le Bruyn, C. *Travels into Muscovy.* 1737.

Lortholany, A. *Le Mirage Russe en France au 18-ème siècle.* Paris, 1951.

Luppov, S. P. *Istoriya stroitel'stva Peterburga v pervoi chetverti 18-ovo stoletiya.* M–L, 1957.

Maikov, L. N. *Rasskazy Nartova o Petre velikom.* St P, 1891.

Mayerburg, A. *Relation d'un voyage en Moscovie.* Leyden, 1688.

Monas, S. "Anton Divier and the Police of St Petersburg", in *For Roman Jakobson.* The Hague, 1956.

Mottley, J. *The History of the Life of Peter the Great, Emperor of Russia,* 3 vols. 1739.

Nagreevsky, N. *Pyetr velikiy v Karlsbade.* Riga, 1909.

Neplyuev, I. I. *Zapiski,* ed. A. S. Suvorin. St P, 1893.

O'Brien, C. B. *Russia prior to Peter the Great, the Regency of Tsarevna Sophia.* Berkeley, 1942.

Russia under Two Tsars. Berkeley, 1952.

Olearius, A. *The Voyages and Travels of the Ambassadors sent by Frederick Duke of Holstein to the Great Duke of Muscovy.* 1662.

Oliva, J. *Russia in the Era of Peter the Great.* Englewood Cliffs, 1962.

Perry, J. *The State of Russia under the Present Tsar.* 1716.

Peter. Letters and papers, ed. Andreev. St P–M, 1897. (Abbreviated *Corr.*)

Pogodin, M. *17 pervykh let v zhizni Petra velikovo.* M, 1875.

Posohskov, I. *Kniga o skudosti i bogatstve.* M, 1911 ed.

Posselt. M. *Der General und Admiral Franz le Fort.* Frankfurt-a-M, 2 vols. 1866.

Predtechensky, A. V. *Peterburg petrovykh vremyen.* M–L, 1948.

Pylaev, M. Y. *Stariy Sankt Peterburg.* St P, 1887.

Russkaya Starina, 1870–1917.

Saint-Simon, duc de. *Mémoires,* vol. xxxi. Paris, 1920 ed.

Sakharov, I. P. *Zapiski russkikh lyudei.* St P, 1841.

Schacht, G. *Briefwechsel der Kurfuerstin Sophie.* Berlin–Leipzig, 1927.

Schuyler, E. *Peter the Great.* 2 vols. 1884.

Shakohvskaya, Z. *Precursors of Peter the Great.* 1964.

Shcherbatov, M. M. *Journal de Pierre le Grand depuis l'année 1698 jusqu'à la conclusion de la paix de Neustadt.* Berlin, 1773. *O povrezhdenii nravov v Rossii.* 1858 ed.

Snegirev, V. L. *Moskovskie slobody.* M–L, 1956.

Sokolov, N. *Raskol v saratovskom krae.* St P, 1888.

Solovyev, S. M. *Istoriya Rossii s drevnykh vremyen,* 29 vols. St P, s.d.

Staehlin-Stocksburg, J. V. *Anecdotes originales sur Pierre le Grand.* Strasbourg, 1787.

Tarle, E. V. *Severnaya voina.* M, 1958.

Timchenko-Ruban, G. I. *Pervye gody Peterburga.* St P, 1901.

Tumansky, F. O. *Sobranie raznykh zapisok i sochinenii o zhizni i deyaniyakh Petra velikovo,* 10 vols. St P, 1787.

Ustryalov, N. *Istoriya tsarstvovaniya Petra velikovo,* 8 vols. St P, 1858.

Villebois, O. *Mémoires secrètes.* Brussels, 1853.

V'yukov, A. I. *Rasskazy o staroi Moskve.* M, 1958.

Waliszewski, K. *Peter the Great,* 2 vols. 1897.

Weber, F. C. *The Present State of Russia.* 1722.

Whitworth, C. A. *An Account of Russia as it was in the year 1710.* Strawberry Hill, 1758.

Wittram, R. *Peter I Czar und Kaiser.* 2 vols. Göttingen, 1964.

Young, I. *Russia in the First Half of the Eighteenth Century. Cambridge History of Modern Europe,* vol. vii.

INDEX